Developing Notetaking Skills in a Second Language

Developing Notetaking Skills in a Second Language combines theoretical perspectives with an analysis of empirical classroom studies and offers a detailed discussion that increases pedagogical awareness of factors impacting second language (L2) notetaking performance and instruction.

Based on original research and including descriptions of classroom practices and samples of student work, the book provides insights on a range of topics relevant to L2 notetaking. The book emphasizes the challenges that many students from different international backgrounds face when taking notes in an L2 and outlines a five-stage pedagogic cycle for notetaking that can be applied to any listening text. It also explores the dialogic potential of notes for stimulating class discussion about notetaking strategies.

This book will be of great interest for teachers, academics, scholars, and postgraduate students in the fields of applied linguistics, L2, and foreign language education. It will also be a useful resource for those in charge of teacher education and postgraduate TESOL, L1, and L2 listening researchers and psycholinguists.

Joseph Siegel is an Associate Professor of English at Stockholm University and Örebro University, Sweden. He teaches TESOL methodology, linguistics, and applied linguistic research methods courses. Among his research interests are second language listening pedagogy, notetaking, pragmatics, and teacher education.

Routledge Research in Language Education

The *Routledge Research in Language Education* series provides a platform for established and emerging scholars to present their latest research and discuss key issues in Language Education. This series welcomes books on all areas of language teaching and learning, including but not limited to language education policy and politics, multilingualism, literacy, L1, L2 or foreign language acquisition, curriculum, classroom practice, pedagogy, teaching materials, and language teacher education and development. Books in the series are not limited to the discussion of the teaching and learning of English only.

Books in the series include:

Attitudes to English Study among Japanese, Chinese and Korean Women
Motivations, Expectations and Identity
Edited by Yoko Kobayashi

Second Language Pragmatics and English Language Education in East Asia
Edited by Cynthia Lee

Writing Motivation Research, Measurement and Pedagogy
Muhammad M. M. Abdel Latif

Pop Culture in Language Education
Theory, Research, Practice
Edited by Valentin Werner and Friederike Tegge

TESOL Teacher Education in a Transnational World
Turning Challenges into Innovative Prospects
Edited by Osman (Othman) Barnawi & Sardar Anwaruddin

Communicating Strategically in English as a Lingua Franca
A Corpus Driven Investigation
Janin Jafari

Dual Language Education in the US
Rethinking Pedagogy, Curricula, and Teacher Education to Support
Dual Language Learning for All
Edited by Pablo C. Ramírez and Christian J. Faltis

The Influence of the Foreign Service Institute on US Language Education
Critical Analysis of Historical Documentation
Theresa Ulrich

For more information about the series, please visit www.routledge.com/
Routledge-Research-in-Language-Education/book-series/RRLE

Developing Notetaking Skills in a Second Language
Insights from Classroom Research

Joseph Siegel

LONDON AND NEW YORK

First published 2021
by Routledge
2 Park Square, Milton Park, Abingdon, Oxon OX14 4RN

and by Routledge
52 Vanderbilt Avenue, New York, NY 10017

Routledge is an imprint of the Taylor & Francis Group, an Informa business

© 2021 Joseph Siegel

The right of Joseph Siegel to be identified as author of this work has been asserted by him in accordance with sections 77 and 78 of the Copyright, Designs and Patents Act 1988.

All rights reserved. No part of this book may be reprinted or reproduced or utilized in any form or by any electronic, mechanical, or other means, now known or hereafter invented, including photocopying and recording, or in any information storage or retrieval system, without permission in writing from the publishers.

Trademark notice: Product or corporate names may be trademarks or registered trademarks, and are used only for identification and explanation without intent to infringe.

British Library Cataloguing-in-Publication Data
A catalog record for this book is available from the British Library

Library of Congress Cataloging-in-Publication Data
A catalog record has been requested for this book

ISBN: 978-0-367-36478-6 (hbk)
ISBN: 978-0-429-34725-2 (ebk)

Typeset in Galliard
by SPi Global, India

To Aki, Ken and Hal

Contents

List of figures	viii
List of tables	x
Preface	xi
List of abbreviations	xiii

1	Notetaking: The gateway academic skill	1
2	Previous research on notetaking in L1 and L2 contexts	25
3	Notetaking from the L2 student perspective	51
4	Principles for evaluating L2 notetaking textbooks	87
5	Pedagogic approaches for L2 notetaking	108
6	Embracing dialogic potential of notes: A new line of sociocultural engagement	129
7	Assessing note quality	146
8	Key insights from classroom research and final thoughts	160
	Index	171

Figures

1.1	A sample of the outline method taken from a classroom listening activity about the Space Race	10
1.2	A diagram of the Cornell notetaking system	11
3.1	Three models of translanguaging in notetaking	65
3.2	Notes taken in short bursts, left to right	71
3.3	Notes with spaces	71
3.4	Notes with spaces and summary words	72
3.5	Notes with arrows	72
3.6	Notes with bullet points	73
3.7	Drifting notes	74
3.8	A vertical pattern with arrows	74
3.9	Two columns	75
3.10	A mind map or word web	76
3.11	Study of fishes (Sample A)	77
3.12	Study of fishes (Sample B)	78
3.13	Study of fishes (Sample C)	78
3.14	Study of fishes (Sample D)	78
3.15	Fish eyes (Sample A)	79
3.16	Fish eyes (Sample B)	79
3.17	Fish eyes (Sample C)	79
3.18	Fish eyes (Sample D)	79
3.19	Gene for sight (Sample A)	80
3.20	Gene for sight (Sample B)	80
3.21	Gene for sight (Sample C)	80
3.22	Big sickness (Sample A)	81
3.23	Big sickness (Sample B)	81
3.24	Big sickness (Sample C)	81
3.25	Big sickness (Sample D)	81
3.26	Separation (Sample A)	82
3.27	Separation (Sample B)	82
3.28	Separation (Sample C)	83

3.29	Separation (Sample D)	83
5.1	Illustrations of stages one – four	115
5.2	Swedish students ($n = 199$) views of each stage	119
5.3	Japanese students ($n = 34$) views of each stage	121
5.4	Preintervention notes (Student A)	122
5.5	Postintervention notes (Student A)	122
5.6	Preintervention notes (Student B)	123
5.7	Postintervention notes (Student B)	123
5.8	Preintervention notes (Student C)	124
5.9	Postintervention notes (Student C)	124

Tables

2.1	Four-stage pedagogic sequence for notetaking	41
3.1	Mode of notetaking	54
3.2	Benefits to concentration and organization	55
3.3	Reasons for taking notes	56
3.4	Aspects that affect ability to take "good" notes	57
3.5	Language choice in notes	58
3.6	Teacher potential in notetaking	59
4.1	Evaluation of *Lecture Ready 2 (2nd edition)*	101
5.1	The Pedagogic Intervention	115
5.2	Pre- and post-intervention test text information	122
7.1	A selection of studies that include transfer of information from notes to a task	151
7.2	Studies from L2 notetaking that include explicit evaluation of notes	154
7.3	Methods for assessment of L2 student note quality	155

Preface

As a language teacher, I have always tried to identify systematic structures and patterns that can help second language (L2) students develop and apply their language abilities. Earlier in my L2 teaching career, I was generally more comfortable providing models, examples, correction, and feedback on language production; that is, when teaching the skills of speaking and writing, I felt like I was "doing something," being an active teacher who could demonstrate language use, provide controlled and freer practice opportunities, and supply guidance and counseling to help students improve in those areas. When it came to receptive skills, however, I typically felt like I was underperforming, and I struggled to emulate the same satisfaction when teaching receptive skills. I started to first ask myself (and then colleagues... and then the literature...), is it possible for receptive skills to be demonstrated and taught in the same explicit ways as productive skills? If so, how? Why?

Notetaking is an essential skill that consists of both receptive (listening) and productive (writing, or to a lesser extent, typing), making it a real challenge to teach, especially in an L2. It is ubiquitous in many corners of education, regardless of whether tuition comes in the form of one's first language or an L2. Students need to listen and write things down, either to help them interact with the input they just heard, to preserve the information for later use, or both. Students may also take notes simply to show their teacher that they are paying attention, working hard, and understanding at least some of the information they are hearing.

Notetaking is also an assumed and misunderstood skill. It is assumed that somewhere along the educational line, every student has developed the ability to take accurate, appropriate, and helpful notes. However, the precise timing and location of this development is seldom explored or articulated, leaving teachers assuming that students have acquired notetaking abilities "somewhere else" prior to entering a present course. The skill is also misunderstood in the sense that teachers may assume that once a student writes something in their notes, they have now learned it and know it from that point on, being able to retain and recall it after one encounter.

Teachers often say things like "write down just the main ideas" or "write down any words you don't know," assuming that students have the capabilities to identify and record these points while they simultaneously listen. Even xii *Preface*

students studying in their first language can struggle with these expectations. Imagine how challenging these ambitions can be when listening to academic English in one's L2, as in the case of countless high school and tertiary students worldwide enrolled in various types of English for academic purposes (EAP) and English-medium instruction (EMI) courses.

My interest in academic notetaking while listening is an offshoot of previous work on L2 listening pedagogy. When I asked colleagues in the English language teaching field how they teach listening, I was surprised that many lacked a systematic approach. Whereas the same qualified and talented teachers had step-by-step, justifiable approaches for teaching productive skills, in which they provided models, examples, correction, and feedback, when it came to listening, the same teachers were often at a loss. They might simply play audio texts multiple times, saying something like "you need to concentrate" or "listen harder next time." *Listen harder next time?* I began thinking: "Is this really the best we can do as a teaching field?". What about systematic approaches? What about models? What about corrective feedback? I felt that the receptive skill of listening was simply glossed over, with too much emphasis placed on the student and too little responsibility taken by the teacher. I wanted to explore how we could improve on the idea that listening simply developed through exposure and the answering of comprehension questions. I felt that I as a teacher could do better.

The same line of thinking led to my interest in notetaking and to notes as artifacts of listening comprehension. Just like "listen harder next time" felt like a flawed statement for a teacher to make, assuming that students could indeed listen harder, I was curious about whether my own instructions "Take notes" and "Write down keywords" were assuming too much about the students in my EAP classes. I wanted to find out more about the many ways that notes can be taken and the variety of strategies and techniques that listeners can employ at several levels during notetaking while listening to academic content. It was this line of thinking, of curiosity about possibilities, and frustrations with my own teaching that stimulated this book and the many classroom-based research projects described within.

A special thanks to all of the EAP and EMI teachers and students who contributed.

Abbreviations

CEFR	Common European Framework for Reference of Languages
CLT	Communicative language teaching
EAP	English for academic purposes
EFL	English as a foreign language
ELF	English as a lingua franca
EMI	English-medium instruction
ESL	English as a second language
IU	information unit
L1	first language
L2	second language
ZPD	zone of proximal development

1 Notetaking
The gateway academic skill

Notetaking in everyday life

People have been recording information they want to remember or to be remembered for tens of thousands of years. From the earliest cave paintings that preserved important images to hieroglyphics written in ancient Egypt to shopping lists scribbled on scraps of paper to notes taken on computers in classrooms, all forms of notetaking have served to provide reminders and stimulate recall of events, tasks, and various other types of information. These days, notes play an often-underappreciated role in several aspects of daily life, in personal, professional, and academic spheres.

Once a person can accomplish basic drawing skills, they begin to communicate messages via "notes," as even when a young child draws a squiggly picture and says it shows their mommy and daddy, they are in a sense creating a note: an item that they created to remind them of or to demonstrate something; in this case, their family. As children transition to the school years, they learn to write, and thus "notes" often become a combination of visual images and written words. Upon reaching junior high school, students are exposed to more written information, and their notes, at least for school, typically begin to contain more and more words.

In high school, class content and ideas become more sophisticated and students are often held accountable for information presented in class by the teacher; thus, their notes become more high stakes, as taking and keeping a good set of notes can lead to academic success. From there, students in many countries enter higher education (e.g., community college or university), where they often must rely on their notetaking abilities to cope with the increased information loads that their teachers expect them to learn. Other young people may enter the workforce, where taking notes also plays an important role in preserving information in order to accomplish tasks (i.e., a restaurant server taking orders or a carpenter building a bookshelf to certain specifications).

At home, notes are always useful ways of keeping family members informed ("Just ran to the store to buy milk. Home soon. XO, Mom") and to remind others and/or yourself ("Charge phone before work!"). Generally speaking,

2 Notetaking

people used to rely on these types of notes written on pieces of paper, but with email and text messaging, much information can be sent directly to individuals.

An introduction to second language (L2) notetaking

While notetaking is noticeable in several avenues of life, the high-stakes nature of higher education, the positive impact that quality notes can have on academic success, and the resonance that such success can have on a student's future calls for specific and in-depth consideration of how notetaking skills develop and are utilized in second language (L2) academic situations. Therefore, this book focuses for the most part on notetaking in academic contexts, and higher education in particular, when the notetaker is listening to a lecture that is given in their L2. Attention to notetaking in English for academic purposes (EAP) and academic skills courses meant to assist students in developing skills needed to succeed in typical educational formats in higher education has increased in recent years. (e.g., listening to and learning from lectures, listening during and participating in seminars, and reading lengthy texts). Furthermore, as the number of university-aged students who attend courses in their L2 increases worldwide, having a book that focuses first and foremost on L2 notetaking (as opposed to having the notetaking be a secondary priority to, for instance, listening skills) and discussing research and various viewpoints related to this crucial ability opens up space for development on several fronts, among them, L2 teachers, English medium instruction (EMI) lecturers, applied linguistic researchers, and L2 students themselves.

This first chapter continues by defining notetaking and accounting for a number of related theoretical perspectives before moving on to consider the roles of different cognitive and language skills (e.g., listening, writing) in the notetaking process. It then details differences between first language (L1) and L2 notetaking before outlining the importance of notetaking with a special focus on EMI and English as a lingua franca (ELF) used worldwide. Most research, examples, and discussion throughout the book center on notetaking in either L1 or L2 English learning contexts, and thus EAP and EMI are often in focus. However, most if not all theoretical concepts and practical teaching techniques are applicable to notetaking in L2s other than English. Several other factors that impact the notetaking act, including cultural aspects, method of notetaking (i.e., traditional pen and paper and digital modes), and teacher options are also introduced. After this overview of notetaking, the book continues by narrowing the focus on research investigations of notetaking in both L1 and L2 educational contexts in Chapter Two. Chapter Three provides perspectives on notetaking generated from students themselves and covers individual aspects that affect notetaking.

The subsequent chapter addresses materials used to teach notetaking, including both commercial and authentic instructional and learning materials. Based on a number of observations that illustrate the drawbacks of some teaching materials, pedagogic perspectives and alternatives for note-taking instruction are introduced in Chapter Five. The potential for dialogic elements of notes is the topic of Chapter Six, which includes transcripts of students discussing their notes together, and analysis of those conversations to demonstrate what original analysis of collaborative discussion based on notes reveals. In Chapter Seven, the issue of note quality and how to determine what "good" notes are is debated, including a review of previous and current methods. The final chapter provides a brief summary and shares closing thoughts.

What are notes?

The previous section described some of the many different types and functions of notes in everyday life. All of them serve to preserve messages and transfer information, either to one's self at a later time or to another person. These messages can be communicated in a number of ways, including symbols, pictures, abbreviations, words, or a combination of these and other options; thus, people writing notes have several techniques available to them. Taking notes is a common part of academic life and has been commonplace in higher education for centuries (e.g., Eddy, 2016). Despite the familiarity with the practice of taking notes, many teachers and students may not have considered in-depth what the process of notetaking really consists of and how to interpret and understand the products of notetaking (i.e., the notes themselves).

According to Piolat, Olive, and Kellogg (2005), notes are "short condensations of a source material that are generated by writing them down while simultaneously listening" (p. 292). This definition is accurate and suitable for several reasons and will be adopted in this book. First, emphasis is placed on taking notes while "listening" to content. Of course, students take notes while reading as well, but those notes tend to be jotted in the margins of books or printouts and may include highlighting or underlining as well. In the case of notetaking while reading, students seldom generate entire pages of notes from scratch and typically prefer to mark their textbooks or print outs. The exception is when books are borrowed from a library or classmate and writing directly on the page would be inappropriate.

Second, the phrase "short condensations" accurately describes the act of selecting relevant information from the source material (in higher education settings, typically the lecture format) and recording it in truncated and more concise fashion. This description excludes verbatim transcription of what the speaker says and suggests, while condensing and transcription are two options for notetakers, condensing and/or paraphrasing in notes is often more effective for learning than verbatim recording (although there is conflicting evidence when it comes to "traditional" longhand pen and paper notetaking compared to computerized notetaking; see Chapter Two for research on this topic). Notetakers do not (or at least should not) attempt

4 Notetaking

to write down 100% of what they hear during a lecture, as this is nearly impossible and also detracts cognitive resources from listening and learning.

The "condensations" can manifest themselves in a number of ways. Words are probably the most common way to record notes, at least at the university level. Other possibilities include drawing pictures, writing abbreviations (which can either be commonly accepted abbreviations or a listener's own creations), and using symbols (such as "@" for "at" or "=" for "equal"). Most people probably use a combination of these techniques, with words occupying the most space, as it can be challenging to capture complex ideas, explanations, or opinions with pictures only, for instance, although sometimes images may be preferable depending on the course or content (Morehead, Dunlosky & Rawson, 2019a). "Words" in notetaking are considered to be "all orthographic units with spaces on each side" (Clerehan, 1995). Words can be evident at several locations within a set of notes: headings, the notes proper, and as labels accompanying a picture or diagram.

The simultaneous nature of notetaking while listening is one of the main obstacles that students (regardless of whether they are listening to their L1 or L2) face when trying to record relevant information from lectures for later learning and use. To take notes, several cognitive and physical actions happen in simultaneous or near-simultaneous fashion. As one sits in a lecture hall with pen and paper ready, the lecture begins, and the student must: listen to the speaker, decipher the messages being delivered, try to distinguish between content that needs to be noted and that which does not (which depends on individuals and tasks or goals), decide how to record the notes (e.g., with symbols, abbreviations, whole words), and finally write the notes, all while continuing to listen out for the next potentially noteworthy point. This cycle is recursive and also includes the notetaker making mental connections to their own background knowledge and to previous notes (Jansen, Lakens & Ijsselsteijn, 2017). As technology advances, some students prefer taking notes with computers and to a lesser extent, tablets and apps. In doing so, they may benefit from faster typing than writing speed, but technology can have negative effects on learning and reduced functionality compared to writing notes by hand as well (see Chapter Two).

Regardless of the method that is chosen, this book adopts the view that notetaking is not a single action but rather a staged, recursive process consisting of multiple steps, all of which are crucial and all of which happen in a very compressed time frame. By taking this multistage perspective, L2 teachers and students can begin to understand and appreciate the enormous complexity of the task. When teachers say "take notes," they may think they are giving a simple instruction; however, the reality is they are making significant demands on their students' faculties, particularly when students are asked to take notes while listening to their L2.

To summarize then, notes are typically shorter than their source texts; are taken *while* listening; and can be taken using one or more styles and methods. Furthermore, the general purpose of notes is to preserve information to compensate for memory limitations as well as to stimulate recall of information during later review. When an individual takes notes, they most likely are concerned with the notes being meaningful for *themselves*; that is, they take notes because they want to remember and/or learn something. They are probably less concerned with whether another person, such as a teacher or fellow student, can access the information in the notes, although there are instances when teachers check and/or assign grades to student notes.

What is notetaking?

In practice, notetaking is the act of recording information in a product-oriented manner. In other words, notes are visible and tangible displays of information recorded by a listener regardless of the method or strategies used to take the notes. Theoretical perspectives underlie notetaking styles and functions as well.

Generative and non-generative

Among the many choices notetakers encounter is the choice between copying the speaker's words in their notes or transforming the speaker's message and writing it in their own words. This is essentially the difference between writing verbatim what is heard and listening to an incoming message and paraphrasing it. In generative notetaking, the listener records notes in their own words; that is, they generate their own interpretation of a speaker's message and avoid writing word-for-word what the speaker has said. This type of notetaking involves more cognitive effort on the part of the notetaker because they are forced to perform more mental tasks than copying verbatim; cognitive load is increased (Jansen et al., 2017). Generative notetaking requires that students listen, comprehend, and search their mental lexicon for synonyms and alternative ways of expressing similar ideas. Then they create a message that is similar to but not precisely the same as that to which they are listening. These generative steps are typically beneficial to processing, retention, and learning of information, as the listener invests more cognitive energy when encoding notes (Piolat, Olive & Kellogg, 2005).

In contrast, non-generative notetaking means that the listener does not construct their own interpretation of the speaker's message. Instead, they rely entirely on writing the speaker's own words, either in part or in full. Non-generative notetaking can be viewed as a comparatively mechanical practice that does not ensure thorough attention to or comprehension of the speaker's output, especially when the speaker talks rapidly and the majority of the listener's energy is put in to trying to copy as much as possible in a hectic and rushed manner. In such cases, the act of non-generative notetaking can be detrimental to cognitive processing of meaning.

It is unlikely that anyone takes notes either using generative or non-generative approaches exclusively. Rather, many students will use a combination

6 Notetaking

of the two, often unconsciously. Factors such as the type of information and the kinds of future tasks for which the notes will be used likely effect which approach is taken. When it comes to pedagogic instruction for notetaking, demonstrating and supporting student development in generative notetaking is the more challenging area, as students may need guidance in interpreting, recasting, and reformulating the messages they hear.

Encoding and storage functions

In theory, notetaking serves two distinct functions for the notetaker. The first occurs in the immediate period during which the notes are taken. As the listener processes the information they hear, they make decisions at multiple levels, both unconscious and conscious. The initial level consists of recognizing the spoken acoustic signal as distinct from other auditory sounds (e.g., the hum of a fan or the ring of a mobile phone). Although many people might not think of this first step, all listeners make the quick distinction between human speech that is intended for them and other sounds being emitted in or by their current environment.

The listener then must distinguish the phonemes they hear, chunk the speech stream into meaning units of information, and accumulate the information to build a larger meaningful structure. This part of the process involves bottom-up processing, in which phonemes combine to form syllabus, which create words, chunks, and utterances (e.g., Buck, 2001; Siegel, 2018a). To do so, listeners rely on their knowledge of the phonological system of the target language (Rost, 2002). In addition, top-down processing is necessary, where listeners apply their background knowledge of both topic and genre, as well as their expectations, both at the linguistic and content levels, to establish predictions of what input is to come (Rost, 2002; Brown, 2011). Upon hearing the speaker's actual words, the listener then mentally compares the actual input with their predications and revises understanding accordingly (e.g., Field, 2008; Siegel, 2015, 2016).

As the aural input is being processed, the notetaker must begin to act. After all, their role is not simply as a listener but as a recorder of information, transferring the information from invisible acoustic form to visible, legible form. They are essentially capturing at least some of the content to preserve it for later purposes. However, as discussed previously, the method for recording that information can be non-generative or generative. For the former, students may write down verbatim what they hear without purposeful processing of the information in what sometimes equates to regurgitation. That is, they are simply reproducing the content word for word without necessarily understanding the meaning. This practice is the written equivalent of mindlessly repeating words without considering or knowing what they mean. Without attaching meaning to the notes at the time of listening, the notetaker may struggle to understand the information at a later date: "through encoding, the learner has linked the material to their existing cognitive structure--[they have] made it meaningful" (DiVesta & Gray, 1972, p. 8).

Notetaking 7

The encoding effect begins with the mental processing of the spoken input. Encoding has more in common with generative notetaking than the non-generative form. In generating representations of spoken information in notes that capture the intended meaning but avoid verbatim copying, the notetaker can increase their comprehension and retention of the information. Manipulating the information by means of, for example, paraphrasing, summarizing, using abbreviations, or word substitution, the listener has engaged actively with the input. By linguistically altering information the notetaker hears and expressing it in their own unique ways, assuming their notes represent the original meaning, deeper processing of the information may lead to more stable learning and recall of information. Depth of processing is defined as the "relative amount of cognitive effort, level of analysis, elaboration of intake, together with the usage of prior knowledge..." (Leow & Mercer, 2015, p. 2). It is in this engagement that benefits of the encoding process lie. The notetaker has invested mental energy in understanding and changing the expression of the content. They have not only transformed the spoken word to a written note but have also imparted their own treatment of that information. Assuming the note they have generated is an accurate representation of the source content, they will, in theory, benefit from the encoding effect (although research findings are sometimes conflicting when it comes to full support for the encoding effect; see Chapter Two for further discussion).

Once the information has been recorded in notes, the notes themselves, whether in paper or digital format, serve as an external storage repository of information. The value of this storage effect manifests itself in the availability of information and written signals to stimulate recall of content. The advantages of the encoding function begin to wane over time, as memory begins to lapse. What was easier to recall closer to the listening event begins to fade into vague notions, which can lead a person to forget, misremember, or lack confidence in their recall. The point when recall begins to diminish is precisely the time when notetakers rely heavily on the storage effect. If they have recorded accurately and provided themselves with signals to stimulate recall of content, then the storage effect works as a timely and practical supplement to the encoding effect, with students reviewing their notes to solidify learning.

The storage function of notes can be effective without active engagement at the encoding stage. It is possible for a person to record notes verbatim, understand little at the time, and then review the transcription to come to fuller comprehension. They may, for instance, reread the transcript with the help of a dictionary and/or translation software. In doing so, they would be reading the transcript at a time distinct from the actual listening/notetaking event; thus, they avoid the immense time pressure put on listening and taking notes during academic lectures. They would have time to read and reread the transcript with less anxiety, which would likely increase confidence along with comfort. Furthermore, DiVesta and Gray (1972) point out that if notes are taken with only the storage function in mind (excluding the encoding

8 *Notetaking*

perspective), then notes are typically taken in a rather mechanical way that often fails to aid comprehension and may in fact prove to be a distraction to the lecture content.

When the encoding and storage functions are both used effectively, they create an ideal situation for learning in which the listener takes full advantage to engage with information at two distinct times: in the immediate time frame as they are exposed to the aural input (i.e., encoding) and in the longer term as they revisit their repositories of information (i.e., storage). They would, in a sense, benefit from both the *process* (i.e., the taking of the notes) and the *product* (i.e., the notes themselves) elements of notetaking (Luo, Kiewra, Flanigan & Peteranetz, 2018).

Academic notetaking

While the theoretical perspectives described above apply to all types of note-taking, the main focus of this book is on notetaking in academic contexts. More specifically, its aim is to examine notetaking practices in EAP courses meant to prepare L2 students for academic EMI lectures in which English is the L2 of at least some of the student body. Such lectures take place in high schools, universities, and postgraduate courses in many countries.

In tertiary education, the most consequential goal is knowledge transfer from lecturers to learners (Lau, Cousineau & Lin, 2016). The emphasis in lectures is generally expected to be on the content the speaker wishes to convey to an audience. The presentation of information during a lecture should be orderly and coherent so as to enable comprehension and memory (Dunkel & Davis, 1994). Since the vast majority of university courses are centered on the academic lecture (Lynch, 2011), notetaking in this particular genre of academic life is particularly important as an object of study.

According to L2 research by Flowerdew and Miller (2000), the lecture is viewed as the most important part of university teaching, with one interviewee describing lectures as "the link between the body of knowledge and the students" (p. 121). As such, the ability to take notes of the crucial information delivered during lectures has often been recognized as the "distinguishing characteristic of learning at university" (van de Meer, 2012, p. 13). As students progress through the school system, increasingly more content is delivered verbally by teachers, and students are typically responsible for learning that material and demonstrating their learning via a variety of tasks. To set the context for this type of notetaking, one must envision a single speaker who delivers a set of information in spoken form, often with the help of visual aids, to a group of listeners. The speaker's purpose is to deliver information in a way that facilitates understanding and presents at least some new, previously unknown content to the listeners, who are there to understand, learn, and retain the information in the short term, likely to put it to use after the listening event (e.g., on a recall test or implemented in an academic assignment).

When taking notes in lecture settings, students are often "on their own" to process the information they hear and record notes in ways meaningful to them. In a conversation or in a small class environment, people can interrupt a speaker and ask for repetition, clarification, and/or reformulation; in other words, listeners have socio-affective strategies (e.g., O'Malley & Chamot, 1990; Oxford, 1990, 2017) available to help them overcome misunderstandings and/or to facilitate comprehension. In lecture environments, listeners typically do not have these tools at their disposal, or at least to much less extent than in discussions or conversations. Even if a lecturer encourages participation and interruption, students may feel social pressure to avoid using them. Therefore, academic notetaking does not typically involve interaction with the speaker.

Academic notetaking is also an activity that takes place in isolation. That is, when a student takes notes, they typically do so in the confines of their own learning space and do not interact with other notetakers. As such, the individual notetaker does not engage with others to check accuracy of notes or to fill in missing pieces of information. When the lecture ends, students leave with the waning knowledge in their heads and the information recorded in their notebooks or on their computers. In this way, notetaking can be viewed as an independent activity that does not necessarily demand cooperation with others. Some researchers have begun to investigate how collaboration can replace isolation in notetaking (e.g., Luo, Kiewra & Samuelson, 2016). Chapter Six expands on the notion of using collaboration to combat the isolated feeling and responsibility of taking notes.

To help prepare students for listening and taking notes during lectures in higher education, many teachers encourage students to develop general academic skills, and notetaking is a major strategy for dealing with the massive amounts of information that students are expected to learn. By recording, organizing, reviewing, and otherwise utilizing information in notes, students can improve their learning outcomes. Due to the complexity of the skill, however, teachers may be underprepared in terms of systematic teaching of listening and notetaking, and students may receive little instruction beyond a simplistic "take notes" (Siegel, 2016, 2019). In other words, in the typical classroom, the skill of notetaking is not broken down into subskills that are achievable to teach and to learn. Much so-called instruction related to notetaking is anecdotal and idiosyncratic, meaning it does not employ a systematic or generalizable framework (e.g., Chaudron, Loschky & Cook, 1994).

When it comes to L2 English classes, such as those that focus on EAP, pedagogy has been similarly ignored. Teachers report lacking the training and competence to deliver notetaking instruction in systematic and effective ways (e.g., Siegel, 2019). Furthermore, many English teaching materials for notetaking, along with teacher manuals, are poorly designed and unhelpful, as noted by Hamp-Lyons, (1983). Yet, note-taking is clearly a beneficial skill to have, both in terms of academic progress and in the workforce. Given the worldwide rise in EMI at universities around the world, and the lack of systematic pedagogy for notetaking in the L2 English teaching and learning field, this book aims to promote understanding of factors that affect L2 notetaking for academic purposes, discuss materials and pedagogy, and generally argue for more attention to this underemphasized yet crucial skill.

Styles and formats

Notes can be taken in a number of systems or in no clear system at all. Decisions or preferences related to notetaking style likely depend on several factors, among them the importance of the information to the listener, the amount of information contained, the purpose for using the notes, the newness or novelty of the information, and the relationships between individual items within the notes. For example, if one is simply jotting down a shopping list for the supermarket, there is a good chance that most of the items are known to the notetaker and that many or all of the items are generally of equal importance; thus, a simple list of single words or phrases (e.g., 1 bag of potatoes), all aligned with the left of the paper, would suffice. In an academic lecture, however, the listener will likely make notes of terms and concepts that are new or indicated as significant, either explicitly or implicitly, by the speaker. A hierarchical structure of information will emerge in which some content relates to and/or is subsumed by other subject matter. In this case, relationships can be indicated by indentations, underlining, drawing arrows, and the like.

Among the most well-known and most widely recognized notetaking formats is the outline format. For this format, main headings are listed with a series of indentations to illustrate the relationship between and among items of information. Larger indentations from the left side of the paper indicate increasingly more detailed information. This format often begins with main headings that lead to subheadings, followed by examples (see Figure 1.1). Hamp-Lyons (1983) observes that the outline format is valuable for its ability to "extend to as many levels of generalization as would ever be necessary" (p. 111). Research has suggested that notes in outline form provide two benefits for information retrieval: (1) the structure that

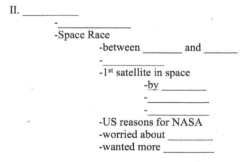

Figure 1.1 A sample of the outline method taken from a classroom listening activity about the Space Race

indicates superordinate to subordinate relationships encourages coherence and (2) each item recorded in notes is linked to at least one other point, thereby creating more global coherence within the notes (Kiewra, Benton, Kim, Risch, Christensen, 1995). From a pedagogic perspective, some teachers either lecturing in their L1 or an L2 provide students with a completed or a skeleton outline that must be filled in during a lecture.

The outline format is often straightforward and can lead both the speaker and the listeners through the information in a predictable manner. A weakness of the outline is its restrictive nature and the challenge of demonstrating relationships between items of information that do not appear close to each other in a given lecture and are therefore separated on the notepaper. Further, many public speakers and lecturers do not speak in the neat, linear fashion represented by the outline format.

A second style of notetaking is the Cornell method (see Figure 1.2), named after Cornell University, where Walter Pauk, an education professor, first introduced it. According to this method (Pauk & Owens, 2014), notepaper is divided into three main sections: a narrow space for keywords and questions down the left-hand side of the paper (the "cue column"); a wider section for notes to the right (the "notetaking column"); and a space for a summary at the bottom of the page. In practice, the listener first takes notes in the "notetaking column." After the listening event, the notetaker then generates questions and extracts keywords, which are written in the "cue column." Finally, the listener is meant to write a brief summary.

This format and learning cycle is meant to engage notetakers with information in a systematic way, offering multiple opportunities to revisit, process, and transfer information. Donohoo (2010) describes a scaffolded process in which the Cornell method can be introduced to students with a goal of their own independent use. Like the outline format, the Cornell method offers a flexible system that can be applied to many genres and various types of subject content. Whereas this format is often the focus of L2 intervention studies (e.g., Tsai & Wu, 2010; Crawford, 2015), L1 university students in

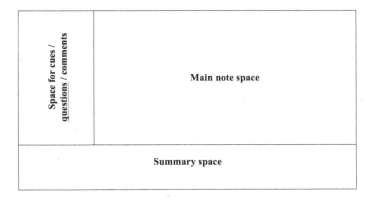

Figure 1.2 A diagram of the Cornell notetaking system (based on Pauk & Owens, 2014)

12 *Notetaking*

Morehead, Dunlosky, Rawson, Blasiman, and Hollis (2019b), only 4% of more than 500 survey respondents reported using the Cornell format.

Hamp-Lyons (1983) provides commentary on several other possible notetaking formats. Among them are the T-formation (p. 118) and the spray chart (p. 120). For the former, the notetaker draws a large capital letter "T" on their paper. The topic or theme is listed at the top of the "T." On the left side, main ideas are listed, and on the right side, specific details and examples are written. This practice allows the notetaker to see the connection between main ideas and supporting details and keeps essential details organized closely with their core topics.

The spray chart is reminiscent of a "mind map" in which the central topic of a lecture is written in the middle of a paper and circled. As the lecture develops, the notetaker draws lines protruding out from the central circle. Main ideas are written directly on top of these lines, and smaller lines with space for supporting details are then drawn under the "main idea" lines. Main idea lines can be numbered so that the notetaker can indicate the sequence of information delivery. This system can be viewed as more random and less structured than the outline, for example, since there is no prescribed order for information to be recorded. In the outline format, the sequence of information is typically clear, with notes at the top of the page having been taken first, and notes at the bottom of the page taken later.

It is important to observe that no single notetaker will use the same style or format of notes on every occasion. Employing one type or another will depend on a number of variables, and many notetakers will be familiar with selecting a style that they are comfortable with and that has generated positive results *in a given situation*. Moreover, notetakers seldom adhere strictly to a formal notetaking style, and jotting notes in margins, or writing additional information outside of the conventions of a given format is common practice (Hamp-Lyons, 1983).

Subskills and impacting factors

Taking notes of any kind can only happen through a sophisticated sequence of events that happens in near simultaneous fashion. This sequence involves cognitive and physical aspects as well as individual language skills, all of which must operate methodically in order to create notes. The level of sophistication of this multifaceted skill is often overlooked and understated when a teacher gives the simplistic instruction "take notes." Such instruction assumes that students already have the ability to do so in effective and efficient ways and therefore many teachers choose to *practice* rather than *teach* notetaking. In order to focus on notetaking from a pedagogic perspective, the subskills and contributing elements that merge during the notetaking process must be identified and articulated. These are all areas where students and teachers could focus their energies in order to develop, maintain, and improve notetaking. The points discussed below are not described in any particular order, although some, such as cognition and listening, typically begin the process and continue throughout, whereas physical factors and writing come later.

Cognitive aspects

Certain subskills involved in notetaking take place only in the mind and are therefore unavailable for direct demonstration or observation. Listening is a precursor to notetaking, and for listening to occur, several cognitive processes, including perception, parsing, and utilization (Clark & Clark, 1977), as well as activation of knowledge sources (e.g., linguistic, pragmatic, discourse, and background) are engaged (Vandergrift & Goh, 2012). When a person listens to a lecture, they must comprehend information and typically employ both bottom-up and top-down listening strategies to do so (e.g., Buck, 2001; Siegel, 2015). They must recognize the input they are listening to so that they can then make decisions about what content to record in notes and how to do so. This ongoing decision-making process occurs throughout the notetaking process and involves the listener differentiating between content that is relevant and important enough to record in notes and that which may be already known (and therefore notes may be redundant) or irrelevant (such as a joke or anecdote the lecturer uses to connect with the audience but which is not relevant to the lecture theme and/or any tasks for which the notes will be used later).

Metacognition

Metacognition includes aspects such as planning for, monitoring, and reflecting on an interaction with language. In terms of notetaking, the planning aspect ideally occurs prior to the notetaking event and includes knowledge of available overall notetaking formats and styles, options for recording individual items in notes (e.g., abbreviation, paraphrasing, etc.), and bringing tools necessary for notetaking (e.g., a pen and paper; a laptop computer with enough battery power to last the duration of the lecture). Organization of and an understanding of the limitations of resources also fall under the planning aspect.

Another metacognitive aspect related to planning is time management. Given the numerous operations that need to happen in rapid succession, the listener would do well to be prepared to engage them all under time pressure. If too much time is spent, for example, on deciding what to write or how to record notes, valuable attention is being diverted from the incoming content, parts of which may be lost due to indecision. The time pressure of taking notes can be relieved through one or more of the following: strong listening comprehension skills; planning about notetaking styles and strategies; practice.

Monitoring comprehension and degree of notetaking success during the actual notetaking event are additional metacognitive aspects that come into play. If, during a lecture, a listener realizes their notetaking strategies are being deployed successfully and they are satisfied that their notes will be useful to them, they should likely elect to continue with their current approaches. However, if they notice that they are not generating the quantity and/or quality of notes that they would like, then they could elect to adapt their approaches and try something new (assuming, of course, they are aware of other options). This monitoring can occur throughout the notetaking session, although the listener may have only brief chances to reflect in this manner due to time constraints and rapidly incoming input. They can also monitor their emotional and anxiety levels, which are particularly significant during the potentially stressful task of taking notes in an L2 through a lecture the content of which may be mostly or completely novel. Finally, monitoring listening and notetaking endurance in an L2 are necessary due to the relatively long time these skills are required during lectures.

Once the notetaking act is complete, the notetaker can read through their notes, consider their comprehension of the lecture, and reflect on their own notetaking performance. They can then identify any areas in which they want to make changes to their approach for the next notetaking opportunity, a consideration that then feeds into another planning stage. This reflective metacognitive stage can be where the notetaker recognizes strengths and weaknesses of their performance and plans to take action to improve (e.g., by increasing exposure to the lecture genre, learning more topic-related vocabulary, and/or adopting different notetaking strategies).

Physical factors

Whereas cognitive and metacognitive aspects operate largely within the mind, physical factors also affect notetaking. When one considers longhand pen and paper notetaking (considered as a traditional approach for the purposes of this book) as well as the more recent development of digital notetaking, having the capabilities to operate these instruments effectively is crucial. Writing and typing speed will drastically affect the quantity, quality, and efficiency of notes. As pointed out by previous research, when taking notes during a lecture, students need to adjust to changes in rate between the speed of the speaker and their own handwriting speed (Peverly, Ramaswamy, Garner, Brown, Sumowski & Alidoost, 2007). Since the notetaker is often under time pressure to complete many tasks almost simultaneously (listen, comprehend, decide what, how, and when to record), having the ability to write and/or type quickly is an advantage. Having this ability would not only generate more notes, but would also give the notetaker confidence in their performance, which could reduce stress and increase attention.

Language skills: Listening

Before notetaking can occur, students need to attend to acoustic signals sent from a speaker through a stream of connected speech (Anderson & Lynch, 1988; Buck, 2001). In terms of lectures, this connected speech stream can be lengthy and uninterrupted, which may cause mental overload and emotional distress related to listening. Several individual processes, including phoneme recognition, morpheme chunking, lexical recognition, and referential procedures, combine on the speech stream throughout listening (Hansen & Jensen, 1994). While some processes are purely aural, visual input may also support the act of listening (Hasan, 2000; Lynch & Mendelsohn, 2002). The multimedia principle put forth by Mayer and Gallini (1990), suggesting that students learn better from words and images than from words alone is certainly a relevant concept in modern lectures. Such support is often available during lectures in the forms of Powerpoint slides, blackboard work, handouts, or references to textbook pages that the student can see. Listening, then, is the successful integration and coordination of these component skills (Rost, Carter & Nunan, 1994; Lynch, 2009). If a student faces challenges at any of these stages of listening, the additional cognitive and physical processes involved in notetaking may be overwhelming and lead to poor notetaking performance.

Language skills: Writing

When the student has listened and identified an item of information they deem worthy of being recorded in notes, their next step is to physically do so by choosing and creating symbols (including alphabetical symbols) to represent that information. Most content in notes is recorded through words, although abbreviations, pictures, charts, and so on are options. When writing (or typing), the notetaker needs to know spelling conventions and sometimes basic grammar in order to reconstruct phrases of varying lengths. Some consideration for how information is organized on the page and notetaking formats can positively influence the writing of notes. For instance, if a notetaker has selected a certain notetaking system, then they can apply it methodically and regularly through writing.

At the production stage, the notetaker needs to decide how and where to record the notes. Should they record a given piece of information verbatim, paraphrase it, or represent it with a picture? If using the outline format, should the given information be a new main heading or a subheading falling under the previous main heading? These types of questions must be addressed, all while continuing to listen.

Language skills: Reading

Reading of notes typically occurs in two different ways. One can happen while the notetaking event is still going on, when the notetaker looks back through the notes they have taken while they are still attending to the present input. They may, for example, flip back a page or two in their notebooks to double check a lecturer's reference to a previously introduced concept or scroll up on their computer to confirm how a new term is spelled. This type of reading may be done in haste and is akin to scanning for certain information for a specific purpose.

16 *Notetaking*

A more holistic type of reading occurs after the notetaking event, when immediate time pressure is not applied. Students read through their notes in order to review content, stimulate recall, and solidify learning. While doing so, they are left only with the notes on the page and their memories to reconstruct the content. As they read, they may add to their notes or identify gaps or questions that they have based on what they have written. Depending on any post-lecture tasks, such as writing a summary, integrating lecture content into a research paper, or preparing for a comprehension test, readers may approach this activation of notes in different ways.

Language choice

The previous sections described what notetaking is, how the process of notetaking occurs at cognitive and physical levels, and the combination of language skills necessary to carry out the multifaceted operation. All of the points presented in previous paragraphs apply to notetaking in both one's L1 or L2. In other words, a person goes through similar processes, from the listening stage to creating notes, irrespective of the language(s) involved.

Linguistic variables that can have large effects on the quantity and quality of notes must also be accounted for. First is the language of input. It may seem a commonsense observation, but when students listen to a lecture in their L1, their comprehension is likely to be higher than if the same lecture content is delivered in their L2. Language choice is also relevant in the actual writing of notes, with some L2 students preferring to translate what they hear and write notes in their L1, while others report that writing notes in the same language that they hear them in (e.g., listening to an English lecture and taking notes in L2 English) is more convenient and less mentally taxing. Translanguaging in student notes is also possible for L2 notetakers, who might blend their languages within the same set of notes (Siegel, 2020). Such students may write most notes in L2 English but use their L1 for information they do not know how to spell in English or that is simpler and clearer for them to record in the L1.

These factors demonstrate how one's language background can affect notetaking behavior and performance. They are also what makes L2 notetaking a unique skill, that it involves the constant interplay between an L2 listener's L1 and L2. *L2 notetaking* for the purposes of this book can involve any one or a combination of the following: when a person listens to their L2 and records information in writing, either in their L1 or L2, in order to stimulate recall after the listening event and/or to use on a post-listening task (e.g., a comprehension test or written summary).

Another consideration is who the audience of notes is. If it is solely for the personal and private use of the notetaker, certain characteristics might be evident in the notes that would not be present if the notes were to be made public in some way. For example, if notes were to be shared with a study group who collaborates after a lecture to review content by combining and revising notes, the individual contributions of each group member may be censored in some way, either consciously or unconsciously, since others beyond the notetaker will be viewing them. Moreover, if the notes are taken for a grade or to submit to the teacher as evidence of attending to lecture content, then the purpose and audience of the notes will likely be taken into account as they are recorded.

Regardless of purpose, audience, and language used to record notes, the act of listening to a lecture in one's L2 poses major challenges that must be overcome even before the act of notetaking can begin. Based on the complex and interrelated combination of macro- and micro-components that comprise lectures, coupled with the fact that many students are listening in their L2, there is no shortage of obstacles to L2 student comprehension in EMI lectures. Among them are the high rate of speech, potentially unfamiliar accents, unknown cultural references, variation in lecturer style, inability to ask for clarification, new terms and concepts, and challenges in taking good notes (e.g., Flowerdew, 1994; Bolton & Kuteeva, 2012; Sheppard, Rice, J., Rice, K, DeCoster, Dummond-Sardell & Soelberg, 2015).

Notetaking within the rise of EMI

The importance and amount of EMI lectures continues to increase as universities worldwide seek to promote internationalization among both the student body and the faculty. With the rise of EMI, student and faculty mobility has increased, allowing for more students to study and for staff to teach in other countries. EMI lectures have become a normal part of academic life for undergraduate students in countries where English is not a native language (e.g., Lynch, 2011; Chang, 2012). This trend has impacted higher education around the world. For example, according to Forsberg's (2018) report in *Universitets Läraren*, nearly 30% of college and university courses in Sweden are conducted in English, and that number is expected to reach 50% within the next 5 years. The trend towards more EMI courses is not unique to Sweden and is common to other parts of Scandinavia as well (e.g., Airey, Lauridsen, Räsänen, Salö & Schwach, 2017). In Asia, countries such as Japan have seen significant increases in the number of universities offering courses and degrees with EMI (Bradford & Brown, 2018).

As EMI has become a priority for global education at the tertiary level, educators and administrators in secondary education are tasked with providing EAP courses meant to prepare L2 English students for EMI. Some universities and colleges also organize and provide EAP bridge courses meant to bridge the gap between secondary and tertiary education in terms of academic English and academic skills. L2 English students who enroll in some universities may be required to pass such prep courses before starting full-time degree courses.

As Dearden (2014) observes, the consequences of using English instead of the L1 on teaching and learning are in need of investigation, and

18   *Notetaking*

Murata (2018) underlines the "relatively unknown territory" (p. 1) of ELF in education. According to respondents in Bolton and Kuteeva's (2012) survey of EMI in Sweden, the English ability of lecturers can vary widely and can have a potentially negative impact, especially on exchange (i.e., non-Swedish) students. In the same report, voices of concern were expressed over teachers whose English includes thick accents that can affect comprehensibility (Bolton & Kuteeva, 2012). Therefore, students must be prepared to cope with listening to and learning from EMI lectures despite the challenges. They can do so, for example, by expanding their use of listening strategies, developing their listening abilities, and increasing their understanding of lecture culture (Flowerdew, 1994). In addition to these general listening endeavors, students can learn and practice specific formats and styles for taking notes in EMI lectures.

Culture and notetaking

Culture is another factor to consider in terms of notetaking practices, expectations in lectures, and EAP/EMI courses. One strand of research has focused on cultural differences related to lecture structure and the roles of the teacher and students in various cultures (e.g., Flowerdew & Miller, 2000). Much of this work has focused on generalizations made between "Eastern" and "Western" views of education. It must be noted that these border on overgeneralizations and should best be interpreted as indicative rather than prescriptive. As cultures blend, as students have multiple experiences with teachers from different parts of the world, as exposure to other cultures increases via the Internet, cultural differences in terms of EMI education are becoming less stark than in the past.

Nevertheless, a typical view of "Eastern" education (for example, Chinese or Japanese) may have the following characteristics: a respectful view of the lecturer, who is not to be questioned; value placed on silence and listening; a group orientation not to disrupt the event (e.g., Flowerdew & Miller, 2000). In contrast, a "Western" view may perceive the lecturer as more of a guide and facilitator than a fountain of knowledge; value is placed on individual interpretation and self-expression; multiple interpretations of the same content may be valued as long as they are justified. These views overlook the fact that other orientations to lecture and lecturer expectations are relevant, and that perspectives from Africa, South America, and elsewhere need to be considered as well, since students and teachers from these continents are also participating actively in EMI.

Technology and notetaking

The development of notetaking preferences and practices have been evolving in recent years, as digital tools such as laptop computers, tablets, and mobile phones have become an integrated part of the classroom learning experience. Notions of traditional pen and paper notetaking are preferred by some for the flexibility and the "authentic" nature of the activity. Some believe that the traditional method aids in their ability to pay attention to input as well as to learn and retain it. For many, there is some unexplainable connection between hearing, feeling a writing instrument in one's hand, and encoding that information in one's own idiosyncratic handwriting. The touch of the pen to paper can indeed be satisfying. Initial research has also suggested that the traditional method generates better results in learning and memory compared to computerized notetaking (e.g., Mueller & Oppenheimer, 2014; see Chapter Two for a synopsis of related research on notetaking and technology).

Various types of digital notetaking are now possible, ranging from typing notes on a physical keyboard to writing notes on a tablet or eWriter with a stylus (e.g., Morehead et al., 2019a). Some students prefer the speed of typing compared to writing as well as the convenience of storing notes electronically, a practice that reduces the chances of notes being lost or damaged. With the advent of cloud sharing, students can save and access their notes from multiple locations as well. Despite these benefits of digital notetaking, some lecturers have put in place rules to limit the use of digital technology in their lecture halls, citing student distraction for both the student as well as those sitting nearby.

In addition to laptops and tablets, a third type of "notetaking" has become common in lecture halls: photos taken with mobile phones or tablets. In some cases, students may rely solely on the photos to be used in place of notes they themselves took. In other cases, the photos form the foundation of notes. This latter use occurs when photos are integrated into a digital notetaking document that also allows for text to be written or typed on or near the photo itself. Photos could also serve the purpose of supplementing notes that the student has taken, either traditionally or digitally. These types of technological advancements may help capture information in the short term but likely also detract from learning and retention if not utilized appropriately. In other words, they may be *too* convenient, tricking the student into thinking they have captured and stored information in an effective way, but in one that glosses over and underutilizes learning opportunities.

Thus far, the discussion of notetaking and technology has only come from the student or listener perspective. Teachers too have a variety of tools to use when delivering their lectures, and often rely on visual aids (in the form of Powerpoint slides, videos, images, and so on). The use of multimodal input can impact a student's lecture comprehension and notetaking ability, and this impact can be positive as is surely intended or can have unintended negative consequences. Students may well benefit from, for example, hearing and reading (on slides) the same message simultaneously. At the same time, listening while watching a series of moving images in a video while trying to write notes could lead to cognitive overload, with the unintended consequence that the main message students are meant to attend to goes unnoticed.

Pedagogic perspectives on notetaking

The myriad and wide-ranging factors discussed so far in this chapter demonstrate the multifaceted skill that is notetaking. And not just in terms of an L2 user's language proficiency and academic competence but also in the organization and production of the speaker as well as technological and cultural concerns. The culmination of these topics leads to one most relevant question upon which to focus the remainder of this book, a central underlying motivation: how can the L2 teacher prepare their students to develop notetaking skills for success in academic contexts where a language other than their L1 is used as the medium of instruction (i.e., EMI)?

Numerous considerations can be taken into account when discussing pedagogy for L2 notetaking (Siegel, 2018b). One is responsibility: who is responsible for teaching learners to take notes? This question leads to further queries: should notetaking skills be developed in L1 contexts, for example, during junior and/or high school years? If so, then do notetaking abilities in the L1 automatically transfer to an L2 context? Or should the L2 EAP teacher be responsible for notetaking *in the L2*? Does the EAP teacher need to *teach* notetaking or merely provide *practice* opportunities?

It seems as if many L2 educators fall into the trap of thinking they teach notetaking when, more likely, they follow a process like this: 1. Play an audio or video text in class; 2. Tell students to "take notes"; 3. Move on to a discussion activity. In such a sequence, the notetaking and the notes are seldom the focus of instruction. Neither the process nor the product of notetaking is utilized to full capacity. Commercial notetaking materials have been published by companies in the English language teaching (ELT) world in an attempt to provide more systematized and specific support for teachers to use in their classes (see Chapter Four for a more comprehensive discussion of commercial materials). Still, scaffolded and pedagogically sound teaching practices for L2 notetaking development are rarely found in EAP classrooms, which is a major drive for this book: to highlight the challenges of teaching students to take notes in an L2, for supporting the development of L2 notetakers, and to attempt to address these issues through classroom research in order to broaden pedagogic options available to teachers, thereby better equipping students for their futures as L2 notetakers.

Chapter summary

This chapter has moved from a broad and general description of what notes are and what notetaking is to focus on notetaking for academic purposes with an emphasis on doing so in an L2. The concepts of notes and notetaking are likely more difficult to pin down and articulate than the average person expects. Almost every adult has, at one time or another, in one of a variety of formats, taken notes. Yet, despite the simplicity we may attach to taking notes, when one stops and considers the immensely complex nature of the skill, one can recognize the numerous challenges that a notetaker can face.

The number and combination of cognitive, linguistic, and physical skills, plus time pressure and L2 obstacles, make lecture listening a challenge for L2 users. EAP instruction and published textbooks have made strides in preparing students to reach their L2 listening comprehension, notetaking, and learning goals in EMI in higher education. However, notetaking is often treated as an assumed skill; that is, teachers do not break it down into manageable sized tasks and subskills that they can teach and that students can develop as discrete learning points. Instead, vague and presumptive missives like "take notes" and "write down keywords" are employed with seemingly little thought to the large and often undeveloped task being asked of students. Given the high stakes of attending and learning from academic lectures, informed and pedagogically sound approaches for teaching notetaking are required.

Now that several factors affecting notetaking have been introduced and a foundation from which the subsequent chapters can proceed has been set, Chapter Two provides an overview of notetaking research involving both L1 and L2 perspectives with a particular focus on how far research has come regarding L2 notetaking in academic contexts. It opens by outlining the various components that make up a lecture, and provides a brief overview of research on the genre of the academic lecture, which has implications for lecture comprehension and notetaking. Chapter Three then discusses notetaking from the L2 student perspective, providing insights on challenges faced and strategies utilized by such students.

The book then takes a more pedagogic focus in Chapter Four by providing a list of criteria for evaluating the usefulness of commercially produced textbooks and providing an illustrative example of such evaluation. Following on this discussion of materials, Chapter Five describes a flexible pedagogic approach to notetaking that can be applied to any text, commercial, semi-authentic, or authentic. Chapter Six examines the potential of using student notes as a dialogic stimulus for student to student learning in terms not only of lecture content but collaboration and notetaking strategies as well. The theme of Chapter Seven is quality of notes and elements that instructors and students need to consider when deciding on the value of notes. Finally, a summary and future research directions are described in Chapter Eight.

Throughout the book, authentic samples of student notes from a range of academic contexts are presented and discussed with the aim of drawing attention to the much needed but currently undervalued, under-researched, and exploratory area of L2 notetaking from a classroom research perspective.

References

Airey, J., Lauridsen, K. M., Räsänen, A., Salö, L., & Schwach, V. (2017). The expansion of English-medium instruction in the Nordic countries: Can top-down university language policies encourage bottom-up disciplinary literacy goals?. *Higher Education*, 73(4), 561–576.

Anderson, A., & Lynch, T. (1988). *Listening*. Oxford: Oxford University Press.

22 Notetaking

Bolton, K. & Kuteeva, M. (2012). English as an academic language at a Swedish university: Parallel language use and the 'threat' of English. *Journal of Multilingual and Multicultural Development*, 33(5), 429–447.

Bradford, A., & Brown, H. (2018). Introduction: English-medium instruction in Japanese higher education. In A. Bradford & H. Brown (Eds.), *English-medium instruction in Japanese higher education: Policy, challenges and outcomes* (pp. xvii–xiii). Bristol: Multilingual Matters.

Brown, S. (2011). *Listening myths*. Ann Arbor, MI: University of Michigan Press.

Buck, G. (2001). *Assessing listening*. Cambridge, England: Cambridge University Press.

Chang, Y.Y. (2012). The use of questions by professors in lectures given in English: Influences of disciplinary cultures. *English for Specific Purposes*, 31, 103–116.

Chaudron, C., Loschky, L., & Cook, J. (1994). Second language listening comprehension and lecture note-taking. In J. Flowerdew & L. Miller (Eds.), *Academic listening: Research perspectives* (pp. 75–92). Cambridge: Cambridge University Press.

Clark, H., & Clark, E. (1977). *Psychology and language: An introduction to psycholinguistics*. Orlando, FL: Harcourt Brace Jovanovich.

Clerehan, R. (1995). Taking it down: Notetaking practices of L I and L2 students. *English for Specific Purposes*, 14(2), 137–155.

Crawford, M. (2015). A study on note taking in EFL listening instruction. In P. Clements, A. Krause, & H. Brown (Eds.), *JALT2014 conference proceedings* (pp. 416–424). Tokyo: JALT.

Dearden, J. (2014). *English as a medium of instruction: A growing global phenomenon*. Oxford: University of Oxford Press.

DiVesta, F. & Gray, S. (1972). Listening and note taking. *Journal of Educational Psychology*, 63(1), 8–14.

Donohoo, J. (2010). Learning how to learn: Cornell notes as an example. *Journal of Adolescent and Adult Literacy*, 54(3), 224–227.

Dunkel, P., & Davis, J. (1994). The effects of rhetorical signaling cues on the recall of English lecture information by speakers of English as a native or second language. In J. Flowerdew & L. Miller (Eds.), *Academic listening: Research perspectives* (55–74). Cambridge: CUP.

Eddy, M. D. (2016). The interactive notebook: How students learned to keep notes during the Scottish enlightenment, *Book History*, 19(1), 86–131.

Field, J. (2008). *Listening in the language classroom*. Cambridge: Cambridge University Press.

Flowerdew, J. (1994). Research of relevance to second language lecture comprehension-an overview. In J. Flowerdew & L. Miller (Eds.), *Academic listening: Research perspectives* (pp. 7–29). Cambridge: Cambridge University Press.

Flowerdew, J. & Miller, L. (2000). Chinese lecturers' perceptions, problems and strategies in lecturing in English to Chinese-speaking students. *RELC*, 31(1): 116–138.

Hamp-Lyons, L. (1983). Survey of materials for teaching advanced listening and note-taking. *TESOL Quarterly*, 17(1), 109–122.

Hasan, A. S. (2000). Learners' perceptions of listening comprehension problems. *Language Culture and Curriculum*, 13(2), 137–153.

Hansen, C., & Jensen, C. (1994). Evaluating lecture comprehension. In J. Flowerdew & L. Miller (Eds.), *Academic listening: Research perspectives* (pp. 241–268). Cambridge: Cambridge University Press.

Jansen, R., Lakens, D., & Ijsselsteijn, A. (2017). An integrative review of the cognitive costs and benefits of note-taking. *Educational Research Review*, 22, 223–233.

Kiewra, K., Benton, S., Kim, S., Risch, N., & Christensen, M. (1995). Effects of note-taking format and study technique on recall and relational performance. *Contemporary Educational Psychology*, 20, 172–187.

Lau, K., Cousineau, J., & Lin, C.-Y. (2016). The use of modifiers in English-medium lectures by native speakers of Mandarin Chinese: A study of student perceptions. *Journal of English for Academic Purposes*, 21, 110–120.

Leow, R., & Mercer, J. (2015). Depth of processing in L2 learning: theory, research, and pedagogy. *Journal of Spanish Language Teaching*, 2(1), 69–82.

Luo, L., Kiewra, K., & Samuelson, L. (2016). Revising lecture notes: How revision, pauses, and partners affect note taking and achievement. *Instructional Sciences*, 44, 45–67.

Luo, L., Kiewra, K. A., Flanigan, A. E., & Peteranetz, M. S. (2018). Laptop versus longhand note taking: Effects on lecture notes and achievement. *Instructional Science*, 46(6), 947–971.

Lynch, T. (2009). *Teaching second language listening.* Oxford: Oxford University Press.

Lynch, T. (2011). Academic listening in the 21st century: Reviewing a decade of research. *Journal of English for Academic Purposes*, 10, 79–88.

Lynch, T., & Mendelsohn, D. (2002). Listening. In N. Schmitt (Ed.), *An introduction to applied linguistics* (pp. 193–210). London: Arnold.

Mayer, R., & Gallini, J. (1990). When is an illustration worth ten thousand words? *Journal of Educational Psychology*, 82, 715–726.

Morehead, K., Dunlosky, J., & Rawson, K. A. (2019a). How much mightier is the pen than the keyboard for note-taking? A replication and extension of Mueller and Oppenheimer (2014). *Educational Psychology Review*, 31(3), 753–780.

Morehead, K., Dunlosky, J., Rawson, K., Blasiman, R., & Hollis, R. (2019b). Note-taking habits of 21st century college students: Implications for student learning, memory, and achievement. *Memory.* 27(6), 807–819.

Mueller, P., & Oppenheimer, M. (2014). The pen is mightier than the keyboard: Advantages of longhand over laptop note taking. *Psychological Science*, 25(6), 1159–1168.

Murata, K. (2018). Exploring EMI in higher education from an ELF perspective: Introduction. In K. Murata (Ed.), *English medium instruction from an English as a lingua franca perspective* (pp. 1–12). London: Routledge.

O'Malley, J., & Chamot, A. (1990). *Learning strategies in second language acquisition.* Cambridge: Cambridge University Press.

Oxford, R. (1990). *Language learning strategies: What every teacher should know.* Boston, MA: Heinle & Heinle.

Oxford, R. (2017). *Teaching and researching language learning strategies* (2nd edition). New York: Routledge.

Pauk, W., & Owens, R. (2014). *How to study in college* (11th edition). Boston, MA: Wadsworth Cengage Learning.

Peverly, S. T., Ramaswamy, V., Brown, C., Sumowski, J., Alidoost, M., & Garner, J. (2007). What predicts skill in lecture note taking?. *Journal of Educational Psychology*, 99(1), 167–180.

Piolat, A., Olive, T., & Kellogg, R. (2005). Cognitive effort during note taking. *Applied Cognitive Psychology*, 19, 291–312.

Rost, M. (2002). *Teaching and researching listening.* Essex, England: Longman.

Rost, M., Carter, R., & Nunan, D. (1994). *Introducing listening.* London: Penguin.

24 Notetaking

Sheppard, B., Rice, J., Rice, K., DeCoster, B., Dummond-Sardell, R., & Soelberg, N. (2015). Re-evaluating the speaking and listening demands of university classes for novice international students. *ORTESOL Journal*, 32, 1–12.

Siegel, J. (2015). *Exploring listening strategy instruction through action research.* Basingstoke, UK: Palgrave Macmillan.

Siegel, J. (2016). A pedagogic cycle for EFL note-taking. *English Language Teaching Journal*, 70(3), 275–286.

Siegel, J. (2018a). Top down and bottom up listening strategies. In J. Liontas (Ed.), *TESOL encyclopedia of english language teaching.* Hoboken, NJ: Wiley.

Siegel, J. (2018b). Notetaking in ELT: Highlighting contrasts. *TESOL Journal*, 10(1), 1–5.

Siegel, J. (2019). Collaborative action research on notetaking: Simultaneous cycles. *The European Journal of Applied Linguistics and TESOL*, 9(1), 77–100.

Siegel, J. (2020). Appreciating translanguaging in student notes. *ELT Journal*, 74(1), 86–88.

Tsai, T., & Wu, Y. (2010). Effects of note-taking instruction and note-taking languages on college EFL students' listening comprehension. *New Horizons in Education*, 58(1), 120–132.

Van de Meer, J. (2012). Students' note-taking challenges in the twenty-first century: Considerations for teachers and academic staff developers. *Teaching in Higher Education*, 17(1), 13–23.

Vandergrift, L., & Goh, C. (2012). *Teaching and learning second language listening.* New York: Routledge.

2 Previous research on notetaking in L1 and L2 contexts

Several strands of notetaking research

Previous research on notetaking comprises four distinct strands: one that focuses exclusively on L1 notetaking; another than involves L1 and L2 notetaking and comparisons thereof; a third that concentrates on L2 notetaking and related instructional practices; and a relatively new strand that investigates how digital innovations impact notetaking with heavy emphasis on L1 contexts. All four strands are relevant to notetaking in EAP and EMI to greater or lesser extents. Moreover, all of these avenues contribute in different, albeit sometimes rather obvious ways, to the collective knowledge base on notetaking. Within these stands, studies have focused on the encoding and storage functions, on habits, preferences, and intentions of students, on pedagogic interventions aimed at improving performance, on the impact of technology, and on the use of notes for post-listening tasks. This last area stands in contrast to research on notes themselves (i.e., studies that have investigated note quality per se rather than examining the extent to which those notes were used on a different task, such as a post-listening comprehension test or writing activity).

While notetaking is invariably linked to listening proficiency and comprehension, which are especially important for L2 students attending EMI lectures, scholarly and pedagogic works on L2 listening typically only gloss over notetaking and fail to recognize the complexity and multifaceted nature of the skill. In Oxford's (1990) practitioner-friendly book on language learning strategies, notetaking is mentioned as one cognitive strategy for listening. However, notetaking is not discussed in detail and is treated as an "assumed" skill; that is, when an L2 teacher tells students to "take notes", the assumption is that the student is already aware of and proficient in the multiplicity of subskills as well as the various elements, factors, and choices involved (see Chapter One). Little pedagogic advice on notetaking is provided. In the same year, O'Malley and Chamot (1990) also briefly mention notetaking but fail to problematize the skill in any meaningful way for students, teachers, or researchers. Later influential works on L2 listening pedagogy and research (e.g., Flowerdew & Miller, 2005; Field, 2008) fail to mention notetaking. While notetaking is discussed briefly in more recent

26 *Previous research on notetaking*

works (e.g., Vandergrift & Goh, 2012; Graham & Santos, 2015), the concept remains treated as a "given" and is not adequately covered in relation to skill complexity. Pedagogic options for L2 notetaking do not seem to be priorities, as if EAP teachers already know what to do. Scaffolded and clear pedagogic options are absent. In fairness to these works, space constraints may have restricted the authors' capacity to allocate more attention to notetaking. For teachers and students, particularly those working in EAP, more work (both research and practice-oriented) would prove helpful.

Before reviewing literature on lecture notetaking, it is important to consider the contexts in which the activity takes place. Therefore, the subsequent section provides an overview of research into the academic lecture genre and related issues, after which the chapter summarizes studies conducted in L1 contexts, those that compare L1 and L2 notetakers, intervention studies from L2 contexts, and finally, those from the developing avenue of research that focuses on technology and notetaking, mostly in L1 environments.

EMI lectures: The genre and norms

Various lecture styles have been identified and detailed through previous investigations. These include the reading style, conversation style, and rhetorical style (Dudley-Evans & Johns, 1981, cited in Dudley-Evans, 1994) and the memorization, reading aloud, and fresh talk styles (Goffman, 1981, cited in Chang, 2012). However, interactive lecturing has become the prominent method of lecturing, which includes more dialogue between lecturer and audience and more reactionary responses from the lecturer (e.g., Chang, 2012).

The genre of the university lecture, however, is neither a uniform nor an objective domain, and the same applies to EMI lectures. A typical lecture generally consists of a variety of different phases and/or segments arranged in one of several different ways. The selection and sequence of these segments likely depends on discipline, content, and individual lecturer style (the following subsection expands on different parts of a lecture). In addition, lectures are "value-laden discourses" (Lee, 2009, as cited in Lynch, 2011, p. 81) in which lecturers, through their choice of expressions, timing, sequencing, et cetera, evaluate and appraise the information they share with students. That is, the lecturer's personal views will, at least at times, be evident in their choices of expression, which can, in turn, affect student comprehension and interpretations of value of the information. Both the structure of the lecture and the individual speech moves that build up the structure and content can affect notetaking in either positive or negative ways, and these effects likely vary by individual student.

Lecturers operating in EMI environments do not always make accommodations for their L2 English user audiences. An extreme example comes from Griffiths and Beretta (1991), who analyzed English lectures given by the same teachers to three groups of students: (1) L1 English users; (2) high-proficiency L2 English users; and (3) low-proficiency L2 English users.

Results showed that the teachers made no significant modifications to their spoken delivery, rate of speech, pausing patterns, and utterance construction based on the different groups to whom they spoke. In a study focused on physics lectures conducted in both English and Swedish, Airey and Linder (2006) found that the L1 Swedish students comprehended and participated less in the EMI versions of lectures than in the Swedish versions. Students also took fewer notes in the EMI compared to the Swedish lectures, demonstrating that the language in which a lecture is given impacts student confidence, engagement, and learning. More recent studies have focused on particular aspects of lecturers' spoken production, for example, use of questions (Chang, 2012), modifiers (Lau, Cousineau & Lin, 2016), and metaphors (Littlemore, Chen, Koester & Barnden, 2011) during lectures.

Macro and micro components of lectures

Lectures consist of various organizational and linguistic elements that range from broad to specific structures. Previous research has identified and elaborated on overall lecture organizational styles, including the problem-solution pattern and a style that focuses on linking experimental data to theory and vice versa (e.g., Dudley-Evans, 1994). Young (1994) outlined a set of macro-structures in lectures that can serve as a standard pattern of the lecture genre, which includes the following phases: announcing, discourse structuring, interaction, theory or content, examples, conclusion, and evaluation, although the sequence of these components will inevitably vary. Findings from analysis of a lecture corpus showed some consistency for these macro-phases among different disciplines, and Young (1994) suggests that L2 learners preparing for EMI be made explicitly aware of these common structures. It is important to note that these phases are not as clear-cut as an over-simplistic beginning, middle, end structure (such as that often found in academic essays), and that "each strand is interspersed with others, so that what emerges is a continual interweaving of threads of discourse which forms a macro-structure" (Young, 1994, p. 172). Shifts between these phases are typically marked by topic shift markers, which provide a structural basis that can be used to separate a lecture into smaller, more discrete sections or parts. The more explicit these topical shift markers are, the more beneficial they are to notetakers. Conversely, when topical changes are made subtly, they may go unnoticed by members of an L2 audience.

Within each phase, lecturers make specific language choices that affect message delivery and therefore student interpretation and comprehension. At the smallest micro-component level is the phoneme, the individual sounds that the lecturer produces to form clusters, words, utterances, and so on. The speaker's accent, rate of speech, and pausing patterns are important micro-features that affect comprehension. Recent research has moved away from the overall structural features of a lecture (i.e., macro-sections) to focus on specific micro-components lecturers' use. Part of a study by Sheppard, Rice, Rice, DeCoster, Dummond-Sardell, and Soelberg (2015)

28 *Previous research on notetaking*

concentrated on listener perceptions of lecturer output in EMI at the phoneme level (e.g., through reductions such as blending, elision, and deletion). At the utterance level, Chang (2012) investigated the teachers' questioning patterns in EMI lectures and suggests that students be aware of the "underlying logic of the use of questions" (p. 113) in order to maximize their understanding. Another study (Lau, Cousineau & Lin, 2016) explored EMI lecturers' use of pragmatic force modifiers (e.g., actually, just, kind of) and found that student perceptions of pragmatic force modifier usage did not match the lecturers' intended usage, leading to misunderstandings. At the level of utterance, students also need to be able to distinguish relevant from nonrelevant output (e.g., jokes, digressions, asides) unrelated to the main lecture theme (e.g., Flowerdew, 1994).

Based on the complex and interrelated combination of macro- and micro-components that comprise lectures, coupled with the fact that many students are listening in their L2, there is no shortage of obstacles to L2 student comprehension in EMI lectures. Among them are the high rate of speech, potentially unfamiliar accents, unknown cultural references, variation in lecturer style, inability to ask for clarification, new terms and concepts, and challenges in taking good notes. According to respondents in Bolton and Kuteeva's (2012) survey of EMI in Sweden, the English ability of lecturers can vary widely and can have a potentially negative impact, especially on exchange (i.e., non-Swedish) students. In the same report, voices of concern were expressed over teachers whose English includes "thick" accents that can affect comprehensibility (Bolton & Kuteeva, 2012). Students must be prepared to cope with listening to and learning from EMI lectures despite the challenges. They can do so by, for example, expanding their use of listening strategies, developing their listening abilities, and increasing their understanding of lecture culture (Flowerdew, 1994). And in order to both facilitate comprehension (e.g., via the encoding effect described in Chapter One) and to create an effective repository of content knowledge to use for recall, review and other future tasks, notetaking can be a powerful strategy for students.

A review of review articles

Several review articles have focused on notetaking research in recent decades. These works have examined large batches of papers on the topics of L1 and L2 notetaking, aiming to provide overviews of the current state of research at a specific point in time, give teachers the most up to date thinking on the topic, and outline directions for future research. Two such papers (Dunkel, 1988a; Crawford, 2016), written almost 30 years apart, are worth examining in terms of where they overlap and where they differ. Doing so helps us understand how far L2 notetaking research has come as well as issues that still plague this specific area of L2 teaching and learning.

Dunkel's (1988a) review of the literature focuses first on findings from L1 research and considers the ways in which those findings may be applicable to the relatively (at that time) new area of L2 academic notetaking. The paper reports findings from L1 research over the previous six decades that demonstrate the positive effects of both the process and the product of notetaking have on learning and recall, highlighting in particular the combination of note*taking* and review (i.e., encoding and storage) that leads to the strongest and most stable learning. As Dunkel (1988a) observes, the act of notetaking presents itself as appealing to students and teachers alike (p. 14). She raises the issue of whether encouraging findings from L1 research will transfer to notetaking in the L2 and points out the dearth of research comparing notetaking in these two contexts. At the end of her article, Dunkel (1988a) provides a list of axioms of good notetaking and pedagogy, including showing notetakers different styles that are more or less suitable for different types of information, recognizing lecture signposts, and understanding overall lecture organization, many of which resonate for teachers and notetakers today.

Crawford's (2016) summary of the field adopts a more pedagogically focused perspective, although it, like Dunkel's (1988a), also highlights the process (i.e., encoding) and product (i.e., storage) functions of notes and the findings that research has contributed to understanding the two areas. The fact that both authors cover the same ground almost three decades apart suggests that the issues of exactly how and to what extent encoding and storage aid listeners, especially those operating in an L2, are still unresolved. In the nearly 30 years between Dunkel's (1988a) article and Crawford's (2016) piece, a number of important developments have taken place in relation to L2 notetaking. One expansion has been the increase in intervention studies in EAP courses in which teachers aimed to explicitly target notetaking through pedagogic change. The second has been the availability of digital notetaking, something that had not come about at generally accessible levels when Dunkel wrote her review. Regarding the former, Crawford (2016) reports that several studies conducted in a variety of contexts (e.g., Hayati & Jalilifar, 2009, Iran; Tsai & Wu, 2010, Taiwan, and Crawford, 2015, Japan) have all demonstrated improvements in student notetaking proficiency following an instructional period. On the topic of digital notetaking, citing several L1 studies, Crawford (2016) emphasizes that despite the ability to type more words verbatim, the processing and paraphrasing that often occurs when writing notes by hand typically leads to better learning and retention.

L1 notetaking research has also generated meta-analysis articles, and these too shed light on issues that potentially impact L2 notetaking. Kobayashi (2005), for instance, in his review of 57 notetaking versus no notetaking comparison studies, reinforces the overall positive effect of notetaking compared to not taking notes, although the effect was modest (p. 253). Also suggested in the article is the notion that more generative notetaking has a positive impact on the encoding effect (p. 254). The next year, Kobayashi (2006a) published a second meta-analysis that focused on the effects of interventions on L1 notetaking and observed a modest effect when comparing notetaking in intervention and nonintervention conditions. In a separate analysis, Kobayashi (2006b) reported that interventions for notetaking

30   *Previous research on notetaking*

yielded greater effects for those with lower school level compared to those with higher levels of education. In general, the takeaway from these L1 meta-analyses and their applicability to L2 notetaking are as follows: (1) that notetaking positively affects learning and recall; (2) both the encoding and storage functions are valuable; and (3) that pedagogic interventions demonstrate improvements to student notetaking performance. Based on this and other work, L2 educators, particularly those working in EAP and EMI preparation, have begun to undertake similar studies involving L2 learners.

While overview articles offer a solid research-based foundation from which to start, particularly in examining what research has elucidated in the past and how those compare to more contemporary reviews, a number of specific issues deserve recognition, either from the L1 or the L2 perspective, or both. Therefore, the following section provides some insight into major areas in notetaking research, covering investigations from both relevant L1 and L2 contexts. Topics covered include student habits, the encoding and storage functions, the effects of pedagogic interventions, and transfer of information from notes to post-listening tasks.

Research on L1 and L2 notetaking

A historical perspective

As pointed out in Eddy (2016), notetaking has been a common practice for centuries, particularly in higher education, and it grew in importance as the demographics of universities began to change in the 1750s. Around that time, students from more working-class and less-privileged families joined those from elite families (Matthew, 1966). Summarizing various studies that focused on notetaking in several European countries, Eddy (2016) reports that varied techniques and approaches to notetaking were taking place in a number of countries, and early notes written in those contexts have become objects of study for historians interested in writing, learning, and academia. Even hundreds of years ago, students were employing techniques such as underlining, annotating, and drawing in their notes (Eddy, 2016). Some notetakers in Scotland in the mid-18th and early 19th centuries employed a systematic three-stage procedure for notetaking that involved: (1) attempting to take notes verbatim by recording as much as possible during a lecture; (2) recopying the original notes for clarity and neatness to improve readability; and (3) editing notes. Some students also worked collaboratively after the lecture to fill in gaps in their notes (Eddy, 2016).

While it might seem intuitive that taking notes during a lecture would lead to better performance on tests of lecture content than not taking notes, that notion was only tested and supported by empirical evidence about 100 years ago (Crawford, 1925). In research involving over 200 L1 English university students studying at universities in the US, Crawford (1925) demonstrated the positive correlation between taking notes and quiz scores. In other words, the better the quality of notes, the better the performance on quizzes.

This research serves to provide evidence for the long-held belief that taking and/or having notes to review leads to better academic performance. Note that Crawford's (1925) early work did not differentiate whether it was the actual taking of notes (i.e., the encoding function) or the reviewing of notes (i.e., the storage function) that proved the more valuable. Other later strands of research developed this distinction, as described below. The following sections provide a more in-depth look at various aspects of notetaking research.

Encoding research

As detailed in Chapter One, the encoding function of the notetaking act serves to engage listeners with aural content and in theory improves learning and recall through the act of transferring information from the spoken to the written format. One strand of research, particularly in L1 contexts, has explored the assumed value of the encoding function. Survey research on L1 student notetaking behaviors (e.g., Morehead, Dunlosky, Rawson, Blasiman & Hollis, 2019a) observes that the most relevant aspects of notetaking that concern encoding are (a) the method students use to record notes (i.e., pen and paper or digital options) and (b) the extent to which students try to organize notes *as they are taken* (p. 2) (in contrast to reorganizing notes after the notetaking event). Findings of the survey ($n = 577$) show that 86% of respondents take notes with a notebook, 46% use a laptop and only 1% ($n = 7$) reported using a tablet. In terms of organization, the bullet list/ outline was the most common answer, at 85%, with rephrasing/paraphrasing at 36%, mapping at 6%, and the Cornell method at 4%. These findings indicate that the linear, top to bottom, sequential nature of bullet points and/or the outline format, along with indentation features to indicate significance and relationships between information (i.e., the main idea-supporting detail-example relationship) remains the preferable organization.

Kobayashi (2005) conducted a meta-analysis of notetaking intervention studies in L1 contexts and found a modest but positive overall effect of interventions on the encoding ability of subjects involved in the studies reviewed. In addition, post-listening test results from L1 students in Morehead et al. (2019b) showed a no-notes group performing at similar levels to those who took notes, findings that draw into question support for the impact of encoding.

As use of English as lingua franca in higher education began to spread rapidly during the 1980s, so too did research agendas begin to examine the relationship of research on academic English usage in L1 contexts to L2 learning and EAP in particular. This new avenue was most likely stimulated by a desire to theorize, justify, and improve the many EAP and English for specific purposes (ESP) courses that were being developed and are now commonplace worldwide. A line of research spearheaded by Patricia Dunkel (e.g., Dunkel, 1988b; Dunkel, Mishra & Berliner, 1989) and others sought to investigate how L1 and L2 notetaking performance was similar and distinct. Dunkel (1988b) showed that both good L1 and L2 notetakers were

32 *Previous research on notetaking*

able to produce notes that compacted large amounts of important information within a small space or a small amount of words/symbols, what Dunkel refers to as "terseness of notations" (1988b, p. 270). The author further states that an approach to write down as much as possible (i.e., writing verbatim) may not result in the effective encoding of lecture content. In Dunkel, Mishra, and Berliner (1989), the researchers examined the influence of short-term memory on encoding of both an L1 and an L2 group of notetakers. Results indicated that encoding without review may not be sufficient to ensure learning and recall regardless of whether the student listens and takes notes in their L1 or L2. In other words, notes need to be reviewed after the notetaking event in order to strengthen their effectiveness.

Clerehan (1995) also investigated the differences between L1 and L2 notetaking performance from a cross-cultural perspective and found that L1 and L2 students recorded important elements in their notes. In addition, both groups used similar encoding strategies, including use of indenting, spacing, numbers, underlining, and bullet pointing. These similarities lead to tentatively conclusions that notetaking instruction conducted in the L1 likely contains universally adaptable strategies and that some overlap in the encoding strategies adopted for L1 and L2 notetaking exists, regardless of student background. However, this study also highlighted important distinctions between L1 and L2 notetakers. In particular, L2 notetakers took fewer notes on the whole, and the L2 group also struggled to differentiate between different "levels" of information (e.g., titles, main headings, definitions, and examples). For example, the L2 group recorded only 19% of main ideas from the lecture material. Somewhat surprisingly, the end of term test scores were almost the same between the L1 and L2 groups, which may have been affected by factors such as working memory capacity and test construction.

In another cross-cultural study comparing L1 and L2 notetaking, this time involving L2 intermediate French learners (Barbier, Roussey, Piolat & Olive, 2006), the extent to which students use similar or distinct techniques when taking notes in their L1 (either Spanish (n = 10) or English (n = 12)) or L2 French was investigated. Analysis of student notes centered on several factors: percentage of words from the source text that appeared in notes; percentage of abbreviated words; percentage of different types of lexical abbreviations; and number of list marks (e.g., bullet points, numbers in a list, stars) (p. 6). As in previous studies comparing L1 and L2 notetaking performance (e.g., Dunkel, 1988b), L1 notetakers took more notes than those working in their L2. Students were found to abbreviate more when taking notes in their L1 than in their L2, a finding that suggests the strategy of abbreviation may be underdeveloped in the L2. This observation implies that students cannot avail themselves of the benefits of abbreviation even in situations when they need it most (i.e., where they face more cognitive challenges by listening and taking notes in the L2). In addition, both the Spanish and English L1 groups organized and structured their notes in similar ways when operating in L2 French.

Specific techniques that fall under the umbrella term *encoding* include writing verbatim, paraphrasing, summarizing, drawing pictures, and using symbols. In particular, paraphrasing and summarizing can help L2 learners engage in deeper processing of information than verbatim writing (e.g., Leow & Mercer, 2015). According to Morehead et al. (2019a), over one-third of university students paraphrase when taking notes in their L1. By encouraging and preparing learners to paraphrase rather than copy content, for example, teachers would be adding an addition layer of activity meant to strengthen information processing and thus, learning and recall. Such activities have been introduced in pedagogic literature specific to L2 notetaking instruction; for example, Siegel (2019a) introduced a three-step teaching sequence that incorporates decisions about what and how to paraphrase as well as practice opportunities. At the same time, paraphrasing likely contributes to the cognitive load notetakers face (Jansen et al., 2017).

The drawing effect, a different type of encoding, has been examined in relation to recall in L1 contexts (e.g., Wammes, Meade & Fernandes, 2016) and findings have demonstrated the positive effects of drawing pictures compared to writing words when vocabulary acquisition is the goal. Drawing generated positive results even when encoding time was decreased and word lists were lengthened (Wammes et al., 2016), suggesting that one's own individualized visual representations make more of an impact on memory than written words. Luo et al. (2018) investigated the impact of longhand and digital notetaking on learning through images and found that more images were included in the notes of the longhand group. Morehead et al. (2019a) point out that the type of content to be learned and its affinity for images may lead students to use one notetaking method or the other.

Storage research

The storage function of notes seems to be robust and appreciated by students. Over 90% of the L1 university students ($n = 577$) in Morehead et al. (2019a) reported that they review their notes and do so mainly by reading through their notes. Other options for making effective use of the storage function include reorganizing, rewriting, and/or summarizing notes. Furthermore, students can test themselves on the content of their notes by, for example, creating their own quizzes or trying memory games. Approximately half of the respondents in Morehead et al. (2019a) reported testing themselves on note content as a form of review. In a survey conducted with high-school L2 English learners in Sweden ($n = 199$) and first reported here, only 24% indicated that they either always or sometimes review their notes at home. Nearly 50% stated that they never reorganize their notes, and the practice of summarizing notes after classes was even less common. It is likely that the stakes for notetaking and learning in the university context investigated by Morehead et al. (2019a) were higher than that of the Swedish high-school students.

34 *Previous research on notetaking*

Research comparing groups of students who reviewed notes and those who did not have shown that note review leads to better recall and test performance; for example, DiVesta and Gray (1972) found that reviewing helped increase the number of words and ideas students expressed on a free recall test, in addition to higher multiple-choice test scores. Perhaps unsurprisingly, Kobayashi's (2006a) review of 33 L1 notetaking intervention studies demonstrated substantial overall effects for both notetaking and reviewing. In an effort to expand upon the opportunities and benefits provided by the storage function, Luo, Kiewra and Samuelson (2016) explored different combinations of note revision, review, and collaborative work on notes following L1 notetaking events. They found that students who revise notes end up recording more notes than those who do not, and that the revision process leads to better learning than simply recopying notes. In addition, they found that revising notes after a lecture is less effective than revising during pauses during the lecture. Further, revising notes in conjunction with a partner leads to more information than revising alone. Whereas the encoding function has received significant attention from researchers in both L1 and L2 contexts, the storage function of notes and student practices for interacting with their notes after the notetaking event in L2 contexts is a relatively unexplored area.

Effectiveness of notes

Several studies have examined the extent to which the act of taking notes is effective on post-listening tasks. These studies have taken place both in L1 and L2 contexts and follow the line of research established by Crawford (1925), who first showed that taking notes leads to better test performance compared to not taking notes. While most of these studies reinforce the usefulness of notes on a variety of tasks in L2 contexts, an exception is Chaudron, Loschky, and Cook (1994). They examined the relationship between notes taken by adult ESL learners in a university course for foreign students and performance on multiple choice and cloze exercises. Findings failed to show a significant effect for notetaking on either performance measure. An additional and perhaps unexpected finding was that overuse of distilling strategies like abbreviation can lead to difficulty in stimulating recall. In other words, the amount and/or type of abbreviations or paraphrases used must be transparent enough to the notetaker to stimulate recall after the listening event. Using too many abbreviations or summarizing in vague terms may lessen the chances that material is remembered accurately. A similar lack of effect of notetaking was found in Morehead et al. (2019b), who reported that non-notetakers performed as well and in some cases better than those who took notes using a variety of methods (i.e., longhand, on laptops, or with eWriters) after listening to a text in their L1 and responding to factual and conceptual questions.

While much research emphasis has been placed on notetaking in higher education, particularly while listening to lectures, some studies have focused on earlier periods in education. Notetaking while reading was the focus of work by Chang and Ku (2015), who conducted a 5-week program on note-taking skills for reading with more than 300 elementary school students in Taiwan. Their pedagogic plan involved the following stages: (1) Highlighting the main idea; (2) Reducing the amount of information; (3) Identifying key words; (4) Organizing information visually; (5) Raising awareness of text structure. They found that teaching students through this pedagogic approach significantly improved their notetaking ability while reading as well as reading comprehension scores. Furthermore, the weakest readers showed the greatest gains following the period of instruction. From theoretical and practical perspectives, notetaking while reading should be easier than while listening, since the reader can see the words, read and re-read at their own speed, and identify certain physical locations in a text, among other reasons. This relationship is likely similar for L2 reading and listening, at least for learners above threshold proficiency and/or age levels. For elementary school students, this may very well be a useful beginning to a successful future of notetaking. As students get older and progress through school, information begins to be delivered more and more through listening, and hopefully notetaking skills learned through interaction with reading texts can be transferred to notetaking while listening.

Working with middle school students in the US, Boyle (2011) found that training in notetaking skills aided the notetaking ability and test performance for both students with and without learning disabilities. Boyle and Forchelli (2014) investigated the importance of notetaking among middle school students in the US in three categories: high achievers, average achievers, and students with learning disabilities. The researchers found major differences in the number and type of notes taken by average achievers and those taken by students with learning difficulties. Differences in test performance between these groups were also evident. These findings suggest that more explicit notetaking instruction and support may be necessary for lower achieving students to keep pace with peers (Boyle & Forchelli, 2014, p. 13). Studies like these, from the early and middle school years of L1 education, indicate the positive effects of notetaking for student performance and the potentially advantageous outcomes from pedagogic intervention and explicit training.

Tsai and Wu (2010) raised the question, in the Taiwanese tertiary context, of which language (i.e., the listener's L1 or the L2) is more effective for taking notes. Their research involved instruction in the Cornell notetaking method along with a language division, in which one group of students took notes in L2 English and the other in L1 Chinese. The English notetakers outperformed the Chinese notetakers leading to a conclusion that notetakers can better capture and record information from a speech when they take notes in the same language to which they are listening. This practice can help listeners record information in ways that are closer to the speaker's intentions rather than facing the possibility of items being "lost in translation" or extra cognitive demands of translating while simultaneously taking notes.

36 Previous research on notetaking

Individual differences in notetaking

Students take notes in diverse ways and for various purposes at different times. The various factors examined by Piolat, Olive and Kellogg (2005), including a variety of listening and notetaking subskills, time pressure, and expected learning outcomes, as well as different contexts and purposes, add up to immense cognitive effort from the notetaker. Gender differences in notetaking were investigated by Reddington, Peverly and Block (2015) in relation to both cognitive (e.g., language comprehension, working memory, and handwriting speed) and motivational factors. This study of 139 undergraduates in the US demonstrated a major advantage for females over males in most categories. The female group recorded significantly more information in their notes and performed better than their male counterparts on measures of working memory, language comprehension, handwriting, and motivation.

Qualitative research by Badger, White, Sutherland and Haggis (2001) aimed to understand a range of factors that impact how students view notetaking. Their interviews with 18 students (six "traditional" students in their first year of university in the UK; six access students who had attended university bridge courses; and six international students) revealed a variety of viewpoints related to both the process and product aspects of notetaking. The process-related reasons for taking notes included aiding with concentration when listening, listening for notetaking cues, and using a variety of notetaking techniques during lectures. Product-oriented reasons typically included preparation for tests and assignments. The researchers noted that differences between the two groups of domestic students and the group of international students in terms of notetaking views and habits were likely due to the fact that the international cohort had taken EAP courses specifically designed for university preparation and that these courses would have included explicit attention to lecture notetaking.

As discussed in Chapter One, several different notetaking formats and systems are used around the world. One branch of notetaking research aims to investigate whether one format of notes (e.g., the outline format) is better than another (e.g., the T-format) for learning and stimulating recall. An early example of this comparative type of study was Kiewra, Benton, Kim, Risch and Christensen (1995), in which three types of notetaking (the participant's own free choice of method, the outline format, and the matrix) were compared to determine whether note format affected note quality and usefulness. Those who took notes in an outline outperformed the other groups on a post-listening writing task. In addition, the study showed that a "flexible" outline format generates more notes than other formats.

Bui and McDaniel (2014) conducted a similar study with L1 English users that compared the effects of two learning aids, namely a skeleton outline of notes and an illustrative diagram, and no learning aid. Both the outlines and diagrams helped improve learning and structural understanding of the lecture content. The authors, however, recognize that the usefulness of the illustrative diagram may be limited to scientific content and may not be flexible enough to extend to other fields, such as the humanities and social sciences, in the same ways as an outline format may be. Outcomes from this study and that discussed in the previous paragraph related to the usefulness of the outline format continue to resonate today, based on Morehead et al.'s (2019a) finding that the bullet list/outline is the most common organizational method employed.

Song (2012) conducted a study with L2 students in which notes taken in either a blank, free format or an outline format were analyzed in terms of collecting information at several levels (i.e., main concepts, supporting details, etc.) and test performance. The study, involving more than 250 ESL students at a university in the US, found that the number of topical ideas in notes, along with note organization, were both strong indicators of listening comprehension. Scores for open-ended listening tasks were better for the outline notetakers than the blank format group.

As Badger et al. (2001) observe, there can be "considerable variation in how [students] conceptualize lectures" (p. 415) and individual differences and preferences related to notetaking should be considered. These authors argue that a "more heterogeneous view of taking notes in lectures" would benefit learners in EAP courses (Badger et al., 2001, p. 406). Instead of providing strict guidelines on any single notetaking format, EAP/EMI teachers might consider notetaking instruction that shies away from prescription but still emphasizes quality (Siegel, 2018a). In an effort to focus less on predetermined notetaking formats and more on the actual content of notes, recent initiatives have promoted structured and systematic excersies that allow learners to take notes according to their individual preferences. For example, Siegel (2018b) has proposed a scheme that involves scaffolded support for the decisions learners need to make about what information to record and how to do so. These explicit activities help students separate information at the utterance level, understand and assign significance to the information, decide whether to record information verbatim or in a simplified form, with students free to choose the overall organization format with which they feel most comfortable or that best fits the lecture content.

How L1 and L2 notetaking differ

There is a complex relationship between the language of the speaker and the language options of the notetaker. As summarized in Barbier, Roussey, Piolat & Olive (2006), the L1 of both the speaker and the notetaker can impact how notes are taken in the L2. Depending on how proficient the listener is in the language the speaker is using, the listener may elect to write some or all of the notes in their own L1 or in the language used by the speaker. This type of translanguaging in student notes (Siegel, 2020a) can make research difficult, and I have not come across many studies (with the exception of Tsai & Wu, 2010) where the language in which the notes were to be taken was determined by the research design. In almost all studies reported on in this chapter, the language of input/lectures was in English, which for some was the L1 and for others an additional language.

Most researchers have not dictated the language in which notes should be taken, possibly for one of several reasons. First, the notes are meant to be meaningful to the notetaker, who is striving to capture and store information in the most effective and efficient way possible *for them*, which may vary by individual. Secondly, there may be a (false) assumption that students take notes in the language to which they are listening (see Chapter Three for further discussion of language choice and translanguaging in student notes). However, when it comes to analysis of notes in EAP research, the expectation may be that notes are written in English, which may disadvantage those who listen and comprehend the English input but find it more convenient to record information either in another language or in a combination of English and another language (i.e., by translanguaging).

Interventions for L2 notetaking

A focus of research for notetaking in L2 English pedagogy seems to accommodate a view that any notetaking skills developed in L1 education do not automatically transfer to L2 English; thus, focused instruction is necessary in the L2. Many of the studies on L2 notetaking involve interventions in which a teacher introduces a specific notetaking format, strategies, techniques, or a pedagogic cycle in hopes of helping students increase their L2 notetaking proficiency. Based on the notions that notetaking improves comprehension, engages listeners, helps concentration, provides material for later use and review, L2 teachers want to incorporate it, particularly for the student populations who need to attend EAP and/or EMI courses in higher education.

However, the best practices for teaching notetaking skills to L2 students are largely unknown. As described by Siegel (2016), much of what teachers claim is notetaking *instruction* is in reality either listening comprehension practice or notetaking *practice*. From an educational standpoint, and a skill acquisition theory perspective in particular, practice is indeed important. Practice, however, typically follows a period of instruction where learners receive input and guidance from a more capable peer or teacher. In skill acquisition, the initial declarative or cognitive stage involves modeling, after which an associative or procedural stage includes focused practice and revision of skills (e.g., DeKeyser, 2007). Much involvement of notetaking in present EAP/EMI courses, based on voices from practicing teachers, neglects the initial teacher-led guidance phases and only targets the practice phase (e.g., Siegel, 2019b). Without adequate training and input in specific notetaking behaviors and strategies, students may be left to use their current approaches and not actually develop as notetakers. Therefore, explicit intervention studies have aimed to examine the effects on notetaking ability and performance.

Hayati and Jalilifar (2009) focused their research on how different formats of notes could impact note quality and listening comprehension performance as measured by simulated TOEFL listening section test scores. Three groups of undergraduate L2 English learners were involved: non-notetakers, uninstructed notetakers, and Cornell notetakers. The first group took no notes and responded to test questions after a lecture. The second took notes in their preferred method. The third group studied the Cornell method of notetaking (e.g., Pauk & Owens, 2014), which formed the intervention. (The Cornell method involves organizing note paper with a section for jotting notes during the lecture and a separate column where main ideas and relevant questions are written, with space for a summary at the bottom of the note page.) This study reinforced the notion that notetaking yields better results than not taking notes on tests of lecture comprehension (e.g., Crawford, 1925). In addition, the intervention involving instruction in the Cornell method resulted in higher scores than the uninstructed notetaker group. Thus, this study demonstrated that the Cornell system, or another systematic approach more generally, may be beneficial when compared to students' sometimes random or idiosyncratic approaches to notetaking.

The Cornell method was also taught as an intervention in a study reported by Tsai and Wu (2010), who also examined the language in which notes are taken (i.e., in L1 Chinese or L2 English). Students were divided into a control (n = 54) and a contrast group (n = 54). These groups were further separated into those who took notes in their own ways and those who received explicit instruction in the Cornell method. Results of listening comprehension tests showed positive results for both the L1 Chinese group and the L2 English group who received the Cornell method instruction compared to the groups who received no notetaking instruction, leading to the conclusion that an intervention can be effective regardless of the language in which notes are taken. The study also found that those who took notes in English according to the Cornell system outperformed Chinese notetakers with the same instruction, suggesting that writing notes in the same language the speaker is using may be beneficial.

In Crawford's (2015) study involving Japanese university EFL learners (n = 21) included an intervention over the course of two semesters and measured student notes for the number of notations, content words, abbreviations, arrows, and highlights. For this research, students received training in various notetaking techniques as well as the Cornell method. Student notes from midterm and final exams were analyzed and showed gains in four of the five categories measured (namely, number of notations, content words, abbreviations, and arrows). A survey that was also part of the study suggests that the notetaking intervention for this group of learners was warranted, as only two students reported receiving notetaking instruction in a prior EFL class. The researcher noted that no control group was involved in the research design (Crawford, 2015, p. 423) and therefore it is difficult to claim with certainty that this specific intervention would be effective compared to others.

Another study from the Japanese university EFL context (Siegel, 2016) (n = 87) introduced a pedagogic cycle focusing on student decisions of: (a) what to take notes on (e.g., differentiating between information that should be recorded in notes and that which is nonessential and can therefore be left out of notes); and (b) when to take notes (e.g., during lecturer pauses or when a speaker is repeating information). The study involved 6 weeks of instruction using skeleton outlines. Each week, the skeleton outline got smaller and expectations for students to complete the outlines increased. Samples of student notes collected before and after the instruction were analyzed for information units (IUs), a measure of note quality commonly used in such investigations (e.g., Dunkel, 1988b; Siegel, 2018b) (see Chapter Seven for further discussion of IUs as evaluative criteria). Findings showed statistically significant increases of IUs before and after the intervention, suggesting that focusing student attention on what and when to take notes has a positive effect on notetaking performance.

The number of students who adopted the outline format on the posttest notes jumped to 69% from the 8% who used outlines on the pretest notes, a finding confirming previous studies (e.g., those involving the Cornell method discussed above) that L2 students can benefit from receiving instruction on the structural organization of notes. On a post-intervention survey, 81% of respondents reported that the instruction was either "useful" or "very useful", and 83% felt that the intervention would help them with lecture comprehension in the future (Siegel, 2016, p. 8). However, since this research did not include a control group, claims about the positive results must be made with caution.

While the interventions described above all took place in Asian EFL contexts, notetaking instruction has been the topic of interest in Europe as well. Research involving upper secondary school (i.e., high school) EAP students in Sweden also supports the potentially positive impacts that notetaking interventions can have. Siegel (2018b, 2019b) and two upper secondary school teachers trialed a four-stage pedagogic sequence used in conjunction with TED Talks for notetaking instruction. The four-stage sequence (see Table 2.1) built on Siegel's (2016) previous work in this area but added stages focusing specifically on *how* notes are taken (i.e., either verbatim or paraphrased), as described in the table below.

Data were collected from pre- and post-intervention samples of student notes as well as comprehension tests after watching TED Talks. Students were allowed to use their notes on the tests. While the comprehension test scores improved slightly from pre- to post-intervention, these increases were minimal and nonsignificant, meaning that they cannot be attributed to the intervention and could be the result of chance alone. Samples of student notes, analyzed for IUs, demonstrated an increase of 7.1 IUs from pre- (6.2) to post-intervention (13.3), a statistically significant increase that can likely be attributed to the intervention.

One weakness of Siegel's (2016, 2018b) studies is the lack of a control group for comparison purposes. That is, while significant gains were made in IU scores, these findings needed to be checked to ensure that gains would be made in comparison to a control group that did not receive the intervention. To build on this study, Siegel (2018b) suggests including a control group in a quasi-experimental research design. In addition, all of the intervention

Previous research on notetaking 41

Table 2.1 Four-stage pedagogic sequence for notetaking (based on Siegel, 2018b)

Stage	Activity	Purpose
1.	Chunking with the transcript (students put a slash (/) on the transcript to indicate IUs)	To help notetakers segment content into meaningful chunks while dealing with rate of speech
2.	Marking the transcript (students use symbols to indicate main and supporting ideas, examples, transitions, redundancies, etc.; then compare and discuss choices with classmates and teacher)	To help notetakers separate information into various levels of importance and to recognize textual features of lectures; to help in the identification of what should be noted and what (probably) should not
3.	Writing verbatim notes (students listen to short segments (30 s–1 min) of the text, write down key words verbatim; then compare and discuss choices with classmates and teacher)	To help notetakers catch and record information in real time; to help them recognize which words are important and which (probably) are not
4.	Simplifying notes (students listen to slightly longer segments (1–2 min), writing verbatim notes when necessary while also trying to write notes in simplified form when possible; then compare and discuss choices with classmates and teacher) (e.g. 'horrible situation' in lecture = 'bad sit' in notes)	To help notetakers practice being efficient and making effective choices when simplifying notes

studies described above featured traditional pen and paper notetaking only, and interventions have seldom if ever been applied to digital notetaking to determine the effects of such instruction on laptop and tablet notetaking.

Kusumoto (2019) attempted an intervention using the pedagogic cycle introduced by Siegel (2018b) with first-year Japanese university EFL learners. For her study, a quasi-experimental research design was used, which included a control ($n = 23$) and a contrast group ($n = 36$). As described in Siegel (2018b), Kusumoto's intervention included 8 weeks of notetaking instruction and practice. Results from pre- and post-intervention tests of listening comprehension showed no significant improvements. Student notes, scored for IUs, showed slight increases from pre- to post-intervention samples, although those increases were minimal and statistically nonsignificant. Kusumoto (2019) speculates that the lack of positive results stemming from the intervention may be related to the gap between the level of the materials used for data collection (i.e., TED Talks) and the student proficiency level (generally around A2-B1 on the CEFR scale). Instead of authentic materials, the author recommends semi-authentic or simulated lecture texts (audio and/or video) in which the teacher can control or adjust factors such as rate of speech and lexical complexity.

42 Previous research on notetaking

While the pre- and post-intervention results did not point to gains that could be attributed to the intervention in terms of test scores or note quality, another part of Kusumoto (2019) involved a survey of student perceptions of the intervention. Roughly 80% of the participants (n = 59) felt that each stage of the intervention helped them understand what the act of notetaking consists of. Furthermore, up to 90% agreed that certain stages, particularly taking notes verbatim (stage 3) and simplifying (stage 4) helped their notetaking ability.

In an effort to address the research design flaw of not including a control group in research involving higher proficiency (approximately B1-C1 on CEFR) learners, Siegel (2020b) conducted a study with control and intervention groups at the intermediate (B1-B2) and advanced (C1) proficiency levels. The intervention and materials used were the same as Siegel (2018b) and Kusumoto (2019). The control groups received no explicit notetaking instruction, while the intervention groups received a 10-week period of scaffolded notetaking instructional cycle. Both groups completed lecture listening and notetaking activities prior to the explicit instruction. Student notes were collected and analyzed for IUs. Regarding the intermediate-level students, both the control and experimental groups showed statistically significant improvements; however, the intervention group registered notably higher t-test and effect size results, which may suggest that the pedagogic intervention may help notetaking ability improve in more effective and time-efficient ways than assuming that students will pick up notetaking by themselves through exposure and practice. The advanced-level intervention group made statistically significant increases in IU scores, whereas the control group did not. Overall, these findings suggest that the intervention can benefit both intermediate- and advanced-proficiency L2 English users.

In all of the studies mentioned previously in this section, the interventions were conducted in L2 English, which may imply that some meaning and intent of instruction was missed by some of the lower-proficiency students. Nekoda (2020) recognized this potential caveat and conducted a small-scale case study to explore the effects that the language of notetaking instruction may have on student performance. In his study, an intervention group received notetaking instruction in L1 Japanese (using L1 Japanese lecture-style texts for notetaking practice) for three sessions, followed by additional notetaking instruction in L2 English for a period of five sessions. Student ability was measured by post-lecture comprehension tests in the L2 before the instruction began, after the L1 instruction and after the L2 instruction. The intervention included use of reflection, abbreviations, linking of concepts and ideas using figures and symbols, and putting information into timelines and charts. Results of the post-listening tests showed that there is a stronger possibility of L1 instruction having a positive impact on notetaking in the L2 than instruction provided in the L2. Based on these results, it would seem that, at least for monolingual classes in which the teacher and students share an L1, instruction in that L1 may prove a more time-efficient strategy when notetaking (and not more holistic exposure to the L2) is the goal.

Research on technology in notetaking

The vast majority of research on notetaking to date has prioritized the traditional pen and paper method of physically writing notes on paper. Since this practice has been commonplace in learning contexts for centuries, and given the intuitive importance of notetaking to the learning process, the attention from applied linguistic researchers is well-justified. With innovations in digital technology in recent years, several new options for notetaking have entered the educational field. The first of these was the laptop computer, which allowed students to type notes into word processing software (e.g., Microsoft Word, Pages, etc.). Later, as tablet computing provided more convenient options (in terms of size and space), devices such as the iPad and Microsoft Surface and other eWriters also became viable options. On a smaller scale, the cell phone industry has also impacted notetaking, as students can type notes and/or take photos of information they want to preserve.

All of these innovations have the potential to replace and/or supplement the traditional notetaking method. Each of the devices mentioned above brings with it advantages in terms of convenience and storage but can also be associated with elements that negatively affect learning, either for notetakers themselves or for students sitting near them in a lecture hall. For students attending lectures, the laptop can be an attractive option, as one can have multiple functions open at the same time (e.g., a PDF of a course reading and a blank document for typing notes). When typing speed and accuracy are up to the task, effective and efficient notetaking can take place. Storage is another advantage of the laptop, especially with cloud computing options, which can help save notes and eliminate situations where a student needs to keep track of multiple loose sheets of notepaper that can easily become disorganized.

However, the temptation to type verbatim what a speaker says may lead to less retention and learning of information than paraphrasing and/or taking notes by hand. Furthermore, the laptop can cause general distraction if the listener surfs the Internet or multitasks while attempting to listen and take notes, options that the longhand notetaker can avoid. In addition, the distractive capacity of computer devices in the classroom has been demonstrated (e.g., Carter, Greenberg & Walker, 2017). Laptop options also lack the flexibility of a pen and paper in the sense that, generally speaking, the laptop notetaker is limited to the default functions of the word processing software they use: typing from right to left, top to bottom, alphabetical and numerical characters only, etc. Options are limited in comparison to the pen and paper method, where one can easily utilize any part of the paper, write in any direction, choose to draw a picture or symbol instead of using letters, and make those decisions in a split second.

Tablets and eWriters are smaller than most laptops, making carrying and storage of the device more convenient. Typing notes is one option for tablets, but newer versions have also incorporated writing utensils that interact with the touchable tablet face. These electronic pencils (e.g., a stylus and the

44 *Previous research on notetaking*

Apple Pencil) have aimed to accommodate those students who like the convenience of taking notes digitally but want the more traditional feel of writing notes by hand on their tablet. In addition, numerous apps have been developed that allow for integration of handwritten notes on typed documents, as well as functions for including photos, videos, and comments in notes. Most tablets also include cameras, so pictures can be substituted for written or typed notes, or a combination thereof can be used. For practical purposes that fit in the palm of one's hand, the cell phone offers many of the same options as the tablet, albeit on a smaller scale, which can affect the efficiency of encoding (i.e., inputting information into a very small and sensitive surface under strict time pressure) as well as review (i.e., reading small text on a palm-sized screen).

Research into how these technological developments may impact notetaking in lectures remains in its infancy, although a handful of studies in L1 contexts have begun to explore these areas. At the same time, digital notetaking in L2 contexts remains a relatively unexplored area of the field.

In L1 contexts

Among the main interests in L1 contexts is whether notetaking with laptop computers is better for learning and recall than the traditional method, which is often slower and requires more physical and mental effort. Bui, Myerson, and Hale (2013) investigated whether taking notes longhand or with a computer produced better results, and whether taking organized notes or transcribing leads to higher scores on immediate and delayed tests of lecture content. Findings showed that students who used the combination of a computer and the transcription strategy scored better than other groups on immediate recall tests. Taking notes in an organized fashion (rather than transcription), both with a computer or longhand, produced the best recall on delayed tests. For students with lower working memory capacity, attempting to transcribe lectures with computers, and the potential amount of information that can be recorded, can lead to better retention (Bui, Myerson & Hale, 2013). These findings support the notion that a laptop provides a viable option for learning, even if a transcription approach to notetaking is adopted, particularly with certain groups of students. A later study produced similar findings and supported the notion that computerized notetaking has promise. In randomized trials, Artz, Johnson, Robson and Taengnoi (2020) showed that computerized notetaking does not necessarily disadvantage learners compared to pen and paper notetaking.

Mueller and Oppenheimer (2014) compared notes taken by hand and those taken with a keyboard. Their study involved 67 L1 English students at Princeton University who took notes while listening to TED Talks, a collection of speeches on a range of topics and often used in notetaking studies as well as EAP courses. Results showed that laptop notetaking generates shallower processing of lecture content, even when distractive features of laptops are eliminated. Students who took notes with computers were outperformed on conceptual questions about lecture content by those who took notes by hand. This difference in performance was ascribed to the laptop notetakers' tendency to transcribe verbatim what the speaker said rather than manipulate and paraphrase the content, a practice which has been theorized to improve recall. The authors point out that processing information and expressing content in the notetaker's own words is likely more effective than a transcription approach, which can be implicitly promoted by the typing speed offered by laptops. As such, evidence exists that supports both modes of notetaking, and a clear advantage has not been unequivocally determined.

In a replication and extension of Mueller and Oppenheimer's original study, Morehead et al. (2019b) failed to replicate the initial findings reported by Mueller and Oppenheimer (2014). Their research, conducted using the same TED Talks as in the original project, found that whether students took notes longhand or with a laptop had no significant impact on impact on factual or conceptual questions answered immediately after the notetaking. Additional findings showed that the quantity of words in notes was greatest for the laptop group and similar between the longhand and eWriter groups. While verbatim overlap between the speaker and the notes was highest for the laptop group, it was not significantly different between the other groups. Luo, Kiewra, Flanigan and Peteranetz (2018) also compared longhand and laptop notetaking and found that laptop notetakers recorded more notes (IU and words) than their longhand counterparts and that longhand notetakers recorded more visual notes (i.e., images). Given these conflicting findings related to technology and notetaking, Morehead et al. (2019b) "argue that the available evidence does not provide a definitive answer to [the question of whether longhand, laptop or eWriter notetaking is preferable]" and recommend caution in making any such claim (p. 773).

However, such research is enticing and has begun to spark the public's interest. The issue of technology in lectures has begun to influence institutional policies for teaching and learning. According to an article in the Wall Street Journal ("I'd be an 'A' student if I could just read my notes", 19 March 2018, https://archive.is/xnAkN), university students in the US continue to struggle with notetaking in university lectures. Lecturer's personal classroom rules as well as school-wide policies have sometimes explicitly banned computers from classrooms in hopes of focusing student attention on lecture content and avoiding distraction. Such policies then leave students with no options but pen and paper notetaking, which may not be their preferred method. This, in turn, could have a negative impact not only learning and retention but also motivation and anxiety levels.

In L2 contexts

While research on L2 notetaking is relatively new, there is a particular dearth of studies involving notetaking and technology in L2 contexts. However, the use of notetaking apps in EFL has been the object of a study by Roy, Brine and Murasawa (2014), who investigated the ways in which EFL learners interacted with various software programs for notetaking in order to determine the extent to which the apps could benefit this learner group.

46 *Previous research on notetaking*

The study involved 10 students using apps such as Evernote, Springpad, and Ubernote to complete the following tasks: text editing, entering content, sharing content and searching and organizing notes. Students were video recorded and interviewed about their experiences in using the various apps. Findings showed that students had positive reactions to the software, yet most tasks took longer than expected despite the supposed convenience of the software. Given that research into notetaking apps, particularly for L2 learners, is at an embryonic stage, and that the range of digital options is constantly evolving, the authors rightly point out that much more research is needed on how apps can help L2 students take, organize, and use notes. Studies and research designs along the lines of Mueller & Oppenheimer (2014), Luo et al. (2018), and Morehead et al. (2019b) should be a priority for notetaking in EAP/EMI contexts in the near future.

Reflecting on research

After commenting on the genre of the academic lecture, this chapter has provided an overview of research on notetaking from both L1 and L2 contexts. The review and the research discussed has substantiated several points that may seem common sense to many: (1) taking notes is beneficial for learning; (2) taking and reviewing notes helps improve test performance; (3) taking notes in one's L1 is typically easier than in an L2. From the angle of pedagogic intervention research, several studies in L2 contexts have demonstrated that teachers strive to teach notetaking in explicit, scaffolded ways in order to break the multifaceted task of notetaking into more manageable parts for teachers to teach and for learners to develop. Digital notetaking, while promising in some ways, remains a somewhat controversial aspect within the field of higher learning more generally and lecture listening specifically, and has only begun to be explored in L2 settings.

In relation to the data collection and analysis methods employed by these studies, an important distinction needs to be drawn between those studies that focus on student *notes themselves* and those that investigate *how the notes are transferred to and utilized on other tasks*. In other words, some of these investigations (e.g., Siegel, 2016) focused exclusively on the notes as objects of study and as evidence of lecture comprehension. Others (e.g., Dunkel et al., 1989; Hayati & Jalilifar, 2009; Mueller & Oppenheimer, 2014) examined how notes were used to answer questions on post-listening tests. A third group of studies combined these two approaches, focusing some investigative efforts on the notes as well as on post-listening tasks (e.g., Dunkel, 1988b; Crawford, 2015; Siegel, 2018b) (see Siegel, Crawford, Ducker, Madarbakus-Ring & Lawson, 2020, for a more comprehensive discussion of these three strands of notetaking research).

This distinction in foci of the different studies is crucial in order to keep perspective on the act of notetaking itself. The notes themselves, more than how they are utilized, can be important objects in need of investigation because the act of encoding is where pedagogic interventions can likely be most effective. Furthermore, the quality of notes in and of themselves becomes less clear when the notes are transferred to an additional task (that is, beside the initial task of taking notes). This opacity stems from the myriad factors that can come in to play when, for example, completing a post-listening test (on which the degree of success may depend on the wording of the questions and/or the content of the questions themselves) or a summary writing task (where the genre of a summary, organizational aspects, as well as writing skills all affect performance).

Key theories of how notetaking helps the learning and retention of information have been elucidated, including the distinction between the encoding and storage functions of notes, and in the case of the former, the difference between generative and non-generative notetaking. Studies on various formats and systems for taking notes as well as individual techniques such as paraphrasing and drawing pictures have been included in order to provide the reader with an appreciation for the multitude of decisions and tools that each notetaker has at their disposal. Methods for how teachers who want to help students develop notetaking abilities in the EAP classroom have been covered from the perspective of pedagogic interventions, and these studies provide several practical options for operationalizing notetaking instruction.

Many of these studies have incorporated groups of varying sizes (some large, like Morehead et al.'s (2019a) 500-plus L1 university students and Song's more than 250 ESL students, and others small, such as Badger et al.'s (2001) group of 18 students in the UK). As such, the research reviewed in this chapter has provided broader information and findings related to how students take notes and how they might be influenced to take and use notes more effectively. In taking a wide perspective, introducing various studies, and expanding on key concepts in notetaking introduced in Chapter One, this chapter has not focused on L2 notetakers as individuals with various preferences, purposes for, and experiences of notetaking. Therefore, the next chapter concentrates specifically on notetaking from the perspective of the L2 student.

References

Airey, J., & Linder, C. (2006). Language and the experience of learning physics in Sweden. *European Journal of Physics*, 27(3), 553–560.

Artz, B., Johnson, M., Robson, D., & Taengnoi, S. (2020). Taking notes in the digital age: Evidence from classroom random control trials. *The Journal of Economic Education*, 51(2), 103–115.

Badger, R., White, G., Sutherland, P., & Haggis, T. (2001). Note perfect: An investigation of how students view taking notes in lectures. *System*, 29, 405–417.

Barbier, M-L., Roussey, J-Y., Piolat, A., & Olive, T. (2006). Note-taking in second language: Language procedures and self evaluation of the difficulties. *Current Psychology Letters*, 20(3), 1–14.

Bolton, K., & Kuteeva, M. (2012). English as an academic language at a Swedish university: Parallel language use and the 'threat' of English. *Journal of Multilingual and Multicultural Development*, 33(5): 429–447.

48 *Previous research on notetaking*

Boyle, J. (2011). Strategic note-taking for inclusive middle school science classrooms. *Remedial and Special Education*, 34(2), 78–90.

Boyle, J., & Forchelli, G. (2014). Differences in the note-taking skills of students with high achievement, average achievement and learning disabilities. *Learning and Individual Differences*, 35, 9–14.

Bui, D., & McDaniel, M. (2014). Enhancing learning during lecture note-taking using outlines and illustrative diagrams. *Journal of Applied Research in Memory and Cognition*, 4, 129–135.

Bui, D. Myerson, J., & Hale, S. (2013). Note-taking with computers: Exploring alternative strategies for improved recall. *Journal of Educational Psychology*, 105(2), 299–309.

Carter, S.P., Greenberg, K., & Walker, M. (2017). The impact of computer usage on academic performance: Evidence from a randomized trial at the United States Military Academy. *Economics of Education Review*, 56, 118–132.

Chang, Y. Y. (2012). The use of questions by professors in lectures given in English: Influences of disciplinary cultures. *English for Specific Purposes*, 31, 103–116.

Chang, W. C., & Ku, Y. M. (2015). The effects of note-taking skills instruction on elementary students' reading, *The Journal of Educational Research*, 108(4), 278–291.

Chaudron, C., Loschky, L., & Cook, J. (1994). Second language listening comprehension and lecture note-taking. In J. Flowerdew & L. Miller (Eds.), *Academic listening: Research perspectives* (pp. 75–92). Cambridge: Cambridge University Press.

Clerehan, R. (1995). Taking it down: Notetaking practices of L I and L2 students. *English for Specific Purposes*, 14(2), 137–155.

Crawford, C. C. (1925). The correlation between college lecture notes and quiz papers. *The Journal of Educational Research*, 12(4), 282–291.

Crawford, M. (2015). A study on note taking in EFL listening instruction. In P. Clements, A. Krause, & H. Brown (Eds.), *JALT2014 conference proceedings* (pp. 416–424). Tokyo: JALT.

Crawford, M. (2016). Lecture notetaking: Questions and answers. *The Language Teacher*, 40 (2), 9–12.

DeKeyser, R. (2007). Skill acquisition theory. In B. VanPatten & J. Williams (Eds.), *Theories in second language acquisition: An introduction* (pp. 97–113). New Jersey: Lawrence Erlbaum.

DiVesta, F., & Gray, S. (1972). Listening and note taking. *Journal of Educational Psychology*, 63(1), 8–14.

Dudley-Evans, T. (1994). Variations in the discourse patterns favoured by different disciplines and their pedagogical implications. In J. Flowerdew & L. Miller (Eds.), *Academic listening: Research perspectives* (pp. 146–158). Cambridge: Cambridge University Press.

Dunkel, P. (1988a). Academic listening and lecture notetaking for L1/L2 students: The need to investigate the utility of the axioms of good notetaking. *TESL Canada Journal*, 6(1), 11–26.

Dunkel, P. (1988b). The content of L1 and L2 students' lecture notes and its relation to test performance. *TESOL Quarterly*, 22(2), 259–278.

Dunkel, P., Mishra, S., & Berliner, D. (1989). Effects of note taking, memory, and language proficiency on lecture learning for native and nonnative speakers of english, *TESOL Quarterly*, 23(3), 543–549.

Eddy, M. D. (2016). The interactive notebook: How students learned to keep notes during the Scottish enlightenment, *Book History*, 19(1), 86–131.

Field, J. (2008). *Listening in the language classroom*. Cambridge: Cambridge University Press.

Flowerdew, J. (1994). Research of relevance to second language lecture comprehension-an overview. In J. Flowerdew & L. Miller (Eds.), *Academic listening: Research perspectives* (pp. 7–29). Cambridge: Cambridge University Press.

Flowerdew, J., & Miller, L. (2005). *Second language listening: Theory and practice.* New York: Cambridge University Press.

Graham, S., & Santos, D. (2015). *Strategies for second language listening.* Basingstoke, UK: Palgrave.

Griffiths, R., & Beretta, A. (1991). A controlled study of temporal variables in NS NNS lectures. *RELC, 22*(1), 1–19.

Hayati, A. M., & Jalilifar, A. (2009). The impact of note-taking strategies on listening comprehension. *English Language Teaching, 2*(1), 101–111.

Jansen, R., Lakens, D., & Ijsselsteijn, A. (2017). An integrative review of the cognitive costs and benefits of note-taking. *Educational Research Review, 22*, 223–233.

Kiewra, K., Benton, S., Kim, S., Risch, N., & Christensen, M. (1995). Effects of note-taking format and study technique on recall and relational performance. *Contemporary Educational Psychology, 20*, 172–187.

Kobayashi, K. (2005). What limits the encoding effect of note-taking? A meta-analytic examination. *Contemporary Educational Psychology, 30*, 242–262.

Kobayashi, K. (2006a). Combined effects of notet-taking/reviewing on learning and the enchancement through interventions: A meta-analytic review. *Educational Psychology, 26*(3), 459–477.

Kobayashi, K. (2006b). Conditional effects of interventions in notetaking procedures on learning: A meta-analysis. *Japanese Psychological Research, 48*(2), 109–114.

Kusumoto, Y. (2019). EFL students' perception of note-taking and the effect of note-taking instruction. *The Kyushu Academic Society of English Language Education Bulletin, 47*, 47–56.

Lau, K., Cousineau, J., & Lin. C-Y. (2016). The use of modifiers in English-medium lectures by native speakers of Mandarin Chinese: A study of student perceptions. *Journal of English for Academic Purposes, 21*, 110–120.

Leow, R., & Mercer, J. (2015). Depth of processing in L2 learning: theory, research, and pedagogy, *Journal of Spanish Language Teaching. 2*(1), 69–82.

Littlemore, J., Chen, P. T., Koester, A., & Barnden, J. (2011). Difficulties in metaphor comprehension faced by international students whose first language is not English, *Applied Linguistics, 32*(4), 408–429.

Luo, L., Kiewra, K., & Samuelson, L. (2016). Revising lecture notes: How revision, pauses, and partners affect note taking and achievement. *Instructional Sciences, 44*, 45–67.

Luo, L., Kiewra, K. A., Flanigan, A. E., & Peteranetz, M. S. (2018). Laptop versus longhand note taking: Effects on lecture notes and achievement. *Instructional Science, 46*(6), 947–971.

Lynch, T. (2011). Academic listening in the 21st century: Reviewing a decade of research. *Journal of English for Academic Purposes, 10*, 79–88.

Matthew, W. M. (1966). The origins and occupations of Glasgow Students, 1740–1839. *Past and Present, 33*, 72–94.

Morehead, K., Dunlosky, J., Rawson, K., Blasiman, R., & Hollis, R. (2019a). Note-taking habits of 21st century college students: Implications for student learning, memory, and achievement. *Memory, 27*(6), 807–819.

Morehead, K., Dunlosky, J., & Rawson, K. A. (2019b). How much mightier is the pen than the keyboard for note-taking? A replication and extension of Mueller and Oppenheimer (2014). *Educational Psychology Review, 31*(3), 753–780.

Mueller, P., & Oppenheimer, M. (2014). The pen is mightier than the keyboard: Advantages of longhand over laptop note taking. *Psychological Science, 25*(6), 1159–1168.

50 Previous research on notetaking

O'Malley, J., & Chamot, A. (1990). *Learning strategies in second language acquisition*. Cambridge: Cambridge University Press.

Oxford, R. (1990). *Language learning strategies: What every teacher should know*. Boston, MA: Heinle & Heinle.

Nekoda, H. (2020). Note-taking instruction using L1 and L2 lectures, *CASELE Journal*, 50, 23–35.

Pauk, W., & Owens, R. (2014). *How to study in college* (11th edition). Boston, MA: Wadsworth Cengage Learning.

Piolat, A., Olive, T., & Kellogg, R. (2005). Cognitive effort during note taking. *Applied Cognitive Psychology*, 19, 291–312.

Reddington, L., Peverly, S., & Block, C. (2015). An examination of some of the cognitive and motivation variables related to gender differences in lecture note-taking. *Reading and Writing*, 28(8), 1155–1185.

Roy, D., Brine, J., & Murasawa, F. (2014). Usability of English notetaking applications in a foreign language learning context, *Computer Assisted Language Learning*, 29(1), 61–87.

Sheppard, B., Rice, J., Rice, K., DeCoster, B., Dummond-Sardell, R., & Soelberg, N. (2015). Re-evaluating the speaking and listening demands of university classes for novice international students. *ORTESOL Journal*, 32, 1–12.

Siegel, J. (2016). A pedagogic cycle for EFL note-taking. *English Language Teaching Journal*, 70(3), 275–286.

Siegel, J. (2018a). Notetaking in ELT: Highlighting contrasts. *TESOL Journal*, 10(1), 1–5.

Siegel, J. (2018b). Teaching lecture notetaking with authentic materials. *ELT Journal*, 73(2), 124–133.

Siegel, J. (2019a). Notetaking in EFL: A focus on simplification. *The Language Teacher*, 43(3), 20–24.

Siegel, J. (2019b). Collaborative action research on notetaking: Simultaneous cycles. *The European Journal of Applied Linguistics and TESOL*, 9(1), 77–100.

Siegel, J. (2020a). Appreciating translanguaging in student notes. *ELT Journal*, 74(1), 86–88.

Siegel, J. (2020b). Effects of notetaking instruction on intermediate and advanced L2 English learners: A quasi-experimental study. *Journal of English for Academic Purposes*, 46. DOI: https://doi.org/10.1016/j.jeap.2020.100868.

Siegel, J., Crawford, M., Ducker, N., Madarbakus-Ring, N., & Lawson, A. (2020). Measuring the importance of information in student notes: An initial venture. *Journal of English for Academic Purposes*, 43, DOI: https://doi.org/10.1016/j.jeap.2019.100811.

Song, M. Y. (2012). Note-taking quality and performance on an L2 academic listening test. *Language Testing*, 29(1), 67–89.

Tsai, T., & Wu, Y. (2010). Effects of note-taking instruction and note-taking languages on college EFL students' listening comprehension. *New Horizons in Education*, 58(1), 120–132.

Vandergrift, L., & Goh, C. (2012). *Teaching and learning second language listening*. New York: Routledge.

Wammes, J., Meade, M., & Fernandes, M. (2016). The drawing effect: Evidence from reliable and robust memory benefits in free recall. *The Quarterly Journal of Experimental Psychology*, 69(9), 1752–1776.

Young, L. (1994). University lectures-macro-structure and micro-features. In J. Flowerdew & L. Miller (Eds.), *Academic listening: Research perspectives* (pp. 159–176). Cambridge: Cambridge University Press.

3 Notetaking from the L2 student perspective

Introduction

The two previous chapters defined and discussed notetaking in general terms, pointed out various purposes for and types of notetaking, and summarized relevant research. In doing so, the chapters have conceptualized notetaking at a somewhat broad level, at times overlooking the myriad options and choices that people make (consciously or unconsciously) when they take notes. As observed in Crawford, Ducker, MacGregor, Kojima and Siegel (2016), "the act of note taking is closely tied to a person's background knowledge, life experience, and personal preferences about information organization" (p. 282). What the more general overviews presented in the first two chapters have neglected is the vast number of idiosyncratic options available to each and every individual who engages in a notetaking act as well as individual perspectives on the role notetaking plays in students' education and future work life. The dual needs of instructing a group of learners in notetaking while at the same time accounting for individual needs and preferences can be a predicament faced by many EAP/EMI teachers (Siegel, 2018a).

Even for something as seemingly simple and straightforward as a shopping list for a trip to the supermarket, the person writing the list chooses a format (e.g., vertical or horizontal list), special indicators (e.g., bullet points, stars, etc.), and an encoding system (e.g., whether to write complete words, use abbreviations or even draw pictures). This multitude of options and personal preferences for how to take or make notes extends to academic lecture notetaking and may have important impacts on note quality and thus on learning and academic performance. Understanding how students view these various options can also inform EMI lecturers and help them in their efforts to support the uptake and learning of information they present.

The vast array of possibilities, individual preferences and habits for notetaking can pose serious obstacles for EAP instructors who attempt to implement or promote a single notetaking system (e.g., the outline format or the Cornell method). Groups or classes are by definition, comprised of individuals who have their own learning styles, preferences, and established habits. Asking students to abandon notetaking patterns that they have become accustomed to, or to adopt wholly unfamiliar practices can be a challenge

52 *Notetaking from the L2 student perspective*

since those learners have likely enjoyed at least some previous success with their current approaches to notetaking in their L1. This hurdle for teachers is especially pertinent for students preparing for or already enrolled in tertiary education, as it may disrupt current successful notetaking practices. In any event, many EAP teachers aim to teach and develop their students' notetaking skills and to do that effectively, teachers should understand learner perspectives, habits, and options.

In order for EAP and EMI instructors to understand notetaking behaviors, the field needs to acknowledge beliefs, practices, and preferences for notetaking at individual levels. This notion is intended to extend from the research findings laid out in Chapter Two to a more personalized level in order to determine how student views converge and diverge regarding the notetaking act and how they prefer to engage in it. As such, Chapter Three first examines survey findings from various L2 contexts and then explores samples of student notes in order to portray the ranging viewpoints and practices employed by students enrolled in EAP courses.

Survey findings first reported here in Tables 3.1–3.6 involved several hundred students from different EFL and ESL backgrounds (e.g., from countries in Africa, Asia, Europe, and North America). These findings are compared and discussed in order to determine similarities and differences in viewpoints from a cross-cultural perspective. Other L2 notetaking survey studies will also be discussed in relation to a variety of topics, which include general notetaking habits and behaviors, views on notetaking, language choice in notetaking, levels of previous explicit notetaking instruction, and how instruction affects ability in the present and for the future. While these survey findings describe groups of students (rather than distinct individuals who make up the groups), they are meant to paint more refined pictures of how different groups may interpret and carry out notetaking. These findings represent generalizations but are at a more precise level than, for instance, "all university students."

Following the survey findings, more specific examples drawn from authentic samples of student notes will illustrate the range of options being used in EAP classrooms, starting with overall structural and organization choices and moving to scrutinize how a single piece of information from a lecture can be recorded in various ways by different students. These depictions substantiate the supposition that there is no "correct" way to take notes but rather a variety of ways, each of which may have advantages and disadvantages depending on contextual factors. All images of notes displayed in this chapter were taken by EAP students, all of whom granted expressed written permission for their anonymous notes to be shared for research purposes.

Survey research

In 2019, a large-scale survey (n = 577) on the notetaking habits of L1 college students in the US was conducted (Morehead et al., 2019). The authors note that "the similarities in reported note-taking habits across [several decades] seem more prominent than do the differences" (p. 10), suggesting that little has changed apart from the introduction of technology to notetaking (e.g., laptops, tablets, and Powerpoint). The most important but least surprising findings from the survey are that a vast majority of students report taking notes when in a classroom, as 96% of respondents reported they take notes, and 88% believe that notetaking is necessary for learning (p. 812). The researchers found that many students are flexible with their notetaking practices, either employing traditional pen and paper notetaking or using a laptop depending on the situation, although pen and paper remains more popular. Approximately half of these L1 students said they had never received explicit instruction for notetaking; however, approximately 60% indicated they would be receptive to such instruction, implying their acknowledgement that such training could be beneficial for performance.

Several of the findings from Morehead et al. (2019) have relevance for L2 teachers and notetakers and can be compared with the views of L2 notetakers in various contexts. In particular, topics such as the importance and popularity of taking notes, the methods by which notes are taken, and the access and exposure to explicit notetaking instruction are issues that have been raised through survey research with L2 notetakers. Several surveys of student habits from L2 contexts provide some insight into how notetaking in the L2 may lead to different views and habits than L1 notetakers.

The following sections include original survey results from seven countries: Cameroon, Indonesia, Japan, Seychelles, Spain, Sweden, and the US. While the results draw on four different continents, the number of respondents from each country ranged widely, mostly due to my personal network of teachers and ability to collect data from each context. The combined number of participants was 742. All respondents were studying in either EAP preparation courses or in EMI contexts, at either high school or university level. They completed an online survey asking about various factors related to L2 notetaking.

By utilizing essentially the same data collection instrument in a variety of contexts, findings can be viewed both at the overall level and based on the national groupings, although it must be noted that not all respondents in a particular country were necessarily citizens of that particular country (i.e., students may have been studying abroad or may have multicultural backgrounds). Results from this large-scale, multicontext survey are displayed in Tables 3.1–3.6. Other relevant surveys are also mentioned in the text for comparative purposes and to offer additional viewpoints to those expressed in the tables. Findings from these and other survey research on L2 notetaking are discussed in an effort to determine where there is general consistency in responses and where responses may diverge depending on context.

Student habits

Crawford et al. (2016) surveyed Japanese university EFL learners ($n = 739$) to determine the habits and preferences in this context. The Japanese respondents reported that, when in high school, over 90% took notes in L2 English

Table 3.1 Mode of notetaking

Survey item	Sweden (n = 272) (%)	Spain (n = 91) (%)	US (n = 48) (%)	Indonesia (n = 44) (%)	Cameroon (n = 18) (%)	Seychelles (n = 13) (%)	Average (%)
I prefer taking notes with pen and paper.	57	73	81	80	88	69	75
I prefer taking notes with a computer or tablet.	25	10	13	16	0	15	13
I have no preference.	18	16	6	5	12	15	12
I think the pen and paper method is more efficient.	68	77	73	66	88	85	76
I think a digital method is more efficient.	32	23	27	33	12	15	24

*Note: Combined *n* = 486 (Japanese respondents did not answer these questions).

Table 3.2 Benefits to concentration and organization

Survey item	Sweden (n = 272) (%)	Japan (n = 256) (%)	Spain (n = 91) (%)	US (n = 48) (%)	Indonesia (n = 44) (%)	Cameroon (n = 18) (%)	Seychelles (n = 13) (%)
I understand the benefits of taking notes.	93	71	88	87	83	89	76
Notetaking helps me concentrate in class.	57	62	66	66	93	89	76
Taking notes helps me understand the class, lecture, or speech content.	58	77	60	77	81	100	84
Taking notes helps improve my organization skills.	58	75	62	73	54	100	92

Table 3.3 Reasons for taking notes

Survey item	Sweden (n = 272) (%)	Japan (n = 256) (%)	Spain (n = 91) (%)	US (n = 48) (%)	Indonesia (n = 44) (%)	Cameroon (n = 18) (%)	Seychelles (n = 13) (%)
The teacher expects me to.	37	32	41	33	36	64	31
It helps me get better grades.	40	22	56	54	57	47	69
It helps me remember content.	83	71	81	88	80	100	73
My classmates take notes, so I do too.	17	14	13	19	20	12	0
They are helpful with tests or homework.	72	75	81	73	84	82	77
It keeps me from getting bored.	30	30	33	29	11	41	8
It's a natural part of school life.	31	20	27	44	45	41	54

Table 3.4 Aspects that affect ability to take "good" notes

Survey item	Sweden (n = 272) (%)	Japan (n = 256) (%)	Spain (n = 91) (%)	US (n = 48) (%)	Indo. (n = 44) (%)	Cam. (n = 18) (%)	Sey. (n = 13) (%)	Average (%)
Speakers accent	27	21	59	46	59	82	46	**52**
Rate of speech	72	55	65	63	55	82	61	**64**
Topic difficulty	47	30	59	58	59	24	38	**45**
My interest in the topic	57	52	58	58	55	47	54	**54**
Time of day	44	13	35	21	16	47	38	**30**
Volume of the speech	29	27	52	45	45	65	15	**40**
Purpose for taking notes	33	45	29	42	36	24	23	**33**
My note taking skills	47	52	55	52	39	24	23	**41**

Table 3.5 Language choice in notes

Survey item	Sweden (n = 272) (%)	Japan (n = 256) (%)	Spain (n = 91) (%)	US (n = 48) (%)	Indo. (n = 44) (%)	Cam. (n = 18) (%)	Sey. (n = 13) (%)
Being able to take notes in English well is an important academic skill.	77	68	71	81	82	94	92
Being able to take notes in my L1 is an important academic skill.	85	77	78	81	79	43	53
Being able to take notes in English well is an important skill to have for my future.	82	68	77	88	86	100	100
Being able to take notes in my L1 well is an important skill to have for my future.	83	77	77	83	82	57	53
Taking good notes in my L1 is difficult.	14	34	10	30	20	72	22
Taking good notes in English is difficult.	21	81	42	39	27	6	0
I need more training in note taking strategies for taking notes in English.	68	33	67	67	72	65	45
I need more training in note taking strategies for taking notes in my L1.	53	29	31	48	57	100	37

Table 3.6 Teacher potential in notetaking

Survey item	Sweden (n = 272) (%)	Japan (n = 256) (%)	Spain (n = 91) (%)	US (n = 48) (%)	Indo. (n = 44) (%)	Cam. (n = 18) (%)	Sey. (n = 13) (%)
My English teacher can help me take better notes.	68	40	76	73	82	89	77
My English teacher helps me take better notes.	32	33	62	62	71	75	68

classes (91%) and content classes taught in L1 Japanese (92%). These percentages dropped, however, when the respondents were asked about notetaking in university, at 56% and 79%, respectively. Nearly 94% of the 408 Japanese students who reported taking notes in university in Crawford et al. (2016) stated that they noted down what the teacher wrote on the board, and 73% wrote down information that their teachers delivered orally.

In terms of post-notetaking engagement, results indicated much less activity, with 50% of students reviewing notes they took in English classes, and only a quarter reorganizing or summarizing notes (Crawford et al., 2016, p. 279). Similar findings come from a survey of EAP students in Sweden (n = 272), who reported lower than ideal levels of engagement with their notes after taking them: 34% said they never review notes; 48% said they never reorganize notes; and 67% said they never write summaries of their notes (first reported here). These numbers related to how students utilize notes after a lecture or class may be disappointing to instructors and also indicative of an area of notetaking, namely review, that could be better supported in the classroom.

When it comes to what and how students record, Japanese students in Crawford et al. (2016) attempt to record notes verbatim (38%), the same percentage as paraphrasing what the speaker says (also 38%). A much more noticeable difference between verbatim and paraphrasing strategies was found with Swedish students (n = 272) (20%–40%, respectively). In other words, paraphrasing strategies seem to be more common among Swedish students than Japanese students. This finding may be related to differences in proficiency levels among the responding students: while both the Japanese and Swedish students were generally the same age (late teenage years), the Swedish students were approximately B1-B2 level on CEFR compared to the Japanese learners, who were approximately A2.

When asked what notetaking means to them, lower intermediate Japanese university EFL students (n = 59) responded thusly: copying what the teacher has written on the board/Powerpoint slides (66%); writing information the teacher said in my notebook (83%); writing new vocabulary words (21%);

and writing questions I want to ask (13%) (Kusumoto, 2019). İpek (2018) surveyed 61 Turkish university L2 English students and found that, prior to an intervention, the majority (98%) struggled to be selective when taking notes and write down only the most important words. Instead, they often tried to write as much as possible because they reported not having cognitive skills in the L2 to differentiate important from relatively unimportant information. Furthermore, 86% felt they needed improvement in order to record notes in their own words (i.e., paraphrase) rather than using a verbatim strategy. Similarly, a majority (91%) felt that their use of abbreviations when taking notes in English was underdeveloped in comparison to their L1 (İpek, 2018, p. 213). Since the notion that extensive verbatim recording may lead to less effective learning (see Chapter Two), and that research has shown paraphrasing to be preferable in many ways, these findings should be taken into account when advising and instructing students on L2 notetaking.

As technology advances, it is certainly having an impact on student habits in relation to notetaking, particularly the accessibility of handouts and slides from lectures and the increasing presence of digital tools for notetaking (i.e., laptops, iPads, etc.). Many students likely rely on handouts uploaded to online learning platforms after lectures and thus may not expend much energy in the notetaking process. Part of Crawford et al.'s. (2016) study that focused on teacher practices found that two-thirds of university teachers (n = 84, a combination of L1 content and L2 language teachers) provided handouts, most often in the forms of either printed Powerpoint slides or blank outlines for students to complete during lectures. This practice may reduce the need for notetaking and even decrease attendance, but the convenience and reliability of handouts and lesson management systems (e.g., Blackboard and Moodle) seems to surpass any potential negative learning outcomes.

Interestingly, when asked about notetaking and student attention in their lectures, some respondents professed that they preferred for students *not* to take notes in order to increase student attention and concentration on the material being delivered (Crawford et al., 2016, p. 280). The notion of distraction also arose in a part of Crawford et al. (2016) that focused on high school students. More than 50% of the 47 Japanese high school students who participated reported that notetaking while listening negatively affected their concentration and comprehension (p. 280). Students cited length of listening passages, topic and lexical difficulties, and anxiety about spelling correctly as inhibitors to notetaking. Issues of concentration relate to cognitive load theory and the ways in which listeners must manage their cognitive resources in a multiplicity of ways during notetaking (Jansen, Lakens & Ijsselsteijn, 2017), factors that may be overlooked by some EAP/ EMI instructors.

Original survey research in L2 contexts

As in Morehead et al. (2019), the use of laptops is beginning to catch up to the traditional pen and paper method, at least in some in L2 contexts.

Table 3.1 reports findings from a survey completed by learners in EAP/EMI courses in several countries related to preferences in the mode of notetaking expressed by the respondents. In other words, do students prefer the traditional pen and paper method or taking notes digitally? As illustrated by the results, a majority of students from every country prefers longhand notetaking and believes it is more efficient than digital options.

Based on this summary of findings related to student habits in a number of L2 contexts, it seems that a number of tentative conclusions can be drawn. A majority of L2 students report taking notes. A mixture of verbatim and paraphrasing techniques is reportedly used, and it seems logical to assume that all notetakers at least at some time combine these two practices. Furthermore, the availability of lecture handouts and slides may reduce the need for notetaking or at the very least affect the style of notetaking (i.e., jotting notes down in the margins of a handout as opposed to writing notes from scratch on a blank piece of paper). The traditional method of handwritten notes remains generally preferable to digital tools, although technology is influencing how notes are taken.

Student views and beliefs

Notetaking in academic lectures is often a voluntary and variable activity. That is, the EMI lecturer does not necessarily check that students are taking notes, nor do they always concern themselves with the quality of those notes. On the other hand, the EAP teacher must be concerned with notes in some way, especially when notetaking is specified as a crucial academic skill to be developed. Since the quantity and quality of notes, the motivations for and influences involved in, as well as the context in which the notetaking act occurs can vary, understanding student views and beliefs can provide useful insights for teachers (both EMI and EAP) and applied linguistic researchers interested in language comprehension and knowledge storage systems.

It has been argued that increasing levels of concentration is among the benefits of notetaking. Table 3.2 reports responses to general questions about whether notetaking aids concentration and organization of information. The percentages listed in Table 3.2 are the combined totals of students who responded *agree* or *strongly agree* to the survey items.

The results displayed in Table 3.2 suggest that many students in various international settings recognize the benefits of taking notes in EAP and/or EMI classes. Interestingly, the capacity for notetaking to aid concentration ranged from 57% for the Swedish students to 93% among the Indonesian learners. Most students also report that notes help them understand course content and improve their organizational skills, although the numbers for the Swedish learners are lower than those from other countries.

Students may take notes for a number of reasons or a combination there of. When it comes to motivation for taking notes, Table 3.3 shows several different factors that influence students' notetaking.

The highest percentage of responses related to reasons why students take notes center on the capacity of notes to help with learning, memory, and success on tests and/or homework. Therefore, it seems learners are engaged in notetaking for worthwhile purposes and for reasons many teachers would hope. While some students indicated that they take notes for reasons such as to relieve boredom, because of peer pressure, or because of teacher expectations, these numbers are notably lower than those for more learning- and performance-focused reasons.

As discussed previously in Chapter One, a number of elements can affect the quality of notes. As exhibited in Table 3.4, students indicated a number of influencing factors, some related to speaker (e.g., accent and rate of speech), some related to the notetaker (e.g., personal interest in the topic) and others related to external factors (e.g., the time of day).

Based on the average percentages displayed in Table 3.4, the main factors affecting student ability to take good notes are rate of speech (average of 64%), students' own topic interest (54%), and speaker accent (52%). Thus, L2 notetakers report that a combination of speaker factors and intrinsic factors affects note quality. Other external and contextual factors such as time of day and volume of speech seem to be less influential on note quality, although they do affect some students.

To summarize these student viewpoints, a majority of students believe that they understand the purpose of taking notes and that taking notes helps them concentrate on lecture content. When asked about their motivations for taking notes, teachers may be happy to learn that students seem to take notes for meaningful purposes (i.e., that they are helpful for academic success) as opposed to peer pressure or because of teacher expectations. Moreover, myriad factors impact the quality of notes taken. Of interest is the fact that there is no single factor that influences note quality. Rather, from a student perspective, a combination of speaker, notetaker, and external factors all affect the degree of difficulty of notetaking.

Language choice in notetaking

Since content in EAP and EMI classes is delivered through the medium of English, students are forced to *listen* to English. However, because the students will likely have at least one other language (their L1) available to them, they have options for the language in which they elect to record their notes, either in the L2 English that they hear, or in their L1, or a combination of both. However, two main types of challenge face notetakers who are listening to and taking notes in their L2: listening comprehension obstacles and the fact that L2 listeners have fewer automatic procedures and techniques for taking notes in the L2 (Piolat, Barbier & Roussey, 2008, p. 114).

Studies have shown that students perceive the task of taking notes in the L2 as more difficult than in their L1. Barbier, Roussey, Piolat and Olive (2006) examined the views of L1 English and L1 Spanish users who were

Notetaking from the L2 student perspective 63

learners of L2 French and reported that both L1 groups indicated taking notes in L2 French was more challenging than in their respective native languages. The L1 English participants reported more difficulty than the native Spanish users. This study also examined samples of notes taken in the L1 and L2 and measured the following characteristics: percentage of words in notes, percentage of words from the source text that appeared in notes (i.e., verbatim overlap), and percentage and type of abbreviations. Not surprisingly, more words appeared in the L1 notes. Students also abbreviated more in their L1, suggesting more ability and flexibility in recording information in the L1 than in the L2. Organizational and structural features of notes seem to transfer from L1 to L2 practices; therefore, the authors conclude that the language in which notes are taken does not impact note structure (Barbier et al., 2006, p. 11), although the amount, content, and quality of the notes does vary between notes taken in the L1 and L2. The authors further emphasize that "students' mastery of notetaking in L2 was not as good as in L1. Not only was cognitive effort greater in L2 than in L1, but also, L2 fluency was lower [resulting in less information in notes]" (p. 122).

Table 3.5 displays findings concerning the language in which notes are taken. As illustrated in Table 3.5, roughly three quarters or more of respondents agree that L2 English notetaking skills are important for academic purposes. In many cases, the expressed importance of L2 English notetaking abilities is either equal to or even more important than L1 notetaking. Along similar lines, a vast majority of students acknowledge that L2 English notetaking skills will be advantageous in their academic and/or work futures, often times slightly more than L1 notetaking. Most groups, with the exceptions of Cameroon and Seychelles, report that taking notes in English is more challenging than doing so in their L1. The largest gap between L1 and L2 notetaking difficutly was reported by the Japanese students, where 81% of students feel taking notes in L2 English is difficult compared to 34% in the L1. When it comes to future notetaking events, a majority of students indicated that they would like to learn more strategies for L2 notetaking. Taken together, these indications that L2 English notetaking is important for academic and work life, that L2 English notetaking is challenging, and that more strategies for and instruction in L2 English notetaking are desirable, explicit, systematic, and scaffolded attention is needed in EAP/EMI classrooms.

Not surprisingly, the vast majority of students acknowledge the important role that notetaking in English plays in learning and academic success. More than 80% of students in Kusumoto (2019) (n = 59) stated that taking notes in English is an important academic skill. This contrasts with only 60% who stated that taking notes in L1 Japanese or another language is an important skill, a finding that demonstrates the prestige with which these students view notetaking in English. Of note, a relatively low number of students (32%) in Kusumoto (2019) describe a desire to learn how to take notes in their native language. However, twice that number (64%) want to learn to take notes in

64 Notetaking from the L2 student perspective

English. This finding seems to suggest that these students place significant value on the ability to take notes in L2 English, even more so than taking notes in their respective L1s. When compared to the findings in Table 3.5, in which the majority of students indicate that notetaking in both their L1 and L2 English are important academic skills, some discrepancies are evident between Kusumoto's (2019) results and those presented above.

Translanguaging perspectives

Some students and teachers may feel that notes should be taken either all in L2 English or all in the L1. However, tolerance for the mixing of languages within a set of notes should be considered, as this would allow the note-taker flexibility and the opportunity to use all of their linguistic resources to accomplish the task. The notion of translanguaging has been in widespread usage in language education and linguistic circles for nearly three decades. Teaching practices to help students maximize their language resources and communicative competence continue to attract attention from educators, particularly in areas where students have access to several languages. When most educators and researchers discuss translanguaging, it is typically in reference to the skills of speaking and, less often, academic writing (e.g., Canagarajah, 2011).

The emphasis on translanguaging in the spoken mode is likely the most prevalent, to which many multilingual users can probably attest. People shift between languages depending on who they are addressing and may incorporate words and phrases from other languages when a good translation is not available, or when memory briefly fails. Canagarajah (2011) defines trans-languaging as "the ability of multilingual *speakers* [emphasis added] to shuttle between languages" (p. 401), highlighting the immediate decisions and output that are involved in spoken interactions. Garcia (2009) describes how multilingual resources can be used to "maximize communicative potential" (p. 140), which would include speaking as well as writing. Conteh (2018) points out that translanguaging includes not only oral texts but the use of different languages in written texts as well. A key question arises: how can translanguaging impact language choice and usage when taking notes?

When a room full of students attends an EMI lecture, they bring with them a variety of linguistic and cultural backgrounds, motivation levels, and notions of the lecture genre. While they all listen to the same spoken output by a lecturer, the content, organization, and quality of their notes varies widely. So too can the languages used to take notes. Some students feel that listening to L2 English and taking notes in English is the most effective method (i.e., listening to and taking notes in the same language is less complicated than alternatives). Others listen and write all of their notes in their L1. A third group mixes languages, perhaps writing most notes in L2 English but using their L1 for information they do not know how to spell in English or that is simpler and clearer for them to record in the L1, or simply

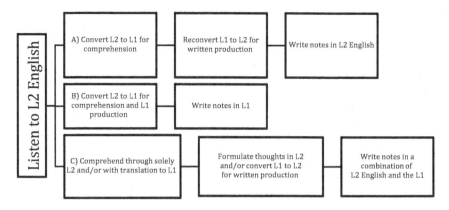

Figure 3.1 Three models of translanguaging in notetaking.

due to L2 fatigue or overload. This third group represents the population who are translanguaging in notes (Siegel, 2020).

Figure 3.1 illustrates three possible paths of how translanguaging can take place at the cognitive, receptive, and productive levels. In path A, the listener translates the L2 input to the L1 for comprehension and then reconverts to the L2 (i.e., the same language as the input) when the notes are written. It is also possible, of course, that learners listen to L2 English and comprehend it as such (e.g., rather than translating to L1), which seems a logical and preferable route. Path B signals a more direct and visible form of translanguaging, where the input is in L2 English but the written output is in the student's L1. In route C, the product of the listening and notetaking is a set of notes that includes both the L1 and L2 English. Regardless of whether notetakers strictly adhere one of these models or use them flexibly and fluidly, so long as valuable information is preserved in their notes, the language(s) that are used to do so should be of less importance. In fact, one could question the extent to which abbreviations, illustrations, and so on in notes are themselves different "languages."

Previous notetaking instruction

Nearly half (47%) of learners (*n* = 739) in Crawford et al. (2016) reported no notetaking instruction in L1 Japanese and 53% reported the same for L2 English courses. More than one-third disclosed that they had received no notetaking instruction whatsoever, regardless of language of instruction (Crawford et al., 2016, p. 279). Siegel (2018b, 2019) used a similar survey with upper secondary school students (*n* = 187) (aged 16–19) in the Swedish EFL context. Approximately 15% had received notetaking instruction in their high school experience, with another 25% indicating that they were uncertain whether they had been taught how to take notes

66 *Notetaking from the L2 student perspective*

(Siegel, 2019, p. 86). The quarter of students who were unsure if they had received instruction is an interesting figure because it suggests that even if teachers intended to and/or actually did include notetaking instruction, that teaching was not recognized as such. The remaining 60% of respondents reported receiving no notetaking instruction in their L2 English courses in lower secondary school.

Findings from this sample were similar when asked about notetaking at the upper secondary school level, with only 18% reporting receiving instruction in their L2 English classes, another 30% who were unsure, and more than half stated they had not received instruction. These results challenge the assumption by some university EFL and EMI lecturers that all, or even most, students have been taught and/or acquired notetaking skills already and therefore, notetaking *practice* (rather than instruction) is needed at the tertiary level.

Given the rather overlooked status of notetaking in EAP courses, it may be logical to assume that notetaking skills were developed in L1 content courses (e.g., science, history, Swedish, etc. taught in L1 Swedish). However, when answering similar questions about notetaking instruction in L1 courses, comparable results were found. Slightly more students (25%) reported that they had received such instruction in L1 courses, 45% said no, and more than a quarter declared they were unsure (Siegel, 2019, p. 87). These findings on notetaking instruction in L1 courses stand in contrast to the assumptions likely made by many EAP teachers that students learn notetaking "somewhere else" and therefore only need to practice (i.e., not learn or develop) notetaking in L2 courses. In other words, explicit and targeted instruction for notetaking in EAP courses seems warranted because a large percentage of students are not reporting (or at least, not recognizing) this instruction elsewhere. These findings from the Swedish context demonstrate a lack of attention to notetaking despite the skill being explicitly stated and implicitly alluded to on the national curriculum for the English subject at the upper secondary school level (Skolverket, 2011).

Impacts of instruction on notetaking ability

Although many students report receiving no explicit notetaking instruction, either in L1 or L2 English courses, learners believe that their teachers can play influential roles in helping the development of notetaking abilities. As reported in Siegel (2018b), 65% of the 187 students responding to a survey agreed that their L2 English teachers could help them improve their lecture notetaking. Disappointingly, only half that number (32%) reported that their teachers actually do provide explicit notetaking instruction on a regular basis. More than three quarters (76%) of students in Kusumoto (2019) reported that they had not learned how to take notes in a formal classroom setting, with the remaining quarter responding that they had received such teaching. Table 3.6 presents original survey results related to the teacher's potential and actual contributions to L2 notetaking development.

Notetaking from the L2 student perspective 67

For all countries represented in Table 3.6, the percentage of students signaling that their L2 English teachers have the capacity to help them take better notes is higher (in Sweden's case, double) than that of students who report that their teachers actually help them take better notes. In other words, these findings may imply that students expect teachers to provide more support, instruction, and practice for L2 notetaking development. They feel the potential exists but is not always acted upon. From the students' perspective, teachers can and should do more to support student notetaking in an L2. Students in other contexts (e.g., Taiwan) have also expressed the desire for more attention to notetaking in an L2 and for better notetaking skills when listening to English, which is a primary concern for international students studying on EMI courses (e.g., Teng, 2011).

Views on pedagogic approaches

The students in Siegel's (2019) study recognized that an explicit notetaking instruction intervention had taken place in their upper secondary EAP courses. Siegel (2019) introduced a four-step approach to notetaking pedagogy in conjunction with authentic materials (e.g., TED Talks) (see Chapter Two for details of the pedagogic intervention and Chapter Five for expansion on notetaking pedagogy). The four-stage sequence activities were meant to bring students from understanding the different chunks of information being offered through the decision-making process and finally to creating an efficient and meaningful record of what they heard. The respective stages were (1) chunking; (2) marking symbols on the transcript; (3) taking notes verbatim; and (4) simplifying notes.

Pre-intervention results for a question about whether they had received explicit notetaking instruction in upper secondary school L2 English classes revealed that 18% said yes, 52% said no, and the remaining 30% were unsure. Asked the same question again following the intervention: 54% said yes, 18% said no, and 28% were unsure. The large change from *no* to *yes* responses indicates that many students acknowledged the explicit emphasis on notetaking instruction, although nearly one third were uncertain if they had received such instruction. This uncertain group may have responded in that way because they had ideas about notetaking that diverged from the pedagogic approach or because they had been absent during key parts of the instruction. Nevertheless, it seems that when an intervention for notetaking is implemented, a majority of students recognize it.

Following the instructional period, Swedish students ($n = 147$) evaluated each stage according to the following aspects: enjoyment, newness, the extent to which it helped notetaking ability, and the extent to which it improved understanding of what notetaking is. The first and second stages (chunking and marking symbols on the transcript) were both rated as more novel than the later stages but also less useful for this particular student group. Stages three and four (taking notes verbatim and simplifying) were rated highly for enjoyment, helping notetaking ability, and increasing understanding of what notetaking is (Siegel, 2019).

Other studies have reported similar findings for these stages. Kusumoto's (2019) study involved similar survey questions, and over 80% of students (n = 59) responded that each of the four stages helped them understand what the notetaking process consists of. As for improving notetaking ability, the following results for each stage were evident: chunking (73% agreed it was helpful); marking symbols on the transcript (76%); writing notes verbatim (87%); and simplifying (90%). Like the findings from Siegel (2019) described earlier, the latter two stages were viewed very positively compared to moderate acceptance of the first two stages. Following the intervention period, 73% of students indicated that they would like even more explicit notetaking instruction for notetaking in English (Kusumoto, 2019).

More than half (62%) of Japanese university EFL learners (n = 87) reported that a similar pedagogic intervention using semi-authentic lecture materials made them more comfortable taking notes in English (Siegel, 2016), and nearly three quarters (73%) reported that the instruction was either "useful" or "very useful" (p. 282). More than seven in ten declared that the instruction would help them in future EMI courses, and that the learning benefits would likely manifest themselves in a number of academic functions: listening to lectures, writing essays and reports, organizing ideas, and preparing presentations (Siegel, 2016, p. 282).

Like the tertiary learners described in Table 3.6 and previous paragraphs, Japanese high school students (n = 47) signaled strong interest in receiving more input and attention from their L2 English teachers in regards to notetaking. More than 60% want to learn more abbreviations and symbols for notetaking, and 70% desire more class time devoted to notetaking. The potential positive impact of teacher guidance was also largely evident in the survey results: 81% want the teacher to show more "model" notes; 87% want the teacher to correct their notes; and 96% want the teacher to give more advice about notetaking (Crawford et al., 2016, p. 281).

Summary of survey findings

The survey results presented and summarized above paint a relatively consistent picture regarding habits and views of L2 students who need notetaking skills for EAP and/or EMI purposes. While the previous sections described and discussed various surveys conducted at different times in a number of different EFL and ESL contexts, the results are relatively consistent. To summarize, students view notetaking in L2 English as skill that likely has a significant impact on academic and work success. There is a clear desire for L2 notetaking instruction to be emphasized in EAP courses in order to help students' develop their abilities. While some students reported receiving notetaking instruction either in L1 or L2 courses, it seems that assumptions that all students have received such instruction are greatly exaggerated.

As such, teachers of EAP and EMI courses would likely be doing their students a service if they included scaffolded notetaking instruction (which may be subject-specific) for L2 learners. In addition, lecturers can take into account the various challenges that listeners face (e.g., accent and rate of speech). In terms of technology, many L2 notetakers have not yet embraced digital notetaking options, although these will likely need to be incorporated in instruction in the future.

The survey as a research tool has been used consistently in the field of L2 teaching and learning for its effectiveness in measuring beliefs, attitudes, preferences, and past behaviors (e.g., Dörnyei, 2003; Burns, 2010). As with all types of data collection, survey research contains inherent flaws that must be acknowledged, and the findings presented and summarized here must be viewed with these caveats in mind. One weakness of survey research is that it is dependent upon self-report data, which can range in accuracy. That is, various types of respondent bias can affect survey data. As Wagner (2015) points out, self-deception bias (when respondents answer in accordance with how they would like to be viewed), prestige bias (responding in ways that will increase their standing in the eyes of teachers and/or researchers), and acquiescence bias (answering in ways they believe researchers want them to; also referred to as the Halo Effect (Brown, 1998)) are potential drawbacks of survey research. In addition, the Hawthorne Effect, in which research participants may respond positively simply because they are taking part in research (Brown, 1998) may have influenced responses. Despite these limitations, surveys have provided insights into the L2 English notetakers' collective mindset and common behaviors, information that can be utilized to implement better and more focused instructional and textual selection practices.

Taking notes in an academic lecture is traditionally viewed as a crucial academic skill for learning at university (e.g., van de Meer, 2012). Teachers (n = 84) who participated in Crawford et al. (2016) "nearly unanimously agreed that notetaking is a useful academic skill and most of them recommended it because it helps students concentrate in class and study for tests" (p. 280). Crucial as it is, notetaking should also be acknowledged as a rather isolating skill. That is, the typical notetaker works alone among a group of other students who are also engaged in solo notetaking, all while listening en masse to the same speaker. The individual rarely has the opportunity to take advantage of socio-affective listening strategies such as asking the lecturer for clarification or extending a confused look with the intention of hearing a repeat or recast of what they heard.

Chances for cooperative notetaking between classmates during a lecture seldom occur, although some L1 researchers are beginning to explore the potential benefits of pauses and collaboration while notetaking (Luo, Kiewra & Samuelson, 2016) (see Chapter Six for small-scale research and pedagogic suggestions aimed at making notetaking more collaborative). This isolating situation leaves the notetaker with only their own cognitive skills to process the incoming input and record notes in the best ways they

70 Notetaking from the L2 student perspective

can. As such, it is crucial for teachers to listen when students voice their views on notetaking and demonstrate the numerous alternatives that are possible.

Now L2 notetaking practices and perspectives garnered from a geographically and culturally diverse sample of EAP/EMI students in both EFL and ESL contexts has been presented, this chapter moves on to illustrate and discuss the various options individual notetakers have when they encode information. That is, while the survey findings inform teachers and researchers at a broader and more general level, the second half of the chapter zeros in on individual practices in terms of overall organizational styles of notes as well as the multiple ways that the same piece of information can be encoded in diverse ways. Authentic samples taken from student notes will be used to illustrate the many configurations, strategies, and techniques that can be employed when taking notes. Rather than dictating any "best" way of taking notes, the purpose of the following sections is to illustrate the creativity and individual variance that are possible in L2 English students' practice.

Illustrating student practices

When given a blank piece of paper and instructed to "take notes," students will inevitably display variations in the ways they organize the information overall as well as in how they elect to jot down each separate entry in their notes. In this second half of Chapter Three, several variations are exhibited in order to illustrate the multitude of ways students tackle the notetaking act. These samples are drawn from Swedish upper secondary school students (ages 16-19) who took notes while listening to a TED Talk given by Prosanta Chakrabarty, a scientist who studies cave fish. The talk is roughly five minutes in length and is generally about Chakrabarty's work investigating the evolution of eyesight in cave fish and how that work can contribute to both eyesight evolution from a historical perspective and improvements to human eye care (a full transcript of the talk is available in Appendix A at the end of the book).

Organizational options

The following figures illustrate the various ways that these students organized their notes at a broad level. Discussion focuses on the organizational strategies rather than the content of the notes, which is the objective in later sections.

A number of students choose to write their notes from left to right, with the notes extending the full width of the paper (see Figure 3.2). In this sample (as well as others in the data set), students write in short bursts of words ranging from one to four, although single words are rather common in Figure 3.2. Each individual segment is separated by a comma and no distinguishing hierarchy of information is discernable, at least to the outsider examining the notes. Relationships between main and supporting ideas as well as examples appear to be nonexistent.

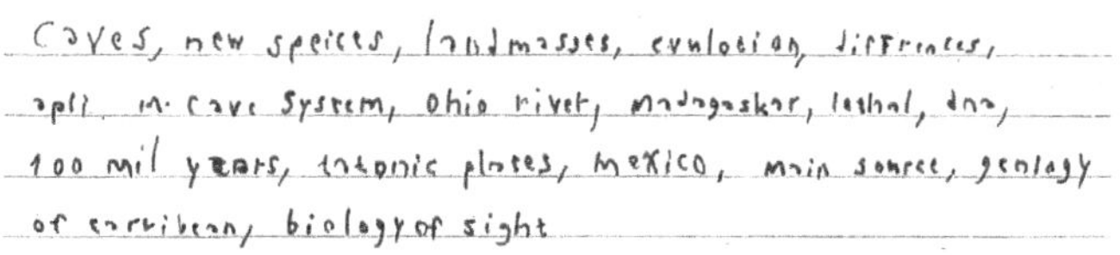

Notetaking from the L2 student perspective 71

> Caves, new species, landmasses, evolution, differences,
> split in Cave System, Ohio river, madagaskar, lethal, dna,
> 100 mil years, tatonic plates, mexico, main source, geology
> of caribbean, biology of sight

Figure 3.2 Notes taken in short bursts, left to right

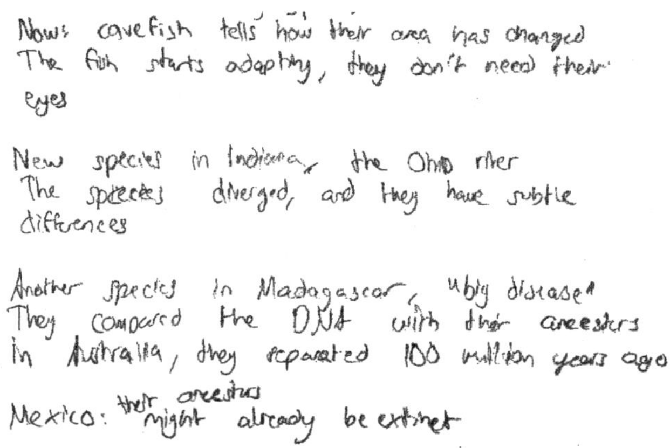

> Now: cave fish tells how their area has changed
> The fish starts adapting, they don't need their
> eyes
>
> New species in Indiana, the Ohio river
> The species diverged, and they have subtle
> differences
>
> Another species in Madagascar, "big disease"
> They compared the DNA with their ancestors
> in Australia, they separated 100 million years ago
> Mexico: their ancestors might already be extinct

Figure 3.3 Notes with spaces

Another student elected to record notes from left to right, similar to those in Figure 3.2. What distinguishes the notes in Figure 3.3 are the spaces intentionally left between short sections of notes. This technique may serve to indicate where a speaker has paused noticeably longer than at other times and/or to show a shift in topic. Spaces could be useful for later revision, either during the notetaking act itself or after the listening event has concluded and the student is reading through and adding information to notes. This sample also includes a few extended and complete sentences; for example, "The fish starts adapting" and "They compared their DNA with their ancestors in Australia." As such, more complete ideas are preserved in these notes than in the previous example, which often listed single words that, by themselves, lack meaning in relation to the topic and may fail to effectively stimulate accurate recall of content.

Like the notes in Figure 3.3, those in Figure 3.4 also illustrate how students can purposefully leave a blank line in between sections of notes. In addition, the notes in Figure 3.4 provide evidence of a unique strategy, namely of adding a single key or summary word that compresses the meaning of that particular section. A review of hundreds of student note samples for this TED Talk revealed this single example of the technique, which seems recommendable as it forces the notetaker to condense their notes even further, a practice that provides an index of sorts, helping make later review more efficient. Thus, this strategy has potential to aid both encoding and storage.

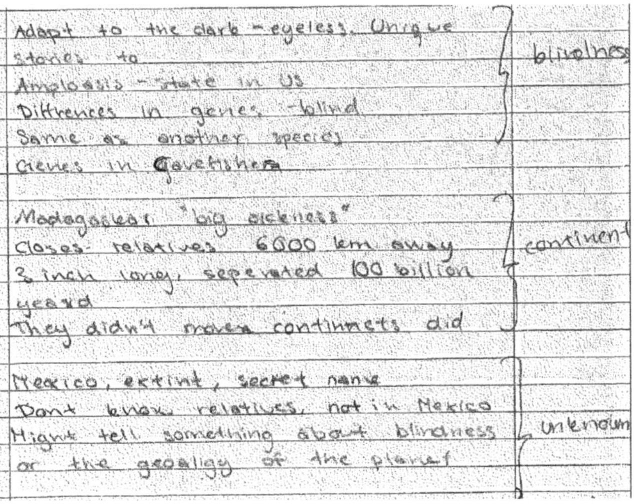

72 Notetaking from the L2 student perspective

Figure 3.4 Notes with spaces and summary words

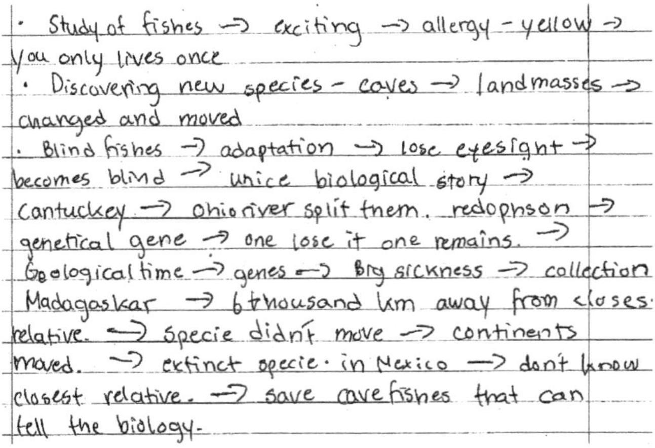

Figure 3.5 Notes with arrows

Figure 3.5 displays another variation in the horizontal, left to right approach. The repeated use of arrows may serve the purpose of presenting an order of topics and/or words the speaker used (i.e., "caves" exist on "landmasses," which have "changed and moved" over time). In some cases, the arrows could represent a cause and effect relationship. As an explicit strategy, use of arrows that is sometimes promoted in L2 English notetaking textbooks (e.g., *Listening & Notetaking Skills—Level 2*, Heinle Cengage Learning). However, the potential overuse of arrows here may render their meaning ineffective. Like other horizontal versions of notes presented

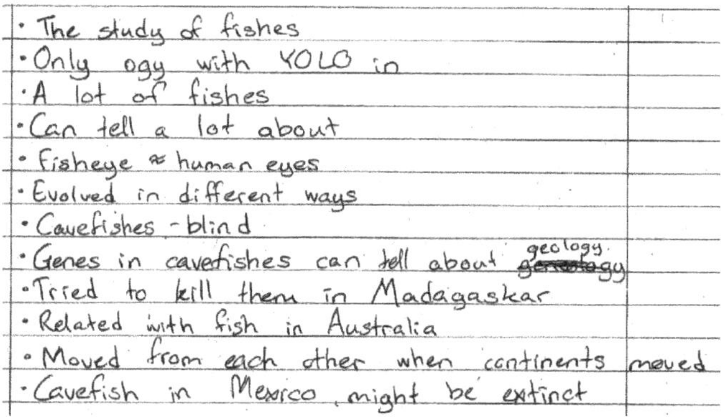

Notetaking from the L2 student perspective 73

```
· The study of fishes
· Only    ogy  with  YOLO  in
· A  lot  of  fishes
· Can  tell  a  lot  about
· Fisheye ≈ human eyes
· Evolved  in  different  ways
· Cavefishes - blind
· Genes  in  cavefishes  can  tell  about  geology
· Tried  to  kill  them  in  Madagaskar
· Related  with  fish  in  Australia
· Moved  from  each  other  when  continents  moved
· Cavefish  in  Mexico , might  be  extinct
```

Figure 3.6 Notes with bullet points

earlier, distinctions between main and supporting ideas are rather difficult to discern since all of the notes are taken in a similar manner (e.g., no bolding or underlining, constant use of arrows, etc.). Bullet points are used initially but are abandoned.

A vertical orientation to the organization of notes is adopted in Figure 3.6, which also includes bullet points on each individual line. The student typically writes at least a few words or a single phrase per line and no spaces between lines are available. Each line seems to attempt to capture a complete idea, although some of these are apparently incomplete and insufficient to stimulate recall (e.g., "can tell a lot about"). This vertical pattern of organization marks a stark contrast to the horizontal left to right versions of notes in Figures 3.2–3.5. Since there is no indentation, highlighting, bolding or any other indication of any hierarchy of importance, the degree of significance of each note entry is unclear.

A similar vertical approach was used by another student who took notes with a vertical orientation, although with x's in place of bullet points. The strategy of recording a single complete idea per line is also consistent between these two samples. Of note is the difference in techniques of using bullet points compared to cross marks or x's. The bullet point involves a single pen stroke or poke while the x, simple as it may be, involves twice as many strokes of the pen. This "x" example displayed a lack of indentation or any other indication of the hierarchical relation between the items.

The notes in Figure 3.7 begin at the upper left corner of the paper and gradually drift towards the bottom right corner. Most of the notes are listed line by line in the center of the paper. This configuration seems to be the result of handwriting speed and control in relation to the rapidly incoming speech. Despite the fact that some indentation is visible, this is likely not purposeful to the overall organization. Assuming the writer is right-handed, they continue to drift to the right as the speech continues without any evident strategy for doing so. In contrast to the previous two samples, no markers

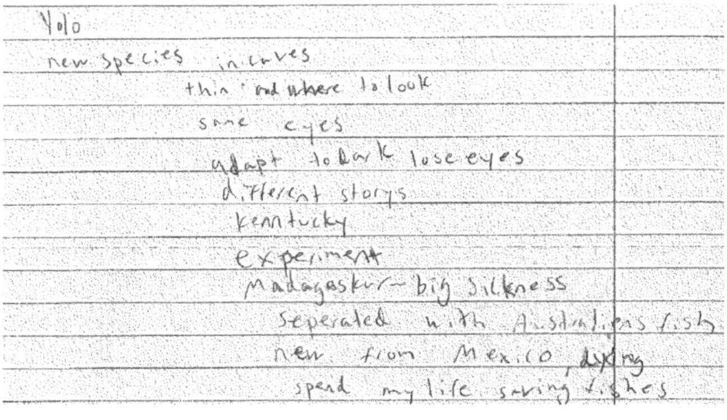

74 *Notetaking from the L2 student perspective*

Figure 3.7 Drifting notes

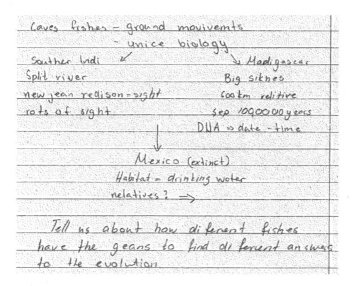

Figure 3.8 A vertical pattern with arrows

(e.g., bullet points or x's) are used to distinguish new ideas. Instead, one infers that new ideas are placed on new lines on the paper.

In Figure 3.8, a more sophisticated vertical pattern is evident, one that combines note items in thematic groups with arrows to indicate the relationship between a broader idea and the examples the speaker used to elaborate on that general idea. The notetaker recognized "unice" (unique) biology" and that the speaker listed and provided details for three distinct geographic examples (Southern Indi (Indiana), Madagascar, and Mexico). This relationship is highlighted through the placement of "unique biology" in an upper central position, connected by arrows with the three examples and related details written below.

Notetaking from the L2 student perspective 75

Figure 3.9 Two columns

The sample in Figure 3.9 shows how students may choose to divide their paper into two vertical columns. This was most likely a decision made prior to the beginning of the presentation and represents a meta-cognitive (i.e., planning) strategy that this notetaker adopts regardless of content or theme. The dividing line down the center of the paper creates shorter spaces in which to write, which may result in two benefits for notetaking efficiency: (1) the notetaker is restrained from writing all the way across the paper from left to right, and (2) after writing notes from the left to the center line, the writer needs to move their hand only half the distance back to the left-aligned starting position in order to continue (i.e., in comparison to writing horizontally across the page and then returning to the left side). All of the note entries begin at approximately the same distance from the starting location, making hierarchical relationships difficult to distinguish. However, the notetaker includes lines (for example, extending "cavefish" to "biology, geology, evolution of sights") and one indented arrow (demonstrating that "cavefish" are one type of "fish").

A mind map or word web is illustrated in Figure 3.10. This type of organizational configuration was seldom seen in the note samples collected, although this structure may be well-known to students and teachers alike, particularly when used for brainstorming or structuring information for productive (i.e., not receptive) purposes. In this case, "study of fishes" is positioned in a relatively central location and circled, clearly demarcating it as the central theme of the content. From that core circle, lines connect to relevant

76 *Notetaking from the L2 student perspective*

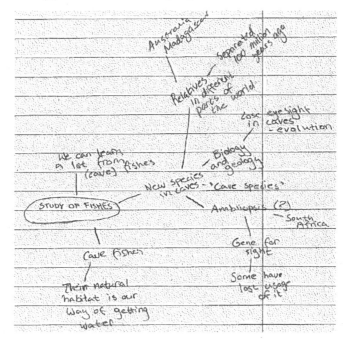

Figure 3.10 A mind map or word web

subtopics, which in turn have lines linking them to more details and examples related to those subtopics. Through the use of these connecting lines, some relationships between more important ideas and supporting details are evident. However, the significance of each subtopic relative to each other is unclear, and the use of the mind map formation neglects the structured lines on the notepaper provided. The mind map format may be better suited for some types of content than others.

Summary comments on organizational options

As evident from the vast array of structuring strategies evident in Figures 3.2–3.10, students produce very distinct sets of notes even when listening to the same content. Many of the strategies employed above may work well for the individual student who took the respective notes. While all organizational frameworks for notes have advantages and drawbacks, from an objective outsider's perspective, some have more weak points than others. From the overview presented above, one key concern is the lack of emphasis on distinguishing the importance of different pieces of information, both in relation to the central theme of the topic and to each other. In other words, it is often difficult to discern a hierarchy of significance from the samples above.

According to Hamp-Lyons (1983): "The crucial skill which [notetakers] must learn is the ability to distinguish levels of generalization: at the very least, they must be able to distinguish the thesis or main topic, from the supports which validate it, from the examples which illustrate them, i.e., three levels of generalization" (p. 119). It is possible, of course, that the notetaker would review their notes and do one of the following: highlight, circle, etc., the set of notes they took to indicate such relationships and/or rewrite their "rough draft" notes in a more orderly and sophisticated manner to demonstrate these relationships.

The purpose in sharing these different versions of notes has been to present an overall view of the many options that students have at their disposal when it comes to organizational practices. Most students probably do not put much thought into "how" they take notes. Instead, they just pick up a pen and paper and begin the task without much preparation or consideration of how they approach notetaking or appreciation for its complexity. Teachers and students alike may wish to consider whether certain organizational principles may be better (or worse) suited for various types of input, lecture styles, or themes.

Whereas this section has focused mostly on how the notes appear on the page, discussion next moves on to individual discrete items in notes and the various ways that these can be recorded, often with similar levels of accuracy.

Same information, different notes

The following section zeros in on specific places within student notes where students have recorded the same information in different ways. Extracts from the transcript of Chakrabarty's talk are listed in **bold**. Below the transcript extracts are images from student notes that illustrate how individual students attempted to record that respective piece of information, with varying degrees of success. In cases where an image may be difficult to read, a typed version of the notes is also included. Discussion of the discrete techniques employed by the students as well as commentary on their presumed effectiveness is also included.

Sample 1: "Ichthyology, the study of fishes"

The following four examples demonstrate different ways that students recorded the following statement: "Ichthyology, the study of fishes." All of these extracts demonstrate students using some similar and some distinct techniques. In Figure 3.11, the student has used an "x" as a symbol indicating a new piece of information (as described above). The meaning of ichthyology (i.e., the study of fish) is stated first, followed by the more scientific term. The student indicates uncertainty about spelling with a question mark.

Figure 3.11 Study of fishes (Sample A)

78 *Notetaking from the L2 student perspective*

The question mark may serve the purpose of marking the item as one to return to in order to check spelling and/or review content.

In Figure 3.12, the technical term is listed first, followed by "Yolo," which is a reference to a joke made by the speaker. The definition (i.e., fish science) comes next. In an interpretive move, the student has replaced "study of" with "science." Ichthyology was likely a new word for most listeners in this activity, and seldom if ever was it spelled correctly in any of the note samples. In Figure 3.12, the student has recorded a phonetic approximation that closely resembles the pronunciation. However, it is spelled incorrectly and no symbols are used to indicate any uncertainty about that point.

Both text and a pictorial representation of a fish were used by the student in Figure 3.13. The picture may well help memory and certainly helps to distinguish this item from the others that are recorded with words. Since the student also wrote the word "fish," the fact that both the word and the picture represent the same item of information means that some redundancy is evident.

The notes in Figure 3.14 show a student who largely prefers pictorial representations to writing notes with words. The "study of fishes" is illustrated through the book image with a fish on the cover. This technique succeeds in capturing the essence of the speaker's utterance but also fails to record the (likely novel and thus probably worthy of being recorded) "Ichthyology." This particular student continued with pictures to represent cavefish and the speaker's advancement to the evolution of their vision.

Figure 3.12 Study of fishes (Sample B)

Figure 3.13 Study of fishes (Sample C)

Figure 3.14 Study of fishes (Sample D)

Notetaking from the L2 student perspective   79

Sample 2: "Now, fish have eyes that are essentially the same as ours"

In Figure 3.15, the notetaker has recorded a roughly verbatim version, capturing the main point that fish eyes and human eyes are basically the same.

Figure 3.16 captures the same content in an arguably more efficient manner by incorporating the arrow symbol to mean "essentially the same as," a technique that saves both pen strokes and space. The word "fish" is also omitted from "fish eyes," likely because the main theme related to fish has been established earlier in the notes and therefore does not need to be repeated here.

Translanguaging is evident in Figures 3.17 and 3.18, as the students recorded in a mixture of L1 Swedish and English. In Figure 3.17, the student wrote "eyes – som våra," which translates to "eyes – like ours." In the second example, "fisk har sam eyes" equates to "fish have the same eyes," with the first three words in Swedish and only the final "eyes" in English. These students have mixed one English word with Swedish words to preserve the meaning, a pattern that corresponds to the discussion of translanguaging earlier in this chapter. Reasons for doing so are open to speculation and invite questions as to the need or desire to mix languages. Interestingly, it is the same English word "eyes" that has been recorded. Nevertheless, the message has been recorded successfully.

Fish eyes- Same as ours

Figure 3.15 Fish eyes (Sample A)

eyes → ours

Figure 3.16 Fish eyes (Sample B)

eyes - som våra.

Figure 3.17 Fish eyes (Sample C) ("eyes – som våra")

Fisk har sam eyes

Figure 3.18 Fish eyes (Sample D) ("Fisk har sam eyes")

80   *Notetaking from the L2 student perspective*

Sample 3: "There's this gene called rhodopsin that's super-critical for sight"

Another scientific term, "rhodopsin," comes up during the presentation, another novel piece of information that students struggled to spell correctly. Some, like that in Figure 3.19, were able to make phonetic approximations of varying accuracy. The equal sign links the gene name with its relevance to the topic, and the phrase "that's super-critical" has been omitted.

The technical term is not included in the notes in Figure 3.20; however, the important adjective "critical" has been noted. This adds some addition information that does not exist in Figure 3.19. That is, the speaker is not simply talking about a "gene for sight" (as described above), but a gene that is not only critical but "super-critical" for vision, which the notes in Figure 3.20 come closer to capturing. The shorter word "eyes" has been substituted for "sight," perhaps due to word length or possibly ease of spelling, with eyes being a higher frequency word.

Among these three examples, the significance of this gene, as emphasized by the speaker, is represented best in Figure 3.21. Here, the notetaker has made an attempt at recording the novel term and included the speaker's own adjective "super-critical." Despite the spelling error in "critical," the phonetic approximation "qritikel" seems reasonably transparent.

Sample 4: "This is a new species we described from Madagascar that we named Typhleotris mararybe. That means "big sickness" in Malagasy, for how sick we got trying to collect this species.... Now, I love this species despite the fact that it tried to kill us."

Whereas many students recorded the country name "Madagascar" in their notes, no one attempted to record the scientific name of the species. Instead, most recorded the nickname given to the species by the speaker and his

Figure 3.19 Gene for sight (Sample A)

Figure 3.20 Gene for sight (Sample B)

Figure 3.21 Gene for sight (Sample C)

Notetaking from the L2 student perspective 81

Big sickness - madagascar - tried to kill us

Figure 3.22 Big sickness (Sample A) ("Big sickness – Madagascar – tried to kill us")

Madagascar + Big Sickness   Tried to kill

Figure 3.23 Big sickness (Sample B)

team (i.e., "big sickness"). This is evident in Figures 3.22 and 3.23. These two samples are very consistent, and they both include the speaker's joke or exaggeration "tried to kill us." One noticeable difference between these two examples is the juxtaposition of "big sickness" and "Madagascar," with the former coming first in the first example and the two items being in opposite positions in the second. In Figure 3.23, the notes are taken in the order of introduction by the speaker (i.e., Madagascar first and big sickness next). However, in Figure 3.22 the nickname is written first, followed by the country. Perhaps the repetition of the language "Malagasy" is what prompted the notetaker to record the country. Since several geographic locations are mentioned throughout the presentation, listeners likely recognized their importance to the overall topic.

In Figure 3.24, much of the speaker's output has been omitted with the exception of "species" and "Madagascar." The notetaker has also substituted "disease" for "sickness" when recording the nickname "big sickness." At seven letters, "disease" is slightly shorter than the eight-letter "sickness," although this change would likely not save the notetaker much time. Since the two words are nearly synonymous, for the purposes of capturing the speaker's intention, this substitution seems successful.

Only L1 Swedish and a small picture of a fish are used in Figure 3.25. The "sjuka när de hittar [indeterminate]" translates approximately to "they got sick when they found [indeterminate]." Despite the final word being difficult to decipher, the small fish picture helps to establish that the speaker and his team became sick when they found this type of fish. As this item is written entirely in the L1, it corresponds to the second model of notetaking outlined

Another species in Madagascar, "big disease"

Figure 3.24 Big sickness (Sample C)

+ skjuka när de hittar nysio

Figure 3.25 Big sickness (Sample D)

82   *Notetaking from the L2 student perspective*

in Figure 3.1, where a listener hears their L2, translates in their heads, and then produces written output in their L1 in notes.

Sample 5: "[These species] have been separated for more than 100 million years, or about the time that the southern continents were last together. So in fact, these species didn't move at all. It's the continents that moved them"

Sample 5 represents the longest and most sophisticated of the transcript and note extracts that are examined here. The transcript contains several key pieces of information: (1) that the species are separated; (2) that they have been separated for more than 100 million years; (3) that at that time, the southern continents were joined; (4) that the species did not actively move on their own; and (5) that the species were moved due to reconfiguration of the continents. As such, discussion of note contents also becomes more elaborate.

The notes in Figure 3.26 preserve points 1, 2, and 3. The fact that the species did not actively move or that the continents shifted are not represented in the notes, although they could be inferred, especially within the context of the entire presentation and with the entire set of notes available. The use of the single word "separated" is interesting because it could refer to either the fish species or the continents, or both. The fact that the continents are now in different locations than they were 100 million years ago is, of course, common knowledge, and that may be the reason the notetaker did not see that as important information to record.

Specific countries are listed in Figure 3.27, along with a joining line above which the word "same" is written. This configuration is likely meant to represent the notion that these places were once part of the same continent and/or that the same species lived in these places until the continents moved. The use of the equal sign in this example is noteworthy since it is being used in a rather unorthodox manner. In other words, "Madagaskar + Australien" does not necessary equal "continents moved," although they are examples of places that have moved. This example does not mention the species or

Figure 3.26 Separation (Sample A)

Figure 3.27 Separation (Sample B)

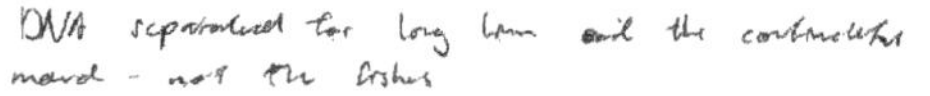

Notetaking from the L2 student perspective 83

DNA separated for long time and the continents moved – not the fishes

Figure 3.28 Separation (Sample C) ("DNA separated for long time and the continents moved – not the fishes")

Separetes 100 million years → Pangea

Figure 3.29 Separation (Sample D)

fish at all, presumably because that has been made clear from previous notes and listening comprehension. The detail of time is also entirely absent. As such, it can be argued that points 1, 3, and possibly 5 have been addressed.

Figure 3.28 is an example that acknowledges points 4 and 5, in particular, the following: "the continents moved – not the fishes." Rather than recording the specific time mentioned (i.e., "more than 100 million years"), this notetaker used a more abstract phrase ("for long time"). While lacking in detail, the phrase expresses the speaker's intention. "DNA," mentioned previously in the talk, is used in place of "species," which can be viewed as an adept choice, since the speaker is in fact more concerned with the fishes' DNA rather than the fish themselves.

The multifunctional "separated" is used in Figure 3.29, and a specific number of years is listed. What makes this example as remarkable is the use of "Pangea." By using this term, the writer acknowledges both the past (when the continents were joined) and the present (that Pangea has separated into the geography of today). Even though the speaker never uses "Pangea" in his presentation, this notetaker made an efficient and effective choice. This word choice demonstrates how background knowledge can have an impact on what and how one records information in notes. It also demonstrates how the notetaker is an intermediary, transferring spoken words through a cognitive filter that results in unique representations of information in notes.

Summary comments on individual samples

The extracts of students notes presented in Figures 3.11–3.29 serve to demonstrate the numerous different yet often equally effective ways that students can record the same piece of information. These examples have demonstrated various techniques at a very precise level: recording verbatim, word substitution, using symbols, drawing pictures, and choice of language. One could argue that, for each specific transcript extract, some of the notes may be better, clearer, or more efficient. Without consulting the notetakers themselves, it is complicated to determine the extent to which these notes could indeed stimulate accurate recall of the lecture content, particularly as more time between the listening and notetaking act passes. While the

84 Notetaking from the L2 student perspective

accompanying commentary has attempted to make objective observations and speculations about the techniques employed, it is not possible to state that any of these techniques are superior to others, particularly when notetaking is used in various contexts in relation to myriad topics.

For EAP and EMI teachers, the take away from the samples of student notes will hopefully be an appreciation for the creativity and wealth of possible strategies that students have at their disposal. Understanding student preferences and offering relevant advice for efficiency can help students maximize the quality and quantity of their notes as well as help conserve cognitive energy to expend on the listening comprehension process. Teachers may wish to target specific techniques illustrated in this chapter through explicit and purposeful notetaking practice in the classroom (e.g., practice for word substitution, utilizing background knowledge, creating accurate representations of the relationships between different agents and/or concepts). Classroom activities for these and other notetaking skills and strategies will be covered in Chapter Five.

Chapter summary

This chapter began by presenting survey findings that shed light on various aspects of L2 notetaking from students' perspectives. Results from these surveys, including a large-scale data collection involving students from seven different countries showed how EAP and EMI students share relatively similar views on L2 notetaking; for example, that notetaking ability in English is a crucial academic skill and that specific attention from teachers can be valuable in helping L2 students improve. Authentic samples from student notes illustrated the many options that students have both in terms of organizational tactics and methods for recording individual pieces of information. Despite notetaking being an individualized activity, one that many students do in their own idiosyncratic ways, when it comes to classroom teaching in EAP and EMI preparation courses, teachers are often challenged to teach groups of varying sizes in uniform ways using identical materials. Textbooks and other commercial materials for EAP notetaking instruction have been around for decades but have recently begun to receive more attention from materials writers and teachers, interest likely sparked by the rise of EMI courses and the subsequent need for L2 notetaking instruction. Chapter Four delves into commercial materials for notetaking and provides a framework for and detailed example of textbook evaluation.

References

Barbier, M.-L., Roussey, J.-Y., Piolat, A., & Olive, T. (2006). Note-taking in second language: Language procedures and self evaluation of the difficulties. *Current Psychology Letters*, 20 (3), 1–14.

Brown, J. D. (1998). *Understanding research in second language learning*. Cambridge: Cambridge University Press.

Burns, A. (2010). *Doing action research in English language teaching: A guide for practitioners.* New York, NY: Routledge.

Canagarajah, S. (2011). Codemeshing in academic writing: Identifying teachable strategies of translanguaging. *The Modern Language Journal*, 95(3), 401–417.

Chakrabarty, P. (2016, February). Clues to prehistoric times, found in blind cavefish [Video file]. Retrieved from https://www.ted.com/talks/prosanta_chakrabarty_clues_to_prehistoric_times_found_in_blind_cavefish/transcript?language=en.

Conteh, J. (2018). Translanguaging. *ELT Journal*, 72(4), 445–447.

Crawford, M., Ducker, N., MacGregor, L., Kojima, S., & Siegel, J. (2016). Perspectives on note taking in EFL listening. *JALT Postconference Publication-JALT 2015*, Tokyo: JALT, pp. 277–284.

Dörnyei, Z. (2003). *Questionnaires in second language research: Construction, administration, and processing.* Mahwah, NJ: Lawrence Erlbaum.

García, O. (2009). Education, multilingualism and translanguaging in the 21st century. In A. Mohanty, M. Panda, R. Phillipson & T. Skutnabb-Kangas (Eds.), *Multilingual education for social justice: Globalising the local* (pp. 128–145). New Delhi: Orient Blackswan.

Hamp-Lyons, L. (1983). Survey of materials for teaching advanced listening and note-taking. *TESOL Quarterly*, 17(1), 109–122.

İpek, H. (2018) Perceptions of ELT students on their listening and note taking skills. *International Online Journal of Education and Teaching (IOJET)*, 5(1), 206–217. http://iojet.org/index.php/IOJET/article/view/281/226.

Jansen, R., Lakens, D., & Ijsselsteijn, A. (2017). An integrative review of the cognitive costs and benefits of note-taking. *Educational Research Review*, 22, 223–233.

Kusumoto, Y. (2019). EFL students perception of note-taking and the effect of note-taking instruction. *The Kyushu Academic Society of English Language Education Bulletin*, 47, 47–56.

Lim, P., & Smalzer, W. (2014). *Listening & notetaking skills, Level 2.* (4th ed.). Boston: National Geographic Learning and Heinle Cengage Learning.

Luo, L., Kiewra, K., & Samuelson, L. (2016). Revising lecture notes: How revision, pauses, and partners affect note taking and achievement. *Instructional Sciences*, 44, 45–67.

Morehead, K., Dunlosky, J., Rawson, K., Blasiman, R., & Hollis, R. (2019). Notetaking habits of 21st century college students: Implications for student learning, memory, and achievement. *Memory*, 27(6), 807–819.

Piolat, A., Barbier, M. L., & Roussey, J. Y. (2008). Fluency and cognitive effort during first-and second-language notetaking and writing by undergraduate students. *European psychologist*, 13(2), 114–125.

Siegel, J. (2016). A pedagogic cycle for EFL note-taking. *English Language Teaching Journal*, 70(3), 275–286.

Siegel, J. (2018a). Notetaking in ELT: Highlighting contrasts. *TESOL Journal*, 10(1), 1–5.

Siegel, J. (2018b). Teaching lecture notetaking with authentic materials. *ELT Journal*, 73(2), 124–133.

Siegel, J. (2019). Collaborative action research on notetaking: Simultaneous cycles. *The European Journal of Applied Linguistics and TESOL*, 9(1), 77–100.

Siegel, J. (2020). Appreciating translanguaging in student notes. *ELT Journal*, 74(1), 86–88.

Skolverket (Swedish Ministry of Education). (2011). Curriculum for English at upper secondary school. Retrieved from https://www.skolverket.se/undervisning/

gymnasieskolan/laroplan-program-och-amnen-i-gymnasieskolan/amnesplaner-i-gymnasieskolan-pa-engelska

Teng, H. (2011). Exploring note-taking strategies of EFL listeners. *Procedia Social and Behavorial Sciences*, 15, 480–484.

Van de Meer, J. (2012). Students' note-taking challenges in the twenty-first century: Considerations for teachers and academic staff developers. *Teaching in Higher Education*, 17(1), 13–23.

Wagner, E. (2015). Survey Research. In B. Paltridge & Phakiti, A. (Eds.). *Research methods in applied linguistics* (pp. 83–100). London: Bloomsbury.

4 Principles for evaluating L2 notetaking textbooks

Introduction

Textbook evaluation has been a standard practice among language teachers for years. To assist teachers in understanding how to view materials in an objective way and to focus their attention on relevant elements of commercial materials, principles, prompts, and questions for such evaluation have been presented in pedagogic literature (e.g., Sheldon, 1988; Tomlinson, 2010). As pointed out by Harwood (2010), all evaluation checklists are at least to some extent dependent on context and student and teacher needs. As such, they should be viewed more as guides to help inform decisions but are typically created for awareness-raising and illustrative purposes.

By using such evaluation checklists and prompts as baseline measures, teachers and/or course planners can consider the strengths and weaknesses of commercial textbooks in comparison to each other. Thus, they can make informed decisions about which materials to use for their courses. While this type of evaluation may be commonplace with four-skills, integrated-skills, or skill-specific (e.g., speaking) textbooks, it has not been applied extensively to commercial notetaking materials. The lone exception I have found is Hamp-Lyons (1983), published in the early 1980s, in which eight notetaking textbooks were examined.

As the number of EAP and EMI courses has expanded, L2 notetaking has become more prominent and is often explicitly stated in the goals of such courses, particularly EAP prep and introductory academic skill courses. In response to a growing need for notetaking textbooks and materials in EAP, major publishers have created a number of multilevel series, which are fertile ground for applying evaluative principles specific to the skill of L2 notetaking. The criteria that have been expressed by Sheldon (1988) and others were likely created with the four main language skills (e.g., listening, speaking, reading, and writing) in mind. They struggle to account for the complexity of L2 notetaking, and therefore this chapter promotes and applies a set of evaluation criteria specifically for notetaking textbooks.

On their own, teachers may be unprepared to assess the quality of commercial materials for notetaking. First, many teachers fail to acknowledge the complexity of notetaking and simply assume that instructing learners

88 Evaluating L2 notetaking textbooks

to "take notes" is appropriate and adequate for learners to develop their abilities. Secondly, teacher education may not have prepared educators to understand the myriad subtle and crucial factors and steps that comprise notetaking. In addition, teachers may not recognize that L2 listening comprehension and notetaking in an L2 are distinct skills, and that materials for them need to be examined in isolation for their ability to accurately target their explicit objective. That is, if a textbook claims to teach notetaking, then a majority of the activities and content need to focus on that central goal (i.e., not listening practice in the guise of notetaking practice).

Since it is now widely recognized that notetaking is a tool essential for academic success in lecture learning, combined with the rise in EAP notetaking, a set of principles for notetaking materials evaluation is needed in order for teachers to compare and contrast options and make informed and justified decisions. This chapter presents and discusses a set of 14 criteria for evaluation of commercial L2 notetaking materials, which have been created and organized according to principles for materials evaluation checklist design (e.g., deciding and formulating criteria, incorporating both universal and more specific criteria, etc.) (McGrath, 2016). Instead of focusing on the listening texts that accompany such works (i.e., audio or video texts), this list of prompts incorporates theoretical and practical aspects of *notetaking* (i.e., not *listening*), several of which have been discussed in the preceding chapters. The list of criteria consists of broader questions whose aim is to generate an overview of the coursebook in question as a unified whole. Narrower prompts zero in on the unit, page, and exercise level. This chapter introduces those principles and elaborates on their theoretical underpinnings and importance. In addition, this list is applied to one textbook in order to illustrate its potential use and to provide a model for other teachers to follow.

A case for evaluation of notetaking materials

When teaching any respective language skills or a combination thereof, the goals for the course should be explicitly stated so that students are aware of what they will learn and so teachers know what to teach. When students and teachers are set to begin a course such as "Academic notetaking" or "Lecture listening," the notetaking element may be explicitly stated or implicitly alluded to, but the link between academic listening and notetaking is likely to be recognized in either case. Thus, one would expect objectives distinctly aimed at notetaking development while listening to academic content would be included. If notetaking is a stated or implied goal, then textbooks chosen for the course should, in large part, target notetaking. In a reading class, for instance, one would expect to do large amounts of reading, often in different ways and through various activities and texts. In a writing class, same thing. Notetaking materials, however, have not received the same type of nuanced attention. Many times notetaking skills are assumed and practiced but not explicitly taught, and as such, the objective of developing learners' notetaking abilities in the sense of improving proficiency and adding skills and strategies to the current cache is in danger of being overlooked. Textbooks for notetaking are viewed at times as if they were *listening* materials with the thinking that if the listening texts themselves are appropriate, then accompanying notetaking activities must be as well. However, the ways in which textbooks engage with notetaking deserve attention distinct from that of L2 listening.

Tomlinson (2010) lays out principles of language teaching, which include elements of alignment, development, and transferability. The principle of alignment suggests that the content (i.e., materials, teaching and learning points, etc.) of a course should be in line with the methods and objectives employed in the course. For the purposes of notetaking, if a notetaking textbook is selected, then its content needs to: improve on the learners' current L2 notetaking ability, raise awareness of potential (though not required) options, and foster flexible and adaptive ways to take notes. Regarding development, the textbook must offer new and varied strategies for the student to acquire and not simply provide repeated and non-developmental practice. Because notetaking can be utilized in both L1 and L2 courses, the transferability of organizational strategies, encoding techniques, and review exercises can easily cross over to other academic subjects, EMI or otherwise.

Materials have often been viewed at three distinct levels: approach, design, and procedure (Richards & Rodgers, 2014). At a general level, *approach* refers to the nature of language itself and how teaching and learning can be carried out. The most relevant theories of language for lecture notetaking are arguably the cognitive model and the genre model. The former involves a view of the mind as a computer that performs a system of procedures that process input and generate output (e.g., Atkinson, 2011). Applied to lecture notetaking, this means listening to incoming aural input, processing that input in the mind, and finally creating notes as the output. The genre model is relevant to lecture notetaking because the genre of the academic lecture embodies "norms of language use" (Richards & Rodgers, 2014, p. 25). Among those norms are introductions, definitions, and explanations, along with lecture types such as those that connect theory to practice or cover material in chronological order (see Chapter Two).

In reference to theories of learning and notetaking, the creative-construction hypothesis is relevant, particularly when it comes to generative notetaking. This hypothesis states that learning is not simply a matter of reproducing input but is instead a creative process that involves construction and interpretation of meaning based on input and could help explain, at least at a theoretical level, why a room full of students all listening to the same content produce different notes. The theory of constructivism also pertains to notetaking in that learning comes from a learner's internal meaning-making mechanisms (Williams & Burden, 1997). Since lecture content is processed internally before notes are generated, this theory can also help to explain why different individuals take notes in various ways and with ranging success.

Design involves the specification of content to be taught and learned, as well as the roles adopted by teachers, students, and materials

90 *Evaluating L2 notetaking textbooks*

(Richards & Rodgers, 2014). In practical terms, design involves syllabus-level details, such as teaching and learning objectives and texts to be used for those purposes. *Design* in terms of notetaking textbooks comes into play when examining the lecture texts that have been chosen to correspond with notetaking instruction and practice. In addition, the types and frequency of notetaking tasks, as well as the roles in which those tasks and the corresponding instructions place learners and teachers, are relevant. For example, if the materials allow for teachers to add their own advice or additional techniques for notetaking, this would recognize a valuable role for the instructor in relation to notetaking. If not, then it would seem the materials themselves can do the job sufficiently without teacher input. For learner roles, acknowledgment of individual notetaker differences and incorporating some flexibility would demonstrate that learners are expected to capture ideas in a number of ways rather than to produce "correct" answers.

Procedure is the level closest to actual happenings in the classroom and includes pedagogic activities and techniques. As expressed by Richards and Rodgers (2014), three dimensions are evident at the level of procedure, and all are relevant to notetaking textbook evaluation. The first is the use of teaching and learning activities and exercises; for example, the types of drills, questions, etc. The second is the ways in which the activities are used to practice, in this case, notetaking. The third involves procedures and techniques for how the teacher gives and how learners receive feedback, in this case, on their performance with specific textbook exercises for notetaking, on their notetaking ability, and/or on the quality of their notes.

For the purposes of this chapter, broad questions pertaining to materials evaluation are roughly aimed at the design level (i.e., syllabus, textbook table of contents) and the narrower prompts are at the procedural level (i.e., actual teaching and learning activities and engagement with language itself).

Notetaking: Distinct from listening

Despite academic listening and notetaking being linked by the fact that one needs to listen and comprehend incoming input before taking notes, the two skills are distinct and should be treated as such when it comes to pedagogic approaches and developmental practices. Listening involves a variety of cognitive skills, including the use of top-down and bottom-up processes. When processing input from a top-down perspective, a listener starts with an overall meaning and intention of a message and then processes various pieces of input at increasingly smaller levels: from the message situated within a communicative context, to utterances, chunks, and then individual words and sounds (e.g., Buck, 2001; Siegel, 2018). Schema, which is defined as "a 'package' of prior knowledge and experience that we have in memory and can call on in the process of comprehension (and perception in general)" is also crucial (Lynch & Mendelsohn, 2002, p. 197).

From an opposite yet complementary view, bottom-up processing begins with the actual acoustic input. Phonemes form words, which combine to

Evaluating L2 notetaking textbooks 91

form chunks, and then utterances, and the message emerges from a combination of parts in an upward direction (e.g., Field, 2008; Siegel, 2018). It is generally agreed that listeners rely on both top-down and bottom-up approaches to listening, and the utilization and/or combination of these may depend on contextual factors as well as individual preferences for information processing (e.g., Lynch & Mendelsohn, 2002; Siegel, 2015).

Without successful (at least to some degree) comprehension, taking accurate notes would be impossible. When it comes to textbook activities targeting listening and notetaking, however, there should be clear and distinct differences between the two. Listening activities in textbooks are often based on a comprehension approach (Field, 2008) in which listeners display their ability to answer questions correctly. Common types of listening practice include true-false, gap-fill, matching, and multiple-choice questions. These measure a listener's comprehension, and although in a notetaking class students might use the notes they have taken to answer such questions, these activities do not in fact target the notetaking act (i.e., encoding). Instead, the central operations are listening comprehension and/or the transfer of information from notes to the questions. They do not help develop notetaking skills; they only demonstrate the results of notes.

Therefore, teachers should be aware of listening comprehension activities and exercises that are disguised as notetaking practice. In order for activities to have a transparent focus on *notetaking*, they need to engage development of either encoding or storage. Activities that involve practicing various organizational formats, paraphrasing, simplifying, creating and using abbreviations and symbols, and depicting conceptual relationships in notes are examples of textbook exercises that emphasize encoding in notetaking. More storage-related activities would prompt students to utilize notes in a variety of ways and could include fleshing out the meaning of notes, reviewing notes, highlighting and/or underlining after the notetaking act, rewriting and/or reorganizing notes, and summarizing. It is important to observe that none of the activities listed in the previous two sentences involve demonstrating comprehension in the sense of a "correct" or "incorrect" answer. Rather, the focus is on how information is recorded in the moment and used after the fact.

Materials that feature only listening comprehension activities, or have an overwhelming imbalance in favor of such activities, are likely undervaluing and underdeveloping notetaking ability. Evaluating the percentage of each type of activity in any coursebook would be worthwhile so that the teacher can understand the extent to which the focus is on academic listening or notetaking.

Previous evaluations of notetaking materials

The single review article that I have located on L2 notetaking has been Hamp-Lyons (1983) survey of eight textbooks for notetaking. Many of those textbooks were published in the late 1970s and early 1980s. Two of the eight works she selected were actually for L1 users, likely because of the dearth of resources targeting L2 notetaking available at the time. The presence of notetaking materials for L1 users is notable, as it reinforces the notion that even L1 users need support for academic notetaking, suggesting that those listening in their L2 certainly warrant support. In that review article, Hamp-Lyons (1983) provides a list of issues and areas teachers should examine when comparing and selecting notetaking textbooks. Some topics are rather general and apply to any language teaching materials choice: cost, pedagogic accuracy, presence of an answer key, transcript for listening texts, etc. In other words, these topics are relevant to specific-skill textbooks (e.g., listening, speaking, etc.) and to integrated skill textbooks as well. They do not in any way center on the objective of notetaking.

Hamp-Lyon's (1983) criteria, however, do include some items very pertinent for notetaking. Criteria such as that the "course should teach, not only practice, skills," "[should teach] teach note-taking techniques," "[should aim for] completeness (i.e., takes the student from no note-taking ability re. lectures, to performative competence in one course)," and "[should include] model notes (pref. several alternatives)" (Hamp-Lyons, 1983, p. 109–110). This selection of criteria focuses admirably at the core notetaking goal, guiding teachers in some ways to focus their attention on these relevant aspects of textbooks. At the same time, no further elaboration is presented in the paper on how a teacher could judge the quality of the textbook in relation to these topics, and thus, the teacher is left only with their own intuition to interpret and apply these brief points. Further descriptions of and specific details related to these topics would have been helpful. As a result, teachers could struggle to determine whether a particular textbook "teaches note-taking techniques" in appropriate amounts and through appropriate means.

Conclusions from Hamp-Lyons (1983) highlighted several drawbacks in the textbooks. Importantly, none of the books focused on more than a single notetaking method or format (e.g., the outline format or the T-formation chart), meaning that students using the book were exposed to a very limited range among a plethora of organizational and systematic options (see Chapter Three). The author argues for greater variety, stating that the advantage of exposing students to various formats is that "they will later be able to select an appropriate form for a particular lecture" (p. 120). In addition, activities for notetaking development were absent in certain books. Other activities focused only on multiple-choice questions that students answered with the assistance of the notes they took, which is more of a post-notetaking activity than one that engages and develops the encoding of information. Such an exercise is more appropriate for assessment rather than the teaching and development of notetaking skills. On the positive side, some textbooks included aspects that appear in many of today's notetaking materials, including abbreviations and skeleton notes.

The level of difficulty of the listening texts is also commented upon with a view to ensuring that the gap between sheltered EAP notetaking courses and the real-world EMI lecture hall is not so large as to shock students.

In other words, the notetaking texts and materials should not be watered down or simplified too much; features of naturally spoken lectures should be included. While the topic of listening texts is certainly important and affects how teachers and students approach notetaking in the EAP classroom, this book takes the view that the quality of and approaches for notetaking instruction should not be confused with features of listening texts themselves and approaches for teaching listening, despite the two being related.

Broader criteria

The following questions should be used at the level of *design* as described above. Most of them can be answered by reading through the Table of Contents at the beginning of the textbook in focus. In principle, it is important for teachers to understand how notetaking is approached as a broad concept throughout the textbook. Such a view can offer teachers information about textbook strengths and weaknesses and suggest the types of supplementation, in terms of both materials and practice opportunities, that might be necessary.

Point 1: The genre of the academic lecture

As observed by Harwood (2010), the genre of academic material needs to be accurately represented in EAP materials. In this case the genre of EMI academic lectures should be taken into account (Harwood, 2010). With regards to notetaking during academic lectures, commercial textbooks may do well to identify, define, and provide examples of the various parts of an academic lecture. While the presence and sequence of particular elements will vary based on speaker preferences, subject content, and external factors such as time, analysis of lectures has shown that they consistently include several parts, such as introductions, discourse structuring, previews, definitions, concepts, examples, evaluations, conclusions, and asides (e.g., Young, 1994; Sheppard, et al., 2015).

Since students may need to adjust their notetaking approaches and techniques depending on which portion of a lecture they are listening to, it would benefit them from having some organizational understanding of different aspects of the lecture as well as conceptual understanding of what the lecture aims to accomplish at each stage. Furthermore, being aware of linguistic or rhetorical signals that mark shifts from one part to another would be valuable.

Point 2: Accounting for the typical academic lecture sequence

Many lectures occur within the context of an academic semester and a specific sequence of events leads up to lecture attendance and notetaking. For higher education, that sequence typically begins with the lecturer assigning reading material, which students (hopefully) have completed prior to the

94 *Evaluating L2 notetaking textbooks*

lecture. The purpose of the lecture, then, may be to review, evaluate, emphasize, clarify, contrast, and/or build on the material covered in the pre-lecture reading. Therefore, when students attend the lecture, they often have a preview and/or at least some minimal background knowledge related to the topic. In other words, seldom do students attend a lecture "cold," with no idea of the upcoming content. Instead, they are likely aware of key terms and concepts and have a general notion about the content. They are also probably aware of how that specific lecture fits in with others in the same course. Moreover, any post-lecture task, such as a quiz or summary writing activity, may have already been outlined and thus, the student has an idea of what notes to take in order to assist them with that task.

The extent to which this sequence is replicated in commercial notetaking materials is worthy of examination. This sequence, or something similar, more closely replicates the real-life experience of a notetaker in EMI university courses. At times, this sequence can be inferred from pre-listening and/or brainstorming activities in textbooks, which seek to stimulate a listener's background knowledge and schema. The extent to which textbooks, through their layout and sequencing, acknowledge and attempt to mimic an authentic lecture experience can certainly contribute to the material's value to teachers and students. In this way, the writers would be recognizing the needs of their audience and of the academic context in which they want to succeed (Harwood, 2010). Since students seldom come to a lecture "cold," it would be strange if they are asked to do so with their EAP notetaking practice.

Point 3. Teacher and student roles

This criteria relates to Richard and Rodgers's (2014) *design*, as it aims to understand what roles the materials expect teachers and students to play in the development of notetaking proficiency. In terms of teacher roles, the following questions can be considered: What types of functions must the teacher fulfill (e.g., as a notetaking model, answer checker, practice provider, advice giver, etc.)?; How do the materials create interactional possibilities between teacher and students?; To what extent are the materials "teacher-proof" in the sense that the teacher does not need to provide any pedagogic techniques or knowledge?; Does the material allow for teachers to put their own "spin" on notetaking, or are all decisions pre-determined? When it comes to student roles, one must consider how active the materials allow students to be. Are students to passively accept the notetaking strategies and techniques introduced in the coursebook? Or are they encouraged not only to try and experiment but also to compare and decide for themselves which approaches to encoding and storage might be more appropriate for them and/or the content they are studying? The ways in which the instructions to activities are expressed, and how the activities are arranged, will certainly position learners and teachers in certain ways. Understanding how these positions manifest themselves throughout the book gives some indication of what the materials expect from teachers and students.

Evaluating L2 notetaking textbooks 95

Point 4: A syllabus itself, or "pick and choose"?

Many times, textbooks begin with simpler teaching points, more accessible texts, and lighter demands earlier, which are then built upon and developed as one progresses through the book. In that sense, the textbook could be viewed as a syllabus in itself, in that the writer has carefully planned, selected, and sequenced the content so that each unit supports the next. With that concept in mind, some teachers and course planners may elect to follow a selected course book from beginning to end. An alternative practice would be to pick and choose specific units or pages in the textbook that meet the immediate needs of individuals in or an entire class. In applying this dichotomy to notetaking, one must consider whether various aspects of notetaking are in focus throughout the book so as to warrant a "start-to-finish" approach. The choice may also depend on the current notetaking ability of the class. In other words, if the textbook provides many different elements of notetaking _and_ the class is relatively weak, that combination would suggest utilizing the whole textbook. If however, learners struggle with some particular aspect of notetaking (for example, recognizing lecture signposts, or paraphrasing content), then perhaps those units and/or pages dealing explicitly with the desired skill could be employed.

Point 5: Notetaking-specific goals

Depending on the nature of the EAP coursebook, the Table of Contents contains several types of organizational information. Most contain thematic units to which various language skills, including notetaking, are applied. If it is a general academic skills textbook, headings like "discussion strategies," "presentation strategies," and "listening strategies" may appear. More detailed Tables of Contents also include vocabulary and pronunciation objectives. From a notetaking perspective, it is important to determine whether explicit and distinct notetaking skills and strategies are listed for each unit. From this list, one can get a general overview of the extent to which notetaking is covered from basic steps or whether it is addressed as an "assumed" skill. I would personally be wary of a textbook that fails to articulate specific notetaking-related objectives throughout the book or fails to provide breadth in the sense of notetaking formats and techniques.

Point 6: Building on previous skills, strategies, and techniques

In terms of pedagogical soundness and alignment, one would logically expect that easier aspects of notetaking would come earlier in a textbook. These more straightforward techniques would then be incorporated and reviewed in exercises throughout the book and could also be extended in later chapters. When examining the Table of Contents, it is worthwhile to examine and consider whether the notetaking part of the syllabus is laid out in any type of discernable order. In my experience, many represent a scattershot of notetaking activities, often seemingly arranged at random.

96 *Evaluating L2 notetaking textbooks*

While it is difficult to list sequentially the various notetaking skills, strategies and techniques in an organized fashion in the same way as grammar acquisition or graded reading levels, some logical possibilities exist. For example, beginning with different types of overall organizational formats early in the textbook could then allow the notetaker to choose from these as they apply other more discrete techniques (e.g., abbreviations, paraphrasing) later. An alternative could be focusing on capturing keywords and main ideas early on before focusing on specific pieces of information and how to record them. In an ideal case, the materials writers would provide explanations of why they choose to sequence the notetaking objectives as they did. I suspect in some cases, a notetaking technique may be highlighted simply because it lends itself well to a selected lecture text, a decision which implies that it is the text itself (i.e., not the individual) that dictates how the notes are best taken.

Point 7: Range of systems and techniques

As pointed out by Hamp-Lyons (1983), a range of notetaking systems should be introduced to learners so that they can select the one(s) with which they are the most comfortable. In addition to acknowledging that "one size does not fit all" and catering to learner individuality, having a variety of options at their disposal will help notetakers apply different formats depending on lecture content or speaker style. Most textbooks seem to focus on only a single format and disregard others. Furthermore, given the increase in options for digital notetaking (e.g., with a laptop or tablet), one would expect textbooks to include activities and exercises aimed at notetaking with technology; however, the majority of current textbooks focus on the traditional pen and paper method and neglect digital notetaking.

Point 8: Encoding and storage

In theory, notetaking serves two important functions. One is the encoding function, which occurs as notes are being taken. The physical practice of writing (or typing) notes is thought to aid in learning and retention of that information (see Chapter Two). Encoding can take many forms, including verbatim, paraphrasing, abbreviations, and symbols. After the notes are taken and the listening event is over, the storage function becomes important. This function infers that students revisit their notes to review and/or reorganize and also that students are in fact able to use their notes to stimulate accurate recall of lecture content.

By examining a textbook's Table of Contents, teachers can get indications of the amounts of emphasis (if any) placed on each of these important aspects of notetaking. In many, the encoding function is sufficiently addressed through a range of techniques. However, the storage function is often overlooked, based on the assumption that students intuitively know what to do with their notes after a lecture or class. This assumption may be tenuous, as students may a) seldom revisit their notes after taking them and/or b) not be fully aware of methods for learning from notes (e.g., reviewing, reorganizing, writing summaries, etc.).

The encoding function is linked to L2 listening comprehension and L2 writing, and therefore likely deserves a more prominent role in the content of a course focused on the taking of notes. The various ways in which students utilize their notes for later learning, review, and tasks are more of a general academic skill than one specific to L2 teaching and learning. Students can, for example, reformat, summarize, highlight, and/or test themselves using notes, all activities that likely strengthen learning. At the same time, some acknowledgement of and support for the storage and later use of notes would help provide a more well-rounded course.

More focused criteria

Unlike the broader questions above that focus at the level of design and Tables of Content, the following five prompts can be applied at the procedural level and used to examine specific coursebook units or individual pages.

Point 9: Generative and non-generative

Most notetaking falls into one of two categories or a combination of both. In the generative variety, the notetaker creates their own version of the input they hear (for example, by paraphrasing or using pictures). Non-generative notetaking involves the consistent verbatim recording of what the speaker says. Some research suggests that generative notetaking leads to better comprehension and retention due to the cognitive effort in transferring an aural message into a similar message in written form (but with at least some paraphrasing and/or word substitution) (e.g., Mueller & Oppenheimer, 2014). The majority of notes are likely taken with a combination of these two approaches; for example, if a speaker is talking quickly and using many long words, generative notetaking may be more efficient. For definitions or particularly clear explanations, the non-generative alternative may be advisable. Sometimes verbatim notes are viewed in a negative manner compared to paraphrases or summaries, but taking particular notes verbatim can be a useful skill. Both types offer the notetaker a different tool and deserve to be explored in notetaking materials.

Point 10: Targeting specific stages of notetaking

As discussed previously, the skill of notetaking is multifaceted and complex. It involves a number of stages: listening to and comprehending the L2; making decisions about the significance of content (i.e., is it important enough to write in notes, or is it superfluous?); deciding when to write notes (e.g., when the speaker pauses or begins an aside); deciding how to write notes (e.g., both at the organizational format level and which options for encoding

98 *Evaluating L2 notetaking textbooks*

will be used for each discrete piece of information); and utilizing notes in various ways after the listening event.

It would be unrealistic to expect each page or unit to incorporate all of these aspects at once. However, each notetaking activity should have an explicit purpose that is clear to the teacher and learners. If the purpose is *instructional*, that should be clear and the unit or page should break the specific stage into teachable, learnable, and practicable chunks. If the purpose is notetaking *practice*, this should also be made clear. The distinction between instruction and practice is a crucial one when it comes to notetaking. Many teachers simply encourage practice (e.g., they say "take notes") and assume that student ability will improve through repeated practice opportunities. Such an approach neglects scaffolded teaching and learning. Therefore, teachers should inspect textbooks to ensure that there is an instruction (not just practice) for these various stages.

Point 11: Individual flexibility

Hamp-Lyons (1983) bemoaned the fact that each of the eight books she reviewed offered only a single notetaking format. This dissatisfaction stems from the view that individuals all have their own preferences for how to arrange and take notes. Therefore, exposure to a variety of overall notetaking styles and specific techniques is important as is emphasizing to students that they are developing a range of skills and strategies. They do not need to use the same approaches all the time: individual flexibility and creativity in notetaking should be promoted and strict adherence to a single format or technique avoided.

Many notetaking textbooks include listening comprehension activities. After taking notes, students are prompted to answer questions about the lecture they heard, using their notes to help them do so. A drawback of such activities as they are often portrayed in materials is that each question has a single correct answer. If the question is, "How did Captain Cook get to Australia?", the teacher and/or teacher's book might list "by ship" as the correct answer that corresponded verbatim to the lecture content. However, "by boat," "on a vessel," "by sea," the phrase "by boat" written in the student's L1, and even a hand-drawn picture of a boat all express the same core idea. Thus, flexibility for how each student successfully records a single idea is vital for recognizing and praising notetaking ability. Teaching materials should suggest a range of possible alternatives that express core ideas as well as acknowledge that other options may be possible as well. These alternatives represent a valuable teaching point for notetaking in EAP: that the same piece of information can be successfully recorded in a number of ways (e.g. verbatim, paraphrase, abbreviation, picture). Teachers can even use this range to engage students in discussions of the pros and cons of each technique and illustrate how one technique may be preferable to others in certain cases.

Evaluating L2 notetaking textbooks 99

Point 12: Distinguishing notetaking from listening comprehension

Although listening comprehension and lecture notetaking are intrinsically bound, they are two distinct skills. Activities designed for listening comprehension should be acknowledged for their capacity to measure, at least to some degree, student listening proficiency. Comprehension activities include open questions, matching, multiple choice and the like, where students are required to produce a "correct" answer (see the previous criteria). These should not be disguised as notetaking activities. Exercises that focus on the stages of notetaking mentioned above (choosing and practicing an organizational format, deciding what to record and how, paraphrasing, condensing and/or expanding notes, etc.) need to be included in sufficient amounts. It is not enough for a notetaking textbook to merely include comprehension activities about lectures. The presence of many and various activities that center attention on some explicit stage in the notetaking act would better align with the objective of notetaking. Listening comprehension activities have a place in notetaking materials, but surely they should not be the only exercises included.

Point 13: Incorporation of meta-cognitive, cognitive, and socio-affective strategies

According to O'Malley and Chamot's (1990) seminal work on language learning strategies, three major categories of strategy are used by language learners: meta-cognitive, cognitive, and socio-affective (see Chapter Six for further discussion on language learning strategies in relation to notetaking). All of these categories have been promoted as advantageous to listening comprehension, but they are seldom discussed in relation to notetaking specifically. Meta-cognitive strategies relate to the overall high-level planning, monitoring, and evaluation of learning and interaction with the target language. In terms of notetaking, this can mean being aware of and selecting a notetaking format prior to listening, determining the effectiveness of certain techniques (for example, using abbreviations or paraphrasing), and reflecting on notetaking quality and performance.

Cognitive strategies involve engagement with the actual language one encounters. For notetaking, this can mean various encoding strategies, ways in which notes can be utilized after the notetaking event, as well as predicting upcoming input, recognizing signposts, and writing notes during speaker pauses. Socio-affective strategies can involve collaboration with classmates to fill in gaps in and/or review notes and use of calming techniques when taking notes becomes stressful. Inspecting textbooks in terms of these three strategic categories can help inform teachers of where coverage is and where it may be lacking. If deficiencies are found, then teachers may need to supplement the coursebook to ensure that a range of strategies in these three areas is incorporated.

100   *Evaluating L2 notetaking textbooks*

Point 14: Roles of other language skills

As pointed out previously, notetaking cannot take place without listening comprehension and writing, and thus these three skills are inherently linked. However, other language skills, such as grammar knowledge and reading can also come into play when working with activities in notetaking textbooks. At times, exercises that claim to develop notetaking skills can be completed simply with grammatical knowledge. For example, when materials writers provide a set of skeleton notes accompanied by a box of pre-selected words that students need to use to complete the notes, it is possible for students to recognize the parts of speech of the words and/or their semantic categories and complete the activity. In other words, they may not even need to listen and take notes to succeed in such an exercise. For some activities, students may be able to rely on their background knowledge of the topic to answer comprehension questions and are therefore not obligated to take notes in the first place. Materials writers should consider the extent to which learners may draw on other language skills to complete activities and make purposeful efforts to ensure that *notetaking* is in fact required in order to complete the tasks. Otherwise, students would be developing a different set of strategies for task completion, and emphasis on notetaking would be ignored.

Applying the criteria: An illustrative evaluation

In the following section, one notetaking textbook from a popular international series, namely *Lecture Ready*, is examined in relation to the 14 criteria outlined above. Due to space constraints, a comprehensive evaluation is not possible. Instead, readers should view the evaluation below as demonstrative of how evaluation of notetaking textbooks might proceed and on which elements of the materials to focus.

Lecture Ready 2 (2nd edition) (Sarosy & Sherak, 2013)

Lecture Ready 2 is published by Oxford University Press and, per the description on the back cover, aims to prepare students for listening, notetaking, and academic discussions and presentations. As such, notetaking is not the exclusive focus but it does receive explicit attention in each unit. This is book two in the series and targets CEFR levels B1 and B2. The following is a list of notetaking strategies that are stated in the book's Table of Contents: "Write the most important words; Assess and revise your notes; use an informal outline; Use your notes to summarize the lecture; Use symbols to represent words and ideas; Use abbreviations to represent longer words; Use a visual form; Describe the visuals used in a lecture; Highlight important ideas; Annotate your notes during a lecture; Edit your notes after the lecture; and Review the note taking strategies" (Sarosy & Sherak, 2013, p. v). These notetaking themes and objectives, as well as the specific content, are analyzed in Table 4.1 in relation to the criteria described earlier in the chapter.

Table 4.1 Evaluation of *Lecture Ready 2 (2ⁿᵈ edition)*

Title: Lecture Ready 2 (2nd edition)

Broader criteria	Commentary
1. Genre of academic lecture	There is some acknowledgement of the academic lecture as a genre, and the textbook seems to assume teachers and learners are already familiar with the various components and generic features of the academic lecture. In selected places, such as "language that signals the big picture" (p. 17), "recognizing lecture language for transitions" (p. 31) and "language that signals a definition" (p. 43), specific elements of lectures mentioned. These fall under the category of "listening strategies," and while they do not go into great depth about the role such features ultimately play in lectures, they expose students to samples of lecture output related to the respective element. Transcripts of the lectures are not available in the student book, which would have provided opportunities for identifying various parts of lectures (e.g., introductions, definitions, etc.). However, these may be available from the online student center.
2. Academic lecture sequence	Each unit begins with a picture to stimulate student thinking followed by a short reading connected to the unit theme. Listening strategies are introduced after which notetaking is emphasized through "concept boxes," isolated practice, predictions, notetaking itself and then comprehension exercises. Following the main lecture and notetaking practice, students engage in discussion and presentation activities. Based on this sequence, the textbook closely resembles a typical academic lecture sequence, as it first introduces the unit/lecture theme through pictures and introductory readings. Then the lecture itself is in focus, followed by discussion and debriefing.
3. Teacher and student roles	The role of the teacher seems to be as materials provider, text controller, and answer checker. The teacher is not encouraged (at least based on examination of the student book) to demonstrate model notes or notetaking, or to offer their individual advice on notetaking. Instead, it seems the book is meant to provide the input on notetaking. Students are expected to follow instructions and complete the exercises.
4. Syllabus or selection	Based on the notetaking specific objectives in the Table of Contents, this seems to cater to teachers who want to pick and choose units and/or practice that focuses on a particular aspect of notetaking. If students need support with, for example, summarizing a lecture or focusing on visual aids, teachers can select those specific units and/or activities. From a notetaking standpoint, the textbook organization does not represent a scaffolded syllabus to a great degree.

(Continued)

Table 4.1 (Continued)

102 *Evaluating L2 notetaking textbooks*

Title: *Lecture Ready 2 (2nd edition)*	
Broader criteria	*Commentary*
5. Goals	As demonstrated by the notetaking strategies outlined in the Table of Contents, this book includes a range of goals specific to notetaking. These range from recognizing and recording the most important words to techniques for saving time (e.g., symbols and abbreviations) as well as overall organizational approaches (e.g., the informal outline and visual formats). Several of the objectives, however, are rather universal and related more to general study habits (in either the L1 or L2) than specifically to L2 English notetaking. Examples are "highlighting important ideas" and annotating notes (p. v), which are hopefully study skills students are already aware of. Furthermore, while the crucial goal of making appropriate decisions about what to take notes on is absent from the Table of Contents, most units include exercises in which students examine short lecture transcripts and are asked to make decisions about what (and what not) to take notes on. These exercises are a major advantage for this book.
6. Building upon previous skills, etc.	By starting with "the most important words" in Unit 1, the book establishes what is essentially the core skill in notetaking. After that, however, the order and sequencing of notetaking-related activities does not seem to follow any particular logical or systematic approach, especially for the middle section of the book, where symbols, visual forms, and highlighting appear. No justification is given as to why or how these elements are ordered, and one may assume that they correspond well to the selected lecture texts. The final unit aims to "review the note taking strategies," an objective that serves as a useful book end, acknowledging that the strategies and techniques practiced previously need to be consolidated for better student acquisition.
7. Range of systems and techniques	Two notetaking formats are specifically addressed: the outline format and the "visual form" (p. 59), which involves the use of arrows and plus signs (+) to show relationships. Digital notetaking, either in the form of laptop computers or tablets, is largely ignored in favor of the traditional pen and paper approach.
8. Encoding and storage	Most of the emphasis is on encoding, as evidenced by activities for writing key words and employing symbols and abbreviations. The storage aspect exists to a lesser extent in the forms of summarizing and editing notes following the lecture.

(*Continued*)

More focused criteria	Commentary
9. Generative and non-generative	Two main methods for creating generative notes are neglected in the book, namely paraphrasing and simplification. While students have ample practice in using symbols and abbreviations, these techniques are limited in many cases to single words. As such, there are limits to how much time can be saved in using them and to their value in capturing important information; in other words, it may be difficult to record a full main idea or supporting detail with merely a symbol or abbreviation. Activities focusing on paraphrasing and/or simplifying entire utterances or complete ideas or concepts would be of more value to the generative notetaking act.
	The notion of non-generative notetaking (i.e., recording information verbatim) and its potential benefits when used selectively are, unfortunately, not acknowledged. The book emphasizes that listeners "do not have to write down every word" and explains that noting key words is more efficient. However, the book does not point out that verbatim recording can, in fact, be preferable, for instance, when a lecturer is defining a key term or when the listener struggles to paraphrase (in the event of the latter, recording verbatim and revisiting the information after the lecture can prove a valuable learning experience).
10. Specific stages of notetaking	The textbook includes several elements that engage students with various stages of notetaking. Beginning with listening strategies that raise awareness of lecture language that can benefit the notetaker, crucial decision making processes are developed in activities that involve reading brief lecture transcripts and taking notes based on them (e.g., the *Analyze the notes* and *Describe visuals* sections on p. 71). The *Making predictions* activity (e.g., from p. 72) demonstrates the importance of tapping into subject background knowledge, which can help prepare listeners to take notes.
	The encoding stage is developed in several ways, such as using symbols, abbreviations, and highlighting important ideas. One notable omission, however, is paraphrasing. Examination of the activities reveals very little space devoted to this crucial ability. Furthermore, verbatim notetaking, both as an option and a potentially valuable strategy, has been excluded.
	The post-notetaking stages receive adequate attention. In particular, the following sections recognize that engagement with notes does not end with the notetaking act: *Assess and revise your notes* (p. 9) and *Edit your notes after the lecture* (p. 111). Moreover, in *Annotate your notes during a lecture* (p. 97), students are encouraged to indicate in their notes information that they need to revisit and expand upon after the lecture, without the pressure of time constraints. Inclusion of these sections shows a broad view of notetaking and the value of interacting with notes beyond the original lecture.

(*Continued*)

Table 4.1 (Continued)

Title: Lecture Ready 2 (2nd edition)

More focused criteria	Commentary
11. Individual flexibility	The fact the book includes only two broad notetaking frameworks (the informal outline and the visual form) suggests limited flexibility for the organizational stage. Lists of commonly used abbreviations and symbols may seem constraining in some ways; however, immediately after these lists, students are prompted to come up with their own original abbreviations and symbols; therefore, individual flexibility is promoted at these points.
	Open questions which students respond to with the help of their notes allow for students to construct their own answers and express information in their own ways (i.e., students can respond with single words, phrases, or sentences). Such flexibility is evident in the *Assess your comprehension* portion of each notetaking section. Also in *Assess your comprehension* are self-evaluation questions that encourage students to report their own comprehension and notetaking abilities with regards to each respective lecture.
	At times, the structural frameworks and spaces provided in the book can be restrictive. An example comes from p. 8, in the *Watch the lecture* activity. Key words to guide the notetaking, along with lines provided on the paper, may be useful to some students but also inherently discourage a more open system of notetaking and/or use of sketches or other visuals.
12. Distinguishing notetaking from listening comprehension	Each unit contains specific sections devoted to listening and notetaking strategies, respectively. As such, the two skills are differentiated and each receives sufficient attention. Each section includes explanations, advice and practice activities that target the area in focus, and the listening elements are well integrated to the lecture texts and notetaking activities.

(Continued)

13. Incorporation of strategies	Various types of strategies from O'Malley & Chamot (1990) and Oxford (1990; 2017) are evident to limited degrees and expressly linked to notetaking. The metacognitive strategy of monitoring performance is present in the self-evaluation questions, such as those on p. 9: "I was able to / didn't recognize when the lecture said the topic." Cognitive strategies such as prediction are incorporated in the *Make predictions* sections that encourage students to draw on and apply prior knowledge. The socio-affective strategy of engaging with peers is apparent in the *Assess and revise your notes* activity (e.g., p. 9) in which students are prompted to "compare and discuss your notes with a few other students." Explicit prompts and/or goals to help students make such discussions worthwhile and successful would likely be helpful, but overall, this coverage of various strategies seems sufficient for a textbook focused on academic skills in general.
14. Other language skills	At numerous points throughout the book, students employ various language skills when working with notes. When students read each others' notes (e.g., p. 35), they not only activate their own reading skills but can also learn notetaking techniques and strategies from their peers. Students are explicitly instructed to use their speaking skills when they make verbal summaries of notes (e.g., p. 35). Of course, listening and writing are heavily involved in most of the notetaking work. Interestingly, the book neglects to include any mention of digital notetaking, and instruction, advice, and practice related to notetaking with laptop computers or tablet devices is absent. As such, general computer and typing skills are neglected in terms of their potential for notetakers.

Moving forward

As notetaking continues to gain importance in EAP classrooms and as commercial publishers strive to keep up with demand for teaching and learning materials to support notetaking, it is important for teachers and course planners to focus on the objective of notetaking. Moreover, listening practice and notetaking development are two distinct features of EAP and EMI that both deserve deliberate attention from teaching and learning materials. The list of criteria offered in this chapter is meant to serve as a stimulus to view notetaking materials in the same way other teaching and learning materials are evaluated; that is, in a systematic and objective manner that utilizes pre-determined criteria for evaluation and comparison among competing titles.

In applying the proposed criteria to *Lecture Ready 2*, an illustrative example of notetaking textbook evaluation demonstrated the great strides made in regards to L2 notetaking materials since Hamp-Lyons' (1983) review several decades earlier. It is clear that materials writers are aware of many of the factors that contribute to EAP notetaking and are actively incorporating them into systematic and organized packages that target notetaking development in pedagogic ways (e.g., by introducing a notetaking technique and providing isolated practice opportunities before encouraging students to apply the technique under simulated lecture conditions).

When the outcome of the evaluation process is a relatively positive review of a given textbook, a teacher would be able to justify their choice to students and other stakeholders. They would then likely have a valuable resource in terms of highly controlled and coordinated lecture texts and activities. Among them would be the type of semi-authentic lecture audio and/or video materials that are now commonly included with notetaking textbooks, which may, for example, include split-screen videos with lecturers on one side and PowerPoint slides on the other. In a way, these listening materials aim to make the notetaking experience itself more authentic. However, since the lecturer's output is often scripted and rehearsed, there can be some ecological distance between them and authentic lectures.

Another general drawback of textbooks for notetaking is that the activities contained within them are intrinsically linked to the lecture texts themselves. This means that rather than being applied to a variety of texts on different topics and delivered by different speakers, the teaching points related to notetaking are fastened to the text the materials writer has chosen. The teaching of notetaking, then, is dictated by the materials, and teachers are left to operate as materials providers rather than educators and, presumably, experienced notetakers and pedagogic experts in their own right. When searching for pedagogic approaches for notetaking instruction that are independent of explicitly written textbooks and are applicable to a variety of authentic texts, teachers may need to look beyond textbooks to flexible and adaptable pedagogic cycles, such as the one described in Chapter Five.

References

Atkinson, D. (2011). *Alternative approaches to second language acquisition*. New York: Routledge.

Buck, G. (2001). *Assessing listening*. Cambridge, England: Cambridge University Press.

Field, J. (2008). *Listening in the language classroom*. Cambridge: Cambridge University Press.

Hamp-Lyons, L. (1983). Survey of materials for teaching advanced listening and note-taking. *TESOL Quarterly, 17*(1), 109-122.

Harwood, N. (2010). Issues in materials development and design. In N. Harwood (Ed.), *English language teaching materials: Theory and practice* (pp. 3–32). Cambridge: Cambridge University Press.

Lynch, T., & Mendelsohn, D. (2002). Listening. In N. Schmitt (Ed.), *An introduction to applied linguistics* (pp. 193–210). London: Arnold.

McGrath, I. (2016). *Materials evaluation and design for language teaching* (2nd edition). Edinburgh: Edinburgh University Press.

Mueller, P., & Oppenheimer, M. (2014). The pen is mightier than the keyboard: Advantages of longhand over laptop note taking. *Psychological Science, 25*(6), 1159-1168.

O'Malley, J., & Chamot, A. (1990). *Learning strategies in second language acquisition*. Cambridge: Cambridge University Press.

Richards, J., & Rodgers, T. (2014). *Approaches and methods in language teaching* (3rd edition). Cambridge: Cambridge University Press.

Sarosy, P., & Sherak, K. (2013). *Lecture Ready 2*. Oxford: Oxford University Press.

Sheldon, L. (1988). Evaluating ELT textbooks and materials. *ELT Journal, 42*(4), 237-246.

Sheppard, B., Rice, J., Rice, K., DeCoster, B., Dummond-Sardell, R., & Soelberg, N. (2015). Re-evaluating the speaking and listening demands of university classes for novice international students. *ORTESOL Journal, 32*, 1-12.

Siegel, J. (2015). *Exploring listening strategy instruction through action research*. Basingstoke, UK: Palgrave Macmillan.

Siegel, J. (2018). Top down and bottom up listening strategies. In J. Liontas (Ed.), *TESOL encyclopedia of eglish language teaching*. Hoboken, NJ: Wiley.

Tomlinson, B. (2010). Principles of effective materials development. In N. Harwood (Ed.), *English language teaching materials: Theory and practice* (pp. 81–108). Cambridge: Cambridge University Press.

Williams, M., & Burden, R. (1997). *Psychology for language teachers*. Cambridge: Cambridge University Press.

Young, L. (1994). University lectures-macro-structure and micro-features. In J. Flowerdew & L. Miller (Eds.), *Academic listening: Research perspectives* (pp. 159–176). Cambridge: Cambridge University Press.

5 Pedagogic approaches for L2 notetaking

Introduction

In the previous chapter, a systematic approach to examining L2 notetaking textbooks was presented with two objectives in mind: first, to set in place an objective framework of criteria for analyzing the content and organization of materials with a specific focus on aspects relevant to notetaking; and second, to illustrate how those criteria could be used to examine such materials. The list of criteria highlighted several areas that teachers, course planners, and administrators should consider when evaluating and selecting commercial materials for notetaking instruction. The results of that systematic materials evaluation exhibited many of the strengths of the *Lecture Ready 2* textbook.

However, the evaluation in Chapter Four was of one single textbook. Other materials created and marketed for EAP notetaking instruction may not perform to the same satisfactory standard. If the books selected by Hamp-Lyons (1983) were scrutinized in the same systematic way, with criteria derived from theoretical and practical perspectives on notetaking, the results are unlikely to portray those works in a positive light, particularly in relation to what notetaking entails and demands in current educational climates. For instance, variable L2 English proficiencies of lecturers and students, digital tools for notetaking, online systems for sharing lecture content with learners, and various distractions in the classroom, such as mobile phones and Internet surfing, were factors that teachers and students did not need to deal with decades ago.

When it comes to notetaking textbooks, two main problems tend to arise: one concerning the nature of the materials themselves and the second related to the role of the teacher in L2 notetaking instruction. Textbooks typically come in nicely organized packages consisting of audio and/or video materials and a bound set of materials chronologically synchronized to align with those materials. Activities in the textbooks explicitly rely on the accompanying materials. Without one, the other can be rather useless for teachers and students. The teacher, then, is controlled by the lecture material and activities selected by the textbook creators. Very little flexibility or individual influence is accounted for. The class needs to follow the textbook in order to develop. If listening to lectures on other topics might be relevant

Pedagogic approaches for L2 notetaking 109

to students, the textbook cannot account for that. If they have individual preferences for notetaking, those risk being suppressed by the approach promoted in the textbook.

In terms of the role of the teacher, textbooks provide "fool-proof" materials and guidelines for the classroom. Assuming the teacher guides students through the instructions, activities, and exercises laid out in the textbook, student ability will improve. The teacher is only required to "stick to the plan," and follow the Table of Contents, share correct answers, and move on to the next activity. They do not need to apply themselves in any "teaching" capacity, as it were. Instead, they are basically following a "listen-answer-check" procedure, one student could do on their own with an answer guide. Teaching is left to the materials, and pedagogic principles are not required of the teacher.

Teachers are typically underprepared in language teacher education programs to deal with listening (e.g., Goh, 2005; Graham, 2017), so teachers often lack pedagogic skills and appreciation for how to teach listening. The complexity of notetaking, starting with listening and ending with a written product, is inevitably even more challenging. Textbooks have stepped up to fill this role, although teachers are left to the decisions of the materials writers. The step-by-step activities are typically mirrored in each unit of such textbooks, with the only difference being the lecture text to which they are applied. In theory, these scaffolded steps help prepare learners to succeed when they get to the actual lecture listening and notetaking practice. While these steps are supportive, they are only linked to their respective texts. As such, they may struggle to facilitate generalizable and transferable skills for notetaking.

An ideal solution to these issues would be to have an instructional cycle for L2 notetaking that draws on theories of cognition and comprehension, that follows the natural processes of transferring aural information from lectures into note form, and that can be applied to any listening text the teacher or students select. Such a cycle would provide a systematic approach to notetaking that could be used flexibility for a wide variety of listening materials: podcasts, online lectures, interviews, TED Talks, etc. This chapter aims to address these two issues related to instruction and practice based solely on notetaking textbooks by promoting a five-stage pedagogic cycle that can be applied to any listening text, be it authentic, semi-authentic, or scripted, as in the case of textbook materials.

The chapter begins with an overview of various pedagogic approaches used by teachers in notetaking interventions. Many of these lack sufficient description to be useful for other teachers to transfer to their own classrooms. In other words, when teacher-researchers have reported their notetaking interventions, they have often done so with a lack of precision, meaning their teaching techniques could be interpreted in a variety of ways. Without detailed descriptions of teaching techniques, readers of such research reports may struggle to replicate the pedagogic advice. Next, the chapter summarizes five-stage cycle for L2 notetaking, providing theoretical justification

110   *Pedagogic approaches for L2 notetaking*

for each stage and describing how it can be realized in the classroom in conjunction with TED Talks (although the same principles can be applied to any text). Findings from interventionist action research projects that have utilized the cycle are shared in the forms of pre- and post-intervention note samples as well as student feedback from two separate L2 contexts.

Pedagogic techniques from the research literature

Unlike the teaching of a particular language skill (e.g., speaking or reading), notetaking involves a complex combination of cognitive and physical skills and relies on the interplay of multiple integrated language skills. Teachers are often unprepared to teach notetaking effectively and instead merely provide practice opportunities instead of providing systematic development opportunities for students (Siegel, 2019a). It has been suggested that teacher education often lacks sufficient coverage for L2 listening (e.g., Goh, 2005; Field, 2008; Graham, 2017), leaving teachers to rely on a limited set of teaching techniques. This lack of attention in teacher education is likely even more pronounced for notetaking.

In terms of classroom activities and explicit support for notetaking, many instructors simply tell students to "listen and write important words" or just to "take notes," instructions that assume students already have the cognitive skills to do so in their L2. As one teacher interviewed by Siegel (2019a) stated, "I just tell them to take notes." A second teacher participant pointed out her presumption about students' previous experience with notetaking regardless of whether it is in the L1 or L2: "I assume they already know how to take notes." This belief highlights an important issue surrounding L2 notetaking: who is responsible for helping students develop notetaking skills? And when should such explicit support, instruction and development occur during one's education? These are topics that will be expanded upon in Chapter Eight.

Teachers giving orders to "take notes" may be overlooking the possibility that learners may have neither the listening skills to recognize keywords nor the decision-making abilities about which words to note down (not to mention how to do so in efficient and effective ways). Moreover, scaffolding and support are largely absent and patterns in many EAP classes could result in practice only (i.e., with little teaching and/or learning of notetaking styles, strategies, and techniques). Instead, students are expected simply to be able to perform the entire task well without opportunities to practice in stages. Imagine teachers saying to a class "write an argumentative essay about reducing pollution" or "make a five-minute presentation on a debatable issue" without providing support for producing introductions, using transitions, presenting main ideas and supporting details, and so on. For speaking and writing in particular, structured support is typically provided by teachers, along with models for which to aim. The same developmental awareness and support, however, is often missing for lecture notetaking in EAP.

Teachers interviewed by Siegel (2019a) are likely representative of the broader field of EAP instructors who are tasked with helping students develop L2 notetaking skills but have not been directly equipped to do so during their teacher education programs. One teacher admitted that "I don't feel like I actually teach [notetaking]." The same teacher added that it was challenging for her to know if the students had strengths and weaknesses in notetaking because she never sees their notes. Thus, any type of intervention that involved reviewing student notes, setting models, and providing opportunities for collaboration around notetaking would be potentially helpful to her teaching as well as to her understanding of her students. Another teacher pointed out that even when students take notes, they just copy words from slides or the whiteboard. This scenario means that students are probably not processing to a great extent the language to which they are listening and are not involved in the identification and selection of what information to record. Instead, the teacher is doing that work through their slide design and/or writings on the whiteboard.

Several teacher-researchers have recognized the lack of pedagogic techniques for notetaking and have attempted intervention studies in efforts to introduce novel techniques for notetaking in their EAP classrooms. While Chapter Two summarized the research-based results of such studies (e.g., Hayati & Jalilifar, 2009; Crawford, 2015), the actual teaching techniques, as described in those studies, are recalled and commented upon here. Hayati and Jalilifar (2009) integrated instruction related to the Cornell Method into their teaching and examined the affects that method had compared to an uninstructed notetaking group and a group who took no notes. Upon reading their research paper, little information about the actual in-class teaching techniques is available. Readers are told that "[students] were taught the Cornell note-taking system through a pamphlet" that included information about the recommended format for notes and the "five R's: recording, reducing, reciting, reflecting, and reviewing" (Hayati & Jalilifar, 2009, p. 103).

However, no more specific information is provided, leaving readers to wonder how much class time was spent using the pamphlet, and what precisely teachers and students did when they were practicing aspects like "reducing" and "reviewing." As such, while the study suggests that the Cornell system benefits students, instructions for teachers on how to incorporate it are lacking; in other words, replication for research purposes or implementation in the classroom for pedagogic purposes is not ensured or promoted. I recognize that space limitations and journal priorities may have constrained the researchers' ability to describe more fully the pedagogic elements of their students. Still, as a language teacher and teacher educator, more comprehensive description of these elements would have enhanced my take away from the article.

In another example of underreported pedagogic elements, Tsai and Wu (2010) state that "detailed and explicit note-taking instruction was given to the treatment group" in their study (p. 120). In describing the actual

112 *Pedagogic approaches for L2 notetaking*

pedagogic element, readers learn that the Cornell system was again the focus. In addition, students "were taught how to transform discrete words into meaningful paragraphs in order to properly summarize the main ideas of the passage" (Tsai & Wu, 2010, p. 124). This is undoubtedly an important skill, to be able to generate a summary of a lecture from keywords in notes. Examples and illustrations, along with teacher explanations, would give readers material and inspiration to transfer these techniques into the classroom. Unfortunately, none are provided and readers receive only these cursory descriptions. The authors also mention that "the note-taking process was modeled by the teacher," that teachers answered questions after class, and taught "hands-on techniques" (p. 124), but no further elaboration is provided. Finding out how the teacher modeling took place, what the teacher said during the modeling, along with what the hands-on techniques were and how they were taught, could be potentially valuable in L2 instructors who teach notetaking.

In Crawford's (2015) intervention, the researcher found a number of statistically significant increases related to various aspects of notetaking (e.g., recording of content words, use of abbreviations, arrows, etc.). The description of classroom practice, however, leaves several details unexplained. According the Crawford (2015), "students received training on how to take notes efficiently by making use of such things as abbreviations and symbols and by focusing on content words as opposed to function words" (p. 418). These are indeed crucial steps students can take to improve their notetaking efficiency. Based on this description, however, readers may be unsure how to apply these ideas in their classroom, what to say to students during instruction, how to exemplify the concepts and apply them to a respective text, and how often the focus of instruction is necessary on each particular point (e.g., how and how often students in this project worked with abbreviation).

In an effort to enhance the quality of descriptions of notetaking pedagogy and make them more relevant, tangible, and explicit for language teachers, I have tried in the subsequent section to explain and illustrate in step-by-step fashion how listening and notetaking can be presented in ways that are digestible and meaningful for teachers who are looking for pedagogic techniques. In Siegel (2013), I wrote about the importance of teacher modeling and think alouds for listening instruction: "teacher explanations are indispensable; they provide the listening archetypes that students attempt to emulate. By attempting to mirror their teacher's listening processes, students can develop similar abilities....the ability to articulate and demonstrate mental activities may come easier to some teachers than others. Essentially, instructors must remove themselves from their seemingly effortless comprehension and focus on identifying the linguistic aspects and listening strategies that help them unlock meaning. Teachers need to think about how and why they understood a given text" (p. 134). The same concepts of teachers articulating their thought processes, explaining comprehension, and justifying choices apply to notetaking instruction, where teacher modeling and note samples can provide supportive frameworks for students.

In terms of more explicit and visual representations of instructional practices for notetaking, I aimed to provide a clear and illustrated description of how teachers can incorporate simplification or reduction practice for notetaking in their classes (Siegel, 2019b). A three-phase teaching cycle for simplification was proposed that included warm-up, transition, and real-time phases, each targeting a different facet of the simplification process. Step-by-step procedures and teacher actions are given for each phase in an explicit effort to provide readers with viable and valuable techniques they can immediately transfer to their classrooms should they so choose. I endeavor to avoid vague language or descriptions of notetaking instruction with the view that many teachers do not want to interpret what I mean by "teach simplification" and desire to learn more about precisely what teaching simplification for notetaking means and how it can be conducted. Siegel (2019b) also includes several samples of authentic student notes and accompanying discussion that reflects on the degree of success students had in applying the simplification techniques.

There have been clear attempts to address the gap in pedagogic options for notetaking; however, the descriptions as presented in some papers are often too vague and lack descriptive precision and depth for readers to be able to activate them in their own classrooms. If readers of those studies wanted to incorporate the techniques, they would need to rely on much inference and guesswork. That is how I felt reading the papers, that while I understood the aims of the interventions and their underlying concepts, I was unsure the precise steps I should take in my classroom to replicate the pedagogy that led to the reported positive effects on notetaking. While other publications on L2 notetaking instruction may take a more research-oriented stance, due to the lack of pedagogic knowledge and techniques for notetaking instruction, more "teacher-friendly" descriptions and illustrations of practice would be equally beneficial for the field. As such, I felt motivated to describe in detail how I designed an approach to and taught, in collaboration with colleagues, notetaking through a five-stage pedagogic cycle and illustrate how the cycle can be applied to a TED Talk, with the view that the same principles can be applied to any listening text which teachers and/or students want to tackle as an object of notetaking.

Five-stage pedagogic cycle

The pedagogic cycle described here is based on two previous propositions for notetaking instruction (Siegel, 2016, 2018a). In 2016, I was working in Japan and wanted to provide my EAP students, who were at approximately CEFR A2-B1 proficiency levels, with scaffolded and guided notetaking instruction and practice. I created a system of skeleton notes and recorded myself making a series of short (approximately 5 min) semi-authentic lecture excerpts. Using teacher modeling, peer-to-peer discussion, example notes, and feedback, we spent around 20 min each week on notetaking decisions and samples. Each week of the 6-week instructional period, the

114 *Pedagogic approaches for L2 notetaking*

skeleton notes became more sparse, thereby increasing expectations placed on students. This cycle formed the basis of the five-stage cycle described in Table 5.1. However, the cycle I used in Japan focused solely on the formal outline system of notetaking, and I wanted to offer students less restrictive and more individualized methods for taking notes. In addition, the skeleton notes I was providing for students were linked exclusively to the self-made semi-authentic recordings I had created; therefore, like one of the issues with textbooks mentioned earlier, neither the texts nor the skeleton notes were of much use without the other.

In 2017, I led a project in Sweden focused on notetaking instruction in Swedish upper secondary schools. Student proficiency ranged between B1 and C1, and I felt that only offering the outline format worksheets, as I had done in Japan, would not be appropriate for these students. The highly scaffolded activities were sufficient with Japanese learners at the A2–B1 levels. However, the Swedish students were generally more individualistic and may have resisted the outline format in favor of their individual preferences. Furthermore, use of authentic materials is required at this level of L2 English in Sweden (per official steering documents created by the Education Ministry *Skolverket*) and therefore, I could not match the outline format to the randomness of authentic materials, similar to the problem of notetaking textbooks and their reliance on the texts chosen. A third reason was the generally more advanced proficiency level of the Swedish student group. More flexibility in terms of notetaking performance and types of texts was necessary. In response to those needs, I introduced a pedagogic cycle that could be applied to authentic and scripted materials alike (Siegel, 2018b, 2019a). The stages are displayed in Table 5.1.

Figure 5.1 provides explicit examples of how stages 1–4 were realized in classroom practice using an excerpt of a specific TED Talk on Internet safety. The figure shows four slides that represent classroom demonstrations for stages 1–4. The source material for this illustrative example was the transcript of Gary Kovacs (2012) TED Talk titled "Tracking our online trackers." The specific text referred to in the slides follows:

"Today, what many of us would love to believe is that the Internet is a private place; it's not. And with every click of the mouse and every touch of the screen, we are like Hansel and Gretel leaving breadcrumbs of our personal information everywhere we travel through the digital woods. We are leaving our birthdays, our places of residence, our interests and preferences, our relationships, our financial histories, and on and on it goes."

At each stage, students must engage with the text in different ways. Students first display their chunking and lexical segmentation ability, which is an initial step in the decision-making process. As a notetaker segments the text, they begin to assign priorities and/or importance to each individual chunk. Is this important enough to note down? Can that be decided now, or should I wait until I hear more? Next, in step two, listeners use designated symbols to indicate the importance of certain chunks compared to others that may be relatively irrelevant. In stage three, students move on to

Pedagogic approaches for L2 notetaking 115

Table 5.1 The Pedagogic Intervention (based on Siegel, 2018b)

Stage	Activity	Purpose
1	Chunking with the transcript (students put a slash (/) on the transcript to indicate IUs)	To help notetakers segment content into meaningful chunks while dealing with rate of speech
2	Marking the transcript (students use symbols to indicate main and supporting ideas, examples, transitions, redundancies, etc.; then compare and discuss choices with classmates and teacher)	To help notetakers separate information into various levels of importance and to recognize textual features of lectures; to help in the identification of what should be noted and what (probably) should not
3	Writing verbatim notes (students listen to short segments (30 s–1 min) of the text, write down key words verbatim; then compare and discuss choices with classmates and teacher)	To help notetakers catch and record information in real time; to help them recognize which words are important and which (probably) are not
4	Simplifying notes (students listen to slightly longer segments (1–2 min), writing verbatim notes when necessary while also trying to write notes in simplified form when possible; then compare and discuss choices with classmates and teacher) (e.g., 'horrible situation' in lecture = 'bad sit' in notes)	To help notetakers practice being efficient and making effective choices when simplifying notes
5	Practice with longer stretches (5 min) of lecture texts; then discuss notes with classmates and teacher	To provide holistic practice in more real-life lecture notetaking scenarios; to combine previously practiced sub-skills

1. Chunking	2. Marking the script
"Many of us would like to believe / that the internet is a private place; / it's not. And with every click of the mouse / and every touch of the screen, / we are like Hansel and Gretel, / leaving breadcrumbs of our personal information / everywhere we travel in the digital woods. / We are leaving our birthdays, / our places of residence, / our interests and preferences, /..."	Today, what many of us would love to believe is that the **Internet is a private place; it's not. And with every click of the mouse and every touch of the screen, we are like Hansel and Gretel leaving breadcrumbs of our personal information everywhere we travel through the digital woods. We are leaving our birthdays, our places of residence, our interests and preferences, our relationships, our financial histories, and on and on it goes.
3. Verbatim	**4. Simplifying**
**Internet not private place. leaving personal information everywhere our birthdays, residence, interests and preferences	**Internet not private place Net =/ privat leaving personal information everywhere our info everywher our birthdays, residence, interests and preferences bday, adres, likes

Figure 5.1 Illustrations of stages one – four

116 *Pedagogic approaches for L2 notetaking*

combine listening and writing by focusing on recording verbatim information that they have determined to be valuable. Since several techniques (e.g., paraphrasing simplifying, abbreviating, drawing, etc.) are strategies that can save time at the encoding stage, students are encouraged in step four to express the same information in denser, more compact ways than verbatim recording permits.

Each of the first four stages is based on theories of language and theories of learning. In the first stage, students are required to demonstrate and practice their ability to chunk the speech stream into manageable parts. The concept of chunking has been described as "one of the key mechanisms of human cognition" (Gobet, Lane, Croker, Cheng, Jones, Oliver & Pine, 2001, p. 236). Each chunk "collects a number of pieces of information from the environment into a single unit" (Gobet et al., 2001, p. 236) and the cognitive act of separating language into chunks is essential in the processing of meaning. Chunking is similar to lexical segmentation in listening, which means decoding spoken language by segmenting it into smaller units of meaning; thus, the listener can focus on word recognition and create and comprehend the meaning of the spoken output they hear.

As people become more familiar with common chunks of language, their ability to process them efficiently increases (e.g., McCauley & Christiansen, 2015). Rather than letting the nonstop spoken output from a lecturer or speaker uncontrollably overrun them, the listener in this first activity is meant to indicate where one thought or idea unit begins and ends. This is an important stage in the listening process, which acknowledges that listeners do not process each individual word distinctly but rather that the brain strives to create chunks or common groupings of words, which makes cognitive processing easier (see Chapter Seven for more in-depth explanation of the "information unit"). Students indicate this on a transcript of the speech, and the visual presence of slash marks sets the stage for deciding what is important to take notes on and what is irrelevant or at least of less importance than other chunks in light of the overall gist of the lecture or speech.

Stages two-four involve specific tasks related to recognizing the importance of information, encoding notes, and comparing one's own notes with those taken by the teacher and other students. Stage two in particular draws on skill acquisition theory in which a student gradually learns a skill from a teacher or expert through: (1) a cognitive and declarative stage where learners acquire knowledge about a skill; (2) an associative and procedural stage where scaffolded practice opportunities are provided; and finally (3) an autonomous and automatic stage where the skill can be performed by a learner without support from a teacher (e.g., DeKeyser, 2007). Skill acquisition theory underpins this teacher-led aspect of the pedagogic intervention, where the teacher outlines the symbols to be used (which are arbitrary, so long as symbols are used consistently to differentiate between main ideas, support ideas, and examples or illustrations). In Figure 5.1, a circle identifies the main overarching theme of the TED Talk, a triangle indicates

Pedagogic approaches for L2 notetaking 117

a supporting idea, and wavy lines show specific examples of the fact that "our personal information (is) everywhere." The teacher sets the symbols and demonstrates how to use them. Comparisons and discussion with the teacher and peers also takes place. Over the course of several encounters with this exercise, students gradually become accustomed to demonstrating their ability to distinguish priority levels of information. This skill is more easily demonstrated and explained using visuals on the transcript, but should in theory be encouraged and transferred to the acts of notetaking while listening.

Interaction is also a prominent feature in this pedagogic cycle. For too long, notetaking has been conceived in a rather traditional sense in which the notetaker is isolated from peers and is left to rely solely on their own L2 listening proficiency and notetaking skills. With improved technological support for notetakers (e.g., Powerpoint slides, the sharing of slides through online systems, and handy cameras and recorders), the notetaking act is becoming more inclusive than solitary. In stages two-four, but especially in three and four, sociocultural learning theory and the "zone of proximal development" (ZPD) (Vygotsky, 1987) are incorporated (see Chapter Six for more on collaborative notetaking).

According to Vygotsky (1987), the ZPD is "the distance between the actual development level as determined by independent problem solving and the level of potential development as determined through problem solving under adult guidance or in collaboration with more capable peers" (p. 86). As such, peer-to-peer interaction and dialogue potentially lead to learning as students' progress through the ZPD (e.g., Chaiklin, 2003; Wells, 1999). The main benefits of working within and through the ZPD are that collaborative efforts with more skilled peers lead to the learning of new content, strategies, and skills with the ultimate goal of learners being able to complete tasks more efficiently and effectively on their own (Shabani, Khatib & Ebadi, 2010). When it comes to notetaking, by comparing decisions and formulations of notes with their teacher and classmates, each individual is prompted to explain and justify their choices and methods. Furthermore, they listen to others describe their own decisions and one can compare individual performance and choices with those of others. Students will, in theory, be exposed to alternative strategies for notetaking both at the decision and encoding stages, thereby leading to an expanded strategy repertoire from which notetakers can select and apply various approaches in future notetaking events.

The fifth and final stage is for consolidation and real-time practice. Whereas the four previous stages aimed to break down and target specific aspects of decision-making and encoding, when listening to lectures or other texts, students must be ready to undertake those cognitive and physical operations in real time as they listen. In this sense, stage five focuses on the automatization phase of skill acquisition theory, in which students combine the previously developed subskills in order to replicate how they need to be orchestrated and activated for successful notetaking. The length of the segments can be gradually increased to strengthen student L2 listening and notetaking endurance.

118 *Pedagogic approaches for L2 notetaking*

Throughout the stages, collaboration with peers allows for students to share and learn different notetaking strategies and to consolidate learning of information. This cooperative element is intended to help learners get feedback on their own notetaking performance. Notetaking is often an isolated task. By expanding it to include more interaction and feedback, it becomes more of a sociocultural and cooperative endeavor. Students can get confirmation that they have recognized and decided upon the same information as their peers, which in a sense means they can feel more secure that they have written the "right" information in their notes. If they missed something, their classmates can help them add it to their notes. It is also likely that students will note the same piece of information in various ways. By sharing and discussing these differences, students can get input and tips on how to be more efficient in notetaking in the future.

Findings from classroom research

The five-stage cycle described above has been used in various iterations, both in Sweden and Japan, by multiple teacher-researchers. The initial use of the cycle in Sweden involved two teachers and four classes of upper secondary school studying in English 5 (the first-year required English course). To summarize results from that project (Siegel, 2018b, 2019a), student scores on pre- and post-instructional comprehension tests increased slightly but not to levels of statistical significance. In terms of information units (IUs) on pre- and post-intervention test samples, the post-test notes showed an average increase of 7.1 IUs (briefly, an IU is "smallest unit [of information] one can judge as true or false" (Anderson, 2014, p. 104); a fuller discussion of IUs is available in Chapter Seven). Based on paired-sample t-test analysis, this 7.1 IU increase was statistically significant, suggesting that the improved scores were a result of the pedagogic intervention rather than random chance. Kusumoto (2019) used the same pedagogic cycle and found only minimal increases in listening comprehension test scores. However, when student notes were analyzed, noticeable gains in total words and IUs were found. Many of the results reported in these studies suggest that the pedagogic cycle has a positive effect on the quality and quantity of student notes, but that the quality of notes does not necessarily transfer to multiple-choice tests of lecture comprehension.

These gains in notetaking performance were also corroborated by more longitudinal research, as Siegel (forthcoming) showed. In that study, students completed notetaking activities four months after the course of study had been completed. The research compared IU scores from pre- and immediate posttest notetaking samples with a delayed posttest four months later. T-test analysis demonstrated significant gains between the pre- and immediate-post tests. While scores decreased significantly from the immediate to the delayed posttest, scores on the delayed posttest were still higher to statistically significant levels than those of the pre-intervention test.

Pedagogic approaches for L2 notetaking 119

In a second iteration of the pedagogic cycle (Siegel (2020) summarized in Chapter Two) compared control and intervention groups at both the intermediate and advanced proficiency levels. Results from pre- and post-intervention note samples showed that the intermediate level control group (n = 25) was outscored by the intervention group (n = 19) by an average of 2.45 IUs. The increase in IUs for the advanced intervention group (n = 38) compared to the control group (n = 19) was even more pronounced, at 5.12 IUs on average.

Additional data related to each respective phase of the five-stage cycle were collected via an online survey completed by students at the English 5 and English 7 (an optional English course) levels in Swedish upper secondary schools as well as with first-year university students in Japan. Students responded to questions on the following topics in relation with each of the five stages: the novelty or newness of each stage; their enjoyment of each stage; the usefulness for each stage in their future notetaking endeavors; the extent to which each stage helped their understanding of what notetaking is; and finally, the extent to which each stage helped their notetaking ability. Students responded to these items using a 5-point Likert scale ranging from 1 to 5, where 1 = strong disagreement and 5 = strong agreement. In the tables below, results from *strongly agree* and *agree* have been combined. The remaining percentages of students selected *strongly disagree, disagree,* or *neither disagree or agree*. The Swedish students completed the survey in English, and the Japanese students completed a version that included both English and Japanese translations.

Figure 5.2 summarizes the findings from the Swedish group (n = 199), which reports percentages of students who *strongly agreed* or *agreed* with each respective statement.

As evidenced in Figure 5.2, Simplifying received the highest ratings for helping students understand what notetaking is (84%), potential usefulness

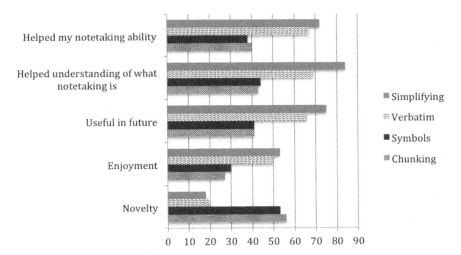

Figure 5.2 Swedish students (n = 199) views of each stage

120 *Pedagogic approaches for L2 notetaking*

on future notetaking tasks (75%), and helping improve notetaking ability (72%). In comparison to the other three stages included on this part of the survey, students firmly recognize the contribution that the Simplification stage makes to improvements in notetaking. Based on the responses for novelty or newness of the activities, many students already seem to be familiar with taking notes verbatim and simplifying. Stages one (chunking) (56%) and two (marking symbols on the transcript) (53%) received the highest ratings for novelty, suggesting that many students were not familiar with these activities prior to the pedagogic intervention.

The results displayed in Figure 5.2 were corroborated through additional questions that asked students which of the five stages were the most and least valuable to them. Simplification scored the highest as "most valuable" (38%), with the Verbatim stage coming next (28%). Interestingly, Stage five Notetaking Practice only received 12% of responses, indicating that students value the explicit and scaffolded instruction, collaborative opportunities, and teacher input afforded by the pedagogic cycle rather than repeated chances to "take notes" with no support. The least valuable stages, from the perspective of this group of students, were symbols (49%) and chunking (32%), a finding that may be explained by the novelty of the activities and/or the relatively high proficiency levels of the Swedish students, who were generally at B1-C1 CEFR levels.

Kusumoto (2019) used the pedagogic cycle with an intervention group of Japanese university EFL learners. In comparison to a control group ($n = 22$), students in the intervention group ($n = 34$) showed very slight increases on lecture comprehension tests following the pedagogic cycle. Total words and number of IUs increased at higher levels, but not to the level of statistically significance. Students in the intervention group also responded to a survey (similar to that described above in Figure 5.2) that focused on how students viewed each stage in terms of helping their understanding of what notetaking is and their notetaking ability itself. Figure 5.3 exhibits results from that survey as percentages.

This group of Japanese students expressed that all of the stages were generally helpful to contributing both to their appreciation for what notetaking is as well as their ability. Even Stage one Chunking (85% and 73%, respectively) and Stage two Writing Symbols (85% and 76%) received relatively high ratings, especially compared to ratings from the Swedish group, whose scores for these stages were typically about 30 percentage points less. This finding may be due to the average lower proficiency of the Japanese learners, who were around A2-B1 CEFR levels. Kusumoto (2019) acknowledges that the pedagogic cycle and the materials to which it is applied may need to be adjusted in order to maximize its effectiveness depending on the proficiency of the group involved. Stage three Verbatim and Stage four Simplification both had the highest scores, this time reflecting the views expressed by the Swedish students.

In response to questions about the most and least useful of the stages, the Japanese students found Stage five Notetaking Practice to be the most valuable (38%), with Simplification second at 32%. The least useful stages were Chunking (50%) and Writing Symbols (29%), findings that are again consistent with those from the Swedish group.

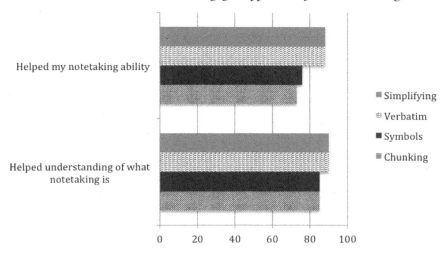

Figure 5.3 Japanese students (*n* = 34) views of each stage

While these studies took place in different geographic locations, among diverse groups in terms of proficiency, and were taught by multiple instructors, findings related to student perspectives would seem to suggest positive contributions of certain stages to notetaking development. The Simplifying stage in particular was reported to be useful for future notetaking tasks, to increase appreciation for what notetaking is, and for contributing to improved notetaking abilities. Some of the earlier stages may need to be revisited or reconceptualized based on student feedback, although the purpose of these stages is to set a mental model for academic listening and to transfer that model of comprehension into the notetaking act. While some students did recognize the value of such precursory steps, more pedagogic development in terms of applying theory and creating classroom activities is needed.

Pre- and post-intervention note samples

The following samples, produced by upper secondary school students in Sweden, illustrate changes in notetaking performance following the pedagogic intervention. Note samples are drawn from students in either the required English 5 course (taken in the first year) or the elective English 7 course (taken in the final year). Students took notes uninstructed for the pre-intervention sample, took part in lessons that included the intervention, and then completed a post-intervention notetaking task. Information on the TED Talks used for the pre- and posttests is available in Table 5.2. Discussion follows each set of note samples.

The first examples (Figures 5.4 and 5.5) show changes in notetaking performance following the pedagogic intervention. The quantifiable difference is obvious, as the notes in Figure 5.5 contain many more words than the

122 *Pedagogic approaches for L2 notetaking*

Table 5.2 Pre- and post-intervention test text information

Speaker	Title	Duration	Rate of speech	Flesch-Kincaid Grade Level*	IUs
Pre-test: Prosanta Chakrabarty	Clues to prehistoric times found in blind cavefish	4:50	157.7 words per minute	9.5	47
Post-test: Aomawa Shields	How we'll find life on other planets	5:26	147.3 words per minute	8.0	46

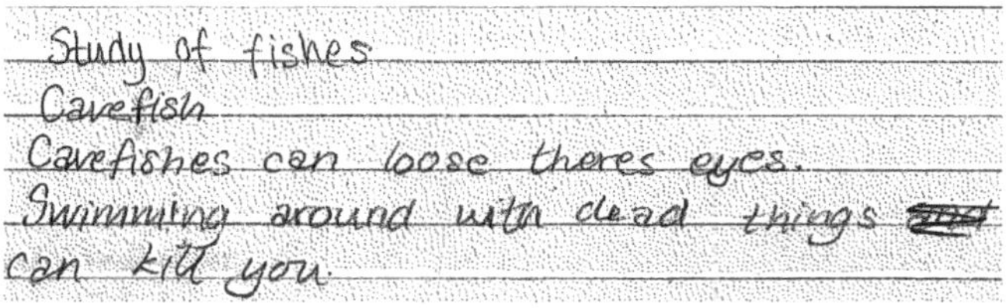

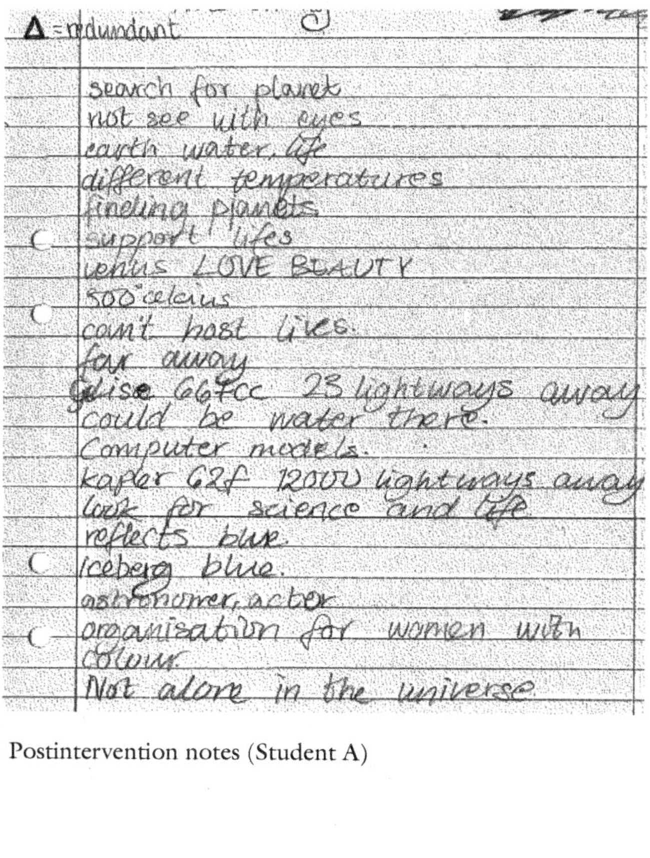

Figure 5.4 Preintervention notes (Student A)

Figure 5.5 Postintervention notes (Student A)

pre-intervention sample. In addition, rather than writing out longer sentences (which may not be an efficient technique) in the post-intervention notes, Student A focused on short bursts or phrases, thereby allowing more of the meaningful lecture content to be recorded. The student also illustrated their awareness of the possibility of redundant information with the small triangle symbol in the upper left corner.

The two examples from Student B (Figures 5.6 and 5.7) show the same vertical orientation and use of lines to indicate relationships between information. However, the amount and terseness (Dunkel, 1988) of the information in the post-intervention sample is much higher. Simple pictures (such as stars, a circle to indicate Earth, and the house with wavy lines to represent the greenhouse effect), absent in Figure 5.6, are clearly evident in Figure 5.7.

In the third sample, that of Student C, the student has succeeded in recording more individual items of information in the post-intervention

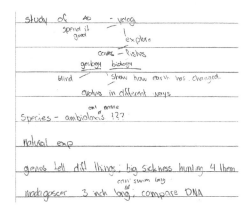

Figure 5.6 Preintervention notes (Student B)

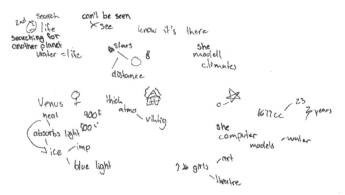

Figure 5.7 Postintervention notes (Student B)

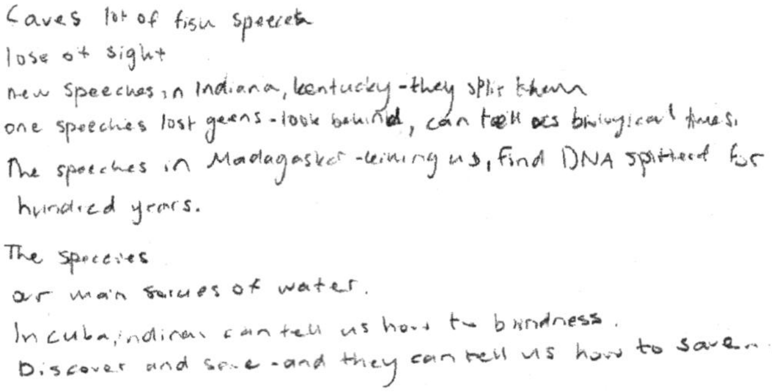

124   *Pedagogic approaches for L2 notetaking*

> Caves lot of fish species
> lose of sight
> new speeches in Indiana, kentucky - they split them
> one speeches lost genes - look behind, can tell des biological times,
> The speeches in Madagaskar - leining us, find DNA splitted for
> hundred years.
>
> The species
> ar main sources of water.
> In cuba, indiran can tell us hort to blindness.
> Discover and save - and they can tell us how to save.

Figure 5.8 Preintervention notes (Student C)

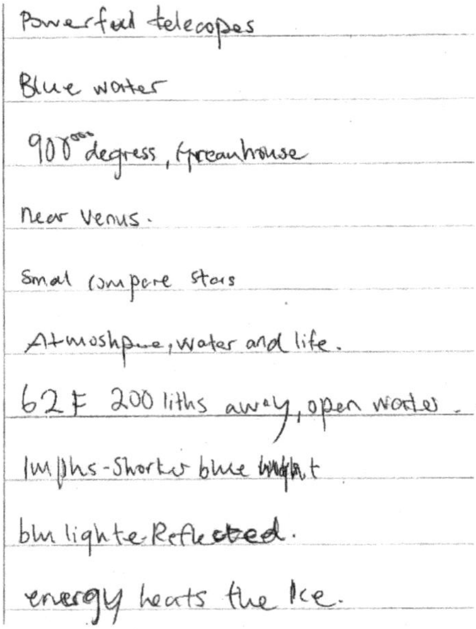

> Powerful telecopes
>
> Blue water
>
> 900 degress, greenhouse
>
> Near Venus.
>
> Small compere stars
>
> Atmoshpue, water and life.
>
> 62 F 200 liths away, open water.
>
> Imphs - Shorter blue wight
>
> blu lighte Reflected.
>
> energy heats the Ice.

Figure 5.9 Postintervention notes (Student C)

notes (Figure 5.9) than pre- (Figure 5.8). Despite there being fewer words
in the second sample, a higher density of information is present. The focus
on decisions to record content words and short phrases rather than complete, grammatically correct sentences is evident.

Building on the cycle

The pedagogic cycle described in this chapter is meant to provide teachers
with a systematic method for acknowledging several stages of the notetaking process, beginning with chunking and lexical segmentation and

concluding with the application of techniques for simplification of information in notes. It has been proposed in response to more abstract and vague descriptions of classroom practice for L2 notetaking in both pedagogic and research literature. Furthermore, quantitative and qualitative findings from classroom research related to the use of the pedagogic cycle have been shared and suggest potential advantages for integrating it into EAP courses.

The cycle, however, should be viewed as a flexible work-in-progress that is malleable rather than set in stone. Notetaking has been around for centuries, but explicit attempts to teach it in systematic ways and apply techniques to L2s are relatively new concepts that need time to develop and to adjust to various contextual parameters. In other words, the core framework of the cycle should be viewed as stable but additions and revisions are inevitably necessary. For instance, the current cycle focuses almost exclusively on the comprehension and segmentation of incoming input and encoding that input in various ways. Additional steps that acknowledge important aspects such as overall organizational principles as well as the use of notes after they are taken (i.e., the storage function) would be valuable. Furthermore, certain stages of the cycle may be of more interest and use to teachers teaching and students learning at different proficiency levels, as mentioned by Kusumoto (2019). Higher proficiency students may skip earlier stages, whereas lower level students may find those early stages valuable in terms of coping with and managing the fast-coming input, which sets the stage for real-time decision-making.

The cycle might also need to be adjusted to accommodate various types of academic texts. Most classroom experience with the cycle to date has taken place in conjunction with TED Talks. While this collection of videos seems very popular with EAP teachers, it is important to note that TED Talks are not typical EMI lectures, and the two genres differ in several ways. The former are usually stand-alone speeches that are well-rehearsed; the latter are situated within a series of lectures, often building on previous sessions and previewing upcoming ones, and, at times, include spontaneous output from the lecturer. Furthermore, one might listen to a TED Talk for enjoyment or general interest, whereas some form of assessment may be linked to EMI and EAP classes.

Genres such as academic class discussions, panel discussions and interviews have not been used, at least to my knowledge, in tandem with the pedagogic cycle. Source texts from other types of online videos (i.e., not TED Talks) or podcasts may be more or less suitable for use with the pedagogic cycle, depending on format, content and organization. However, the overall principles and theories underlying each of the stages remains the same and should at least be partially transferable to other genres and text-types. That is, by emphasizing the chunking of incoming input, making decisions about priorities, and practicing efficient ways to simplify information, notetakers can improve their abilities regardless of genre or text-type.

Unresolved issues about notetaking pedagogy

There are several issues related to notetaking pedagogy that remain unresolved (see Siegel, 2018b), and the pedagogic cycle proposed here does little to address them. A major concern is who is responsible for developing students' notetaking abilities. Would it be easier for L1 content teachers to teach notetaking skills with the view that these skills will then automatically transfer to the L2 lecture hall? Or should EAP teachers be solely responsible for developing L2 notetaking skills from scratch? The answer may depend on the proximity of a student's L1 to English (i.e., that if the L1 is far removed from English, then perhaps L1 notetaking ability can be less helpful). One might also ask when the pedagogic cycle in this chapter would benefit learners the most. One possibility could be in L1 content instruction as early as junior high school. Another option could be in an EAP course meant to prepare students for academic life in EMI contexts. The who and when questions are proposed but not resolved in this book. The pedagogic cycle proposed here provides teachers with an option that can be applied in different ways, at various times, and to a range of texts.

Teachers also have options of promoting a specific notetaking method (such as the Cornell system or the outline format) or to allow each individual student to use the format (or combination thereof) with which they are the most comfortable. Several studies outlined in Chapter Two showed teachers employing the Cornell method. In addition, many L2 notetaking textbooks feature a limit range of organizational options, implicitly promoting certain frameworks. The pedagogic cycle in this chapter has been purposefully designed so as not to emphasize a single format but rather to work flexibly with the format(s) students are comfortable with. As such, the concepts of chunking/lexical segmentation, decision-making, and recording notes either verbatim or through simplification (or more commonly, a combination of these two) can be realized through any and all notetaking formats. The focus here is less on the structure and more on the content, on actually capturing and crystalizing information for later use, regardless of the overall format.

In an issue related to text choice, teachers typically have options of using one or more of the following: an EAP four-skills book, an EAP listening and notetaking book, and/or authentic materials such as online videos or podcasts. The pedagogic cycle in this chapter can be applied to any of these materials options. As described above, it has been implemented with TED Talks with some degree of success. However, it can be applied to the scripted lecture texts that accompany commercially produced textbooks as well. In other words, teachers and students could use a certain textbook as prescribed and laid out by the materials writer and publisher but could also supplement with some or all of the stages outlined in Table 5.1. Such supplementation could compensate for areas identified by textbook evaluation procedures (see Chapter Four) that may be underdeveloped, such as chunking, decision-making, and/simplifying.

Chapter summary

The purpose of this chapter has been to provide teachers with a systematic and flexible approach for notetaking instruction that is described in sufficient depth to be actionable in the classroom. Underlying theoretical perspectives pertaining to each stage have been highlighted in order to provide sound justification for the discrete parts of the cycle. This cycle has been proposed as a viable alternative to teaching L2 notetaking with authentic materials in particular and is meant to augment notetaking textbook activities that are restricted only to those texts selected by materials writers. As such, the cycle opens up notetaking instruction to invite the infinite possibilities of texts available online. Based on a limited range of iterations, findings from classroom research indicate that students view the cycle as valuable and an improvement on previous approaches based only on limited directives like "take notes." However, some aspects of the cycle seem to resonate more or less with different types of students at varying proficiency levels.

The previous and present chapters have focused more on how students can learn and develop L2 notetaking abilities through commercial materials (Chapter Five) and teacher-led instruction (Chapter Five). Another exciting potential forum for students to enhance their notetaking abilities is in collaboration with peers through scaffolded discussions, which is the focus of Chapter Six.

References

Anderson, J. (2014). *Cognitive psychology and its implications* (8th edition). New York: Worth.

Chaiklin, S. (2003). The zone of proximal development in Vygotsky's analysis of learning and instruction. In A. Kozulin, B. Gindis, V. Ageyev, and S. Miller (Eds.), *Vygotsky's educational theory in cultural contexts* (pp. 39–64). Cambridge: Cambridge University Press.

Crawford, M. (2015). A study on note taking in EFL listening instruction. In P. Clements, A. Krause, & H. Brown (Eds.), *JALT2014 Conference Proceedings* (pp. 416–424). Tokyo: JALT.

DeKeyser, R. (2007). Skill acquisition theory. In B. VanPatten & J. Williams (Eds.), *Theories in second language acquisition: An introduction* (pp. 97–113). New Jersey: Lawrence Erlbaum.

Dunkel, P. (1988). The content of L1 and L2 students' lecture notes and its relation to test performance. *TESOL Quarterly*, 22(2), 259–278.

Field, J. (2008). *Listening in the language classroom*. Cambridge: Cambridge University Press.

Gobet, F., Lane, P., Croker, S., Cheng, P., Jones, G., Oliver, I., & Pine, J. (2001). Chunking mechanisms in human learning. *Trends in Cognitive Sciences*, 5(6), 236–243.

Goh, C. (2005). Second language listening expertise. In K. Johnson (Ed.), *Expertise in second language learning and teaching* (pp. 64–84). Basingstoke: Palgrave Macmillan.

Graham, S. (2017). Research into Practice: Listening strategies in an instructed classroom setting. *Language Teaching*, 50(1), 107–119.

128 *Pedagogic approaches for L2 notetaking*

Hamp-Lyons, L. (1983). Survey of materials for teaching advanced listening and note-taking. *TESOL Quarterly*, 17(1), 109–122.

Hayati, A. M., & Jalilifar, A. (2009). The Impact of Note-taking Strategies on Listening Comprehension. *English Language Teaching*, 2(1), 101–111.

Kovacs, G. (2012). Tracking our online trackers (2012, February) [Video file]. Retrieved from: https://www.ted.com/talks/gary_kovacs_tracking_our_online_trackers?language=en.

Kusumoto, Y. (2019). EFL students' perception of note-taking and the effect of note-taking instruction. *The Kyushu Academic Society of English Language Education Bulletin*, 47, 47–56.

McCauley, S., & Christiansen, M. (2015, July). Individual differences in chunking ability predict on-line sentence processing. *CogSci*, 1553–1558.

Shabani, K. Khatib, M., & Ebadi, S. (2010). Vygotsky's zone of proximal development: Instructional implications and teachers' professional development. *English Language Teaching*, 3(4), 237–248.

Siegel, J. (2013). Methodological ingenuity for second language listening. In J. Schwieter (Ed.). *Studies and global perspectives of second language teaching and learning* (pp. 113–139). Charlotte: Information Age Publishing.

Siegel, J. (2016). A pedagogic cycle for EFL note-taking. *English Language Teaching Journal*, 70(3), 275–286.

Siegel, J. (2018a). Teaching lecture notetaking with authentic materials. *ELT Journal*, 73(2), 124–133.

Siegel, J. (2018b). Notetaking in ELT: Highlighting contrasts. *TESOL Journal*, 10(1), 1–5.

Siegel, J. (2019a). Collaborative action research on notetaking: Simultaneous cycles. *The European Journal of Applied Linguistics and TESOL*, 9(1), 77–100.

Siegel, J. (2019b). Notetaking in EFL: A focus on simplification. *The Language Teacher*, 43(3), 20–24.

Siegel, J. (2020). Effects of notetaking instruction on intermediate and advanced L2 English learners: A quasi-experimental study. *Journal of English for Academic Purposes*, 46. DOI: https://doi.org/10.1016/j.jeap.2020.100868.

Tsai, T., & Wu, Y. (2010). Effects of note-taking instruction and note-taking languages on college EFL students' listening comprehension. *New Horizons in Education*, 58(1), 120–132.

Vygotsky, L. S. (1987). Thinking and speech. In R. Rieber & A. Carton (Eds.), *The collected works of L.S. Vygotsky: Vol 1. Problems of general psychology* (pp. 39–285). New York: Plenum Press. (Original work published 1934).

Wells, G. (1999). *Dialogic inquiry: Towards a sociocultural practice and theory of education*. Cambridge: Cambridge University Press.

6 Embracing dialogic potential of notes

A new line of sociocultural engagement

Introduction

When a student takes notes in a lecture setting, they often do so stranded on a proverbial island. The audience focuses on the lecturer's words, and there is typically an unspoken mutual agreement among audience members to remain relatively quiet during the lecture unless the instructor opens the floor for discussion or elicits questions or viewpoints from the audience. The desire for silence among the audience is typically respected and is valuable for many listeners. However, when a student misses or misunderstands a point the lecturer makes, they have several options, many of them less than satisfying. They may (a) put up their hand to ask the lecturer directly, (b) whisper to a neighbor to get the information they need, (c) write a question mark or other symbol in their notes to indicate that they need to return to that point, or (d) simply ignore the information and continue with the ongoing listening and notetaking operations.

Option A is one that many L2 students, particularly when attending lectures with larger groups, would like to avoid, as it could identify them as weaker L2 listeners. Option B happens frequently, with quick, hushed conversations between peers to help one keep up with the lecture content. The third alternative can be valuable but only if the student indeed revisits the point, gaining the missed information from the teacher, another student, the course material, or the Internet. Choice D may happen frequently as well, as the lecturer and thus the listener turn their attention to the next points. These options are each limiting to some extent, whether related to, for example, saving face, concerns about interrupting another student, or worries about missing part of the rapidly incoming input.

As such, the notetaker may feel isolated and bound by their L2 listening and notetaking abilities. This notion of seclusion when notetaking, sometimes the result of lecture organization, management, or classroom structure, can be viewed as an obstacle to the interaction and communicative competences that are stalwarts of the communicative language teaching (CLT) movement (e.g., Richards & Rodgers, 2014). To offset feelings of isolation, anxiety, and pressure during L2 lecture notetaking, underlying theories of sociocultural interaction, learning from peers, and the scaffolding of the notetaking and learning processes can be applied in order to maximize communicative potential and to develop a more interactive notetaking practice.

A relatively new line of research in notetaking has begun to exploit the potential of collaborative work surrounding notes and to examine any positive impacts it may have on notetaking and learning. Luo, Kiewra and Samuelson (2016) explored various models for revising notes from L1 lectures, which included combinations of updating and improving notes during pauses in lectures as well as in collaboration with partners. Among their findings was a modest partner effect, which indicated that revising notes with a partner yielded better and more complete notes than revising alone. Their findings promote collaboration and joint work around the notetaking act for the betterment of all involved. No longer does the notetaker need to sit on the proverbial island alone; instead, teachers can orchestrate activities to prompt such collaboration during classes.

Data collected from the aforementioned study included multiple-choice test scores and completeness scores for student notes. While the study demonstrated positive findings for collaboration, the actual content of the student discussions was less in focus. In other words, Luo et al. (2016) established that collaboration and revision lead to better notes from a product-oriented perspective with students taking notes in their L1. However, from a process-orientation, the actual development of notetaking skills and strategies, along with understanding of material to be learned, that students might share with each other in discussions has not yet been fully understood. The contents of the collaborations were not in focus in this study, and thus further exploration is warranted. Moreover, notions of collaboration around notetaking have yet to be explored in L2 contexts.

The aim of this chapter is to examine the potential for student dialogue based on their notes and notetaking practices in terms of the value of such dialogues and how they might influence student use of notetaking strategies. The chapter begins with an overview of relevant concepts from educational psychology, including sociocultural theory and the zone of proximal development. Using these perspectives as a basis, various taxonomies of L2 learning strategies are introduced with specific relevance to notetaking. These strategy frameworks, which collectively cover mental, physical, and interactive tactics, will be used to examine transcripts of authentic dialogues between EAP students who took notes during formal listening events and then held semi-structured discussions afterward. Findings show that students are able to articulate and share some notetaking strategies, both explicitly and implicitly, and that adding time for student discussions based on notes can be a valuable practice, both in terms of note quality and for future notetaking performance. Discussion of how teachers can facilitate such discussions and the potential positive benefits they generate are presented towards the end of the chapter.

Brief background from educational psychology

Collaboration, learning from peers, and the role dialogue plays in learning and cognitive development are established pillars of educational psychology

Embracing dialogic potential of notes 131

and became well-known through Vygotsky's (1934/1987) ideas related to sociocultural theory for learning and teaching and the "zone of proximal development" (ZPD). Wells (1999) observes that the contributions of Vygotsky in psychology and Halliday (1993) in linguistics have both had profound effects in the field of education and also points to the central role of linguistic discourse in learning and teaching. Wells (1999) expanded on ideas from both Vygotsky and Halliday and elaborated on the notion of dialogue inquiry and ways it can be used to facilitate learning in a variety of subjects (e.g., science, language, building machinery, running a business, etc.). Several of the ideas expressed by Wells (1999) and the researchers who inspired his work can be applicable to the development of notetaking abilities.

The framework for a sociocultural approach to teaching and learning can be viewed as placing a central focus on one's ZPD, which is defined by Vygotsky (1978) as "the distance between the actual development level as determined by independent problem solving and the level of potential development as determined through problem solving under adult guidance or in collaboration with more capable peers" (p. 86). In other words, working with others who have and bring different strengths to a particular task can stimulate development and learning in individuals in ways that working alone cannot (Shabani, Khatib & Ebadi, 2010). This mediation often occurs through social dialogue with others (Oxford, 2017). In theory, the skills, knowledge, and insights gained by a person from their participation in collaborative work can then be put to use in future individual work. Wells (1999) states that the ZPD applies to "any situation in which, while participating in an activity, individuals are in the process of developing mastery of a practice or understanding a topic" (p. 333).

When notetakers meet to discuss the content and quality of their notes, along with sharing strategies and techniques they used to record individual pieces of information, the potential exists for the collaborative group to: (a) confirm or revise the content of their notes (i.e., the material to be learned); (b) review and consolidate information; (c) share notetaking strategies for overall organizational approaches; and (d) share notetaking strategies for specific pieces of information. By incorporating the notion of the ZPD and applying it to collaborative discussions around notetaking, I aimed to explore what, if any, notetaking strategies were discussed among groups of peers. This investigation was meant to demonstrate whether time students spend discussing notes has potential to improve note quality and notetaking ability.

Such collaborative discussions facilitate not only reflection and explanation but instruction as well (Wells, 1999, p. 295). For notetakers, a post-notetaking discussion in which they compare their notes with peers, prioritize information, and discuss and justify various ways in which they recorded particular items of information allows for reflective opportunities. In addition, collaborative work can relieve the pressure placed on the lone individual to record all appropriate information on their own. When one notetaker has a unique style or has taken notes of a higher quality than the others,

132 Embracing dialogic potential of notes

it is possible for that student to instruct (or at least advise) the others. Group members could be involved in transformations in terms of "the individual's intellectual functioning and of [their] capacity for effective participation in the activity...[and] of the tools and practices as they are creatively adapted to suit the particular situation and activity in which they are being used" (Wells, 1999, p. 295). Several aspects within these transformations are relevant to notetaking: the cognitive aspects of noticing and prioritizing information, the explicit strategies and techniques for organizing and encoding information, and justifying decisions made about what to take notes on and how to do so.

Whereas Vygotsky emphasized that more expert participants are necessary to provide guidance and support for less capable individuals, when it comes to notetaking discussion groups, a clear distinction between expert and novice (or teacher and learner) may not be clearly delineated. Due to variations in background knowledge of the topic, vocabulary level, exposure to certain genres, and general L2 proficiency, different group members may occupy the role of expert at different times during collaborative discussions. Individual variations in subskills and preferences for notetaking in terms of paraphrasing ability or use of abbreviations, for example, could also contribute to the temporal nature of who has "expert" status. Wells (1999), in expanding on Vygotsky's definition of ZPD, points out that "the ZPD applies potentially to all participants, and not simply to the less skillful or knowledgeable" (p. 331). Furthermore, a designated teacher is not a prerequisite for learning through the ZPD and each member can learn and develop based on the contributions of others (Wells, 1999). The ZPD can also be enhanced by "semiotic artifacts" (Wells, 1999, p. 331), which include written works such as notes.

To establish a successful environment for learning within the ZPD, Wells (1999) suggests that students have opportunities to: "present their work to others and receive critical, constructive feedback...[and] reflect on what they have learned, both individually and as a community" (p. 336). When teachers provide interactive opportunities for students after a notetaking event, they can enable similar possibilities. An approach to classroom discourse that would seem relevant and fitting to adopt for student conversations regarding their notes is "inquiry dialogue," which Chappell (2014) summarizes as: "achieving common understanding through structured inquiry, wondering (playing with possibilities, reflecting, considering, exploring) and discussion that guides and prompts" (p. 4). Main features of inquiry dialogue include its goal of "promoting common understanding and inquiry...[and] building on one another's contributions in order to help develop knowledge and mutual understanding" (Chappell, 2018, p. 99).

The "knowledge" in regards to lecture notetaking can include both knowledge of the lecture content as well as awareness of various strategies and techniques for notetaking. When integrated with notetaking discussions, students could exchange ideas on how to record certain information (e.g., verbatim, paraphrase, abbreviation, picture, etc.) and weigh the pros and cons of each option (i.e., "playing with possibilities"); evaluate their note-taking performance for that particular text and identify areas to improve (i.e., "reflecting"); ponder over the significance of various items of information and their relationship to the central themes of a lecture (i.e., "considering"); and work through a series of questions provided by the teacher (i.e., "discussion that guides and prompts") (see the subsection titled *Suggested Prompts* below for examples).

Within these collaborative discussions, students have opportunities to compare the notes they have taken, reflect on their performance, and discuss various notetaking strategies. Such strategies can be linked to larger frameworks of L2 learning strategies, which are reviewed next and discussed in relation to L2 notetaking.

L2 learning strategies and strategy taxonomies

With Joan Rubin's (1975) seminal article *What the Good Language Learner Can Teach Us*, the idea of understanding strategies used by successful L2 learners was interjected into the field. The pedagogic train of thought expressed in the article was to monitor and articulate the habits and strategies of good learners and facilitate the adoption of those strategies by less proficient and/or less motivated learners. Among the characteristics of good language learners identified by Rubin (1975) are: being a willing and accurate guesser; having a strong drive to communicate and to learn from communication; being uninhibited and unafraid of appearing foolish so long as communication is generally successful; practicing and seeking out opportunities to practice; monitoring one's own performance to determine whether it meets particular standards; and attending to meaning first and foremost, rather than only to grammar or surface meanings. Several of these traits have resonance with L2 notetaking, as students must attend to spoken input, take chances in recording information in notes, utilize a variety of options, monitor progress and adjust approach if necessary, and practice taking in notes in desired formats.

As research into L2 learner strategies went on and "blossomed into a research field in its own right" (Rose, 2017, p. 421), a number of researchers proposed various categories of strategy, often arranged through taxonomies and classification systems. Many of these taxonomies have relevance to the four main language skills (listening, speaking, reading and writing), and strategies can generally be separated into "language *learning* strategies...and language *use* strategies" (Rose, 2017, p. 422, emphasis in original). More specifically, O'Malley and Chamot (1990) proposed a categorization system consisting of three main types of strategy: metacognitive, cognitive, and socio-affective. Metacognitive strategies relate to the executive function of managing resources for learning and involve selectively attending to different parts of a task as well as planning, monitoring, and evaluating performance. Cognitive strategies are needed to interact with, comprehend and produce language in different ways and involve "manipulating [language]

134 *Embracing dialogic potential of notes*

in different ways to enhance learning" (O'Malley & Chamot, 1990, p. 44). Examples of cognitive strategies are making inferences, summarizing, and organizing words and/or concepts in ways to facilitate learning. The third category, socio-affective, covers strategies that either involve interaction or control over affect and emotion.

A more elaborate and extensive strategy framework for L2 learning was put forth by Oxford (1990) and further developed in Oxford (2011, 2017). At a broad level, strategies are separated into direct and indirect types, the former of which Oxford (1990) likens to the "Performer in a play" and the latter the "Director of a play" (p. 14-15). Direct strategies allow L2 learners to work "with language itself in a variety of specific tasks and situations" (Oxford, 1990, p. 14). In this way, the category is similar to the cognitive type proposed by O'Malley & Chamot (1990). Direct strategies are further divided into memory, cognitive, and compensation strategies. Indirect strategies encompass those for coordinating and regulating learning as well as for controlling emotions; therefore, they align with metacognitive and socio-affective strategies (O'Malley & Chamot, 1990), respectively. The three types of indirect strategies are metacognitive, affective, and social. Oxford (1990) emphasizes the combination of the tangible role of the Performer (i.e., direct strategies) and the internal role of the Director (indirect strategies).

Oxford (2011, 2017) further expanded the strategy taxonomy that she put forward by elaborating on and refining the definitions of the categories she had originally proposed in 1990. In her metaanalysis of 33 different definitions of "language learning strategies" and similar terms, Oxford (2017) observed that the definitions cover internal, mental aspects (e.g., thoughts and cognitions), actions (e.g., what learners do), and techniques, devices and tools (e.g., what learners use) (p. 20). Each of these dimensions are realized during the notetaking act, as the notetaker must first process information and then take action in the form of, for example, writing or typing an abbreviation or composing a paraphrase, which they accomplish using a tool of some type, such as a pen, computer, or tablet. Oxford (2017) also emphasizes the process-nature of strategies and that a strategy is "never" defined as a product (p. 29). A process is "a systematic series of actions, changes or functions directed to some end" (Oxford, 2017, p. 29). In regards to notetaking, the notes themselves are the product and notetaking, through a series of strategic choices, is the process by which the notes are produced.

Based on her original definitions of various types of strategy, Oxford (2017) expanded and broadened these notions in several ways. In general, she applied the concept of metacognition to other sub-categories of strategy. That is, the "meta" factor for planning, monitoring, and evaluating strategy use is integrated into other areas, such as "metamotivational strategies" (p. 193) and "metasocial strategies" (p. 199). The revised version of metacognition includes four strategy sets: paying attention to cognition, planning for cognition, organizing learning and obtaining resources for cognition, and monitoring and evaluating for cognition (Oxford, 2017, p. 181). Cognitive strategies were also reorganized thusly: using sense to understand

and remember, activating knowledge, using reasoning, conceptualizing with details, conceptualizing broadly, and going beyond the immediate data (Oxford, 2017, p. 182), and the author illustrates each of these with concrete examples.

Several of these categories and specific examples of strategy use correspond to the notetaking act. In terms of O'Malley and Chamot's (1990) taxonomy, students engage metacognitive strategies when they: (a) plan which notetaking format they will use; (b) weigh pros and cons of different formats; (c) monitor their notetaking performance during the act; and (d) evaluate their notetaking performance after the act. Based on one performance, they may decide to alter their approach to notetaking and/or to learn additional strategies and/or to practice notetaking in the L2 more.

At a broad level, metacognitive strategies (Oxford, 1990, 2017) allow notetakers to plan and select notetaking techniques beforehand, to monitor notetaking progress and evaluate notetaking performance. Cognitive strategies such as grouping and classifying words, using visual images, and organizing information systematically (Oxford, 1990, 2017) all manifest themselves during notetaking. Socio-affective aspects (Oxford, 1990, 2017) such as collaborating with peers, asking a lecturer about a particular concept or item of information, and utilizing positive self-talk (or inner voice), especially when notetaking becomes nearly overwhelming, can help one take notes to the best of their ability.

Notetakers likely use a combination of several direct and indirect strategies as well. They undoubtedly engage their memory strategies as they attempt to transfer spoken output from a lecturer to their notebook or computer. They may employ strategies for representing concepts and ideas in their notes through, for example, images, paraphrases, and/or abbreviations. They may resort to taking notes in the L1, which would likely be a "compensation strategy" under Oxford's (1990) classification, as the student would aim to overcome limitations in L2 writing even if they understand the L2 output of the lecturer. In terms of affective aspects, notetakers need to regulate their anxiety while listening so that they can concentrate on the time-sensitive and often high-stakes operation at hand. Social factors including asking classmates for help in completing notes or asking questions of the lecturer would support students in creating the highest-quality notes possible.

Whereas the taxonomies proposed above are meant to encompass several if not all areas of L2 learning, strategies specific to L2 listening have also been identified. Among the expanding list of such strategies and skills are predicting content, applying world/background knowledge, and identification of chunks (e.g., Graham & Santos, 2015). Richards (1983) outlines micro-listening skills for academic lecture listening in particular; for example, identifying the topic of the lecture, following topic development, identifying relationships between various units of the discourse, and recognizing cohesive markers. Most of these strategies and skills centre entirely on the cognitive act of listening as it occurs inside the listener's mind and therefore do not extend to the close relationship between comprehension and the

136 *Embracing dialogic potential of notes*

generative act of producing content in notes. Therefore, more needs to be learned about how students can positively affect the notetaking abilities and note content of their peers.

With these strategy frameworks in mind, set within the underlying theoretical foundations of sociocultural theory outlined above, I endeavored to analyze conversations that EAP students in Sweden had about their notes and their notetaking performances. This project was meant to address the lack of knowledge about how and the extent to which L2 notetakers might engage in specific strategic activities, as well as to investigate the extent to which peer-to-peer dialogue immediately after notetaking could both improve the quality of the immediate notes as well as stimulate learning about notetaking strategies for future use. In particular, I examined transcripts of conversations in order to identify instances of strategy use that were consistent with the various categories of the strategy proposed by previous authors.

Methodology

To understand the potential for peer-to-peer learning related to L2 notetaking development, short conversations between small groups of students (three-five) were recorded, transcribed, and analyzed. All students were in upper secondary school (high school) in Sweden, taking an elective English course (e.g., English 7). After watching a TED Talk on happiness and how to lead a good life (Waldinger, 2015; https://www.ted.com/talks/robert_waldinger_what_makes_a_good_life_lessons_from_the_longest_study_on_happiness?language=en), students sat in groups and were asked to discuss the notes they took, any similarities and differences in those notes, and the strategies they used to record information. In total 25 students participated in six separate small group discussions, which were digitally recorded by their teachers. The discussions lasted between six and 15 minutes each. These recordings were transcribed and analyzed for contributions from and exchanges between students that align with the taxonomies of language learning strategies proposed by O'Malley and Chamot (1990) and Oxford (1990). Such a qualitative approach to research language learning strategies seems prudent given this lesser-researched area (Rose, 2017), namely discussions surrounding L2 notetaking certainly qualifies.

Findings

While notetaking as a broad concept itself might be defined first and foremost as a memory strategy, findings from an analysis of the student transcripts demonstrate several of the strategy types proposed by O'Malley and Chamot (1990) and Oxford (1990, 2011, 2017) were evident in the student discussions. In some cases, the two taxonomies overlap, and the same speech sample can be interpreted as matching both frameworks. The following section displays and discusses specific transcript excerpts in relation to the strategy frameworks.

Embracing dialogic potential of notes 137

Emergent strategy use

The excerpts below highlight elements of the strategy taxonomies that emerged during the discussions. No alterations or corrections have been made to the student output. Categorizations of the strategies present are included after the respective student output in *[italics]*.

Sample 1

A: 80% wanted to be rich, 50% wanted to be famous.

B: I wrote pretty much the same thing but I didn't write about exact numbers but I wrote... *[metacognitive strategy: reflection]*

C: Yeah me too I didn't write the numbers. *[metacognitive strategy: reflection]*

In Sample 1, students B and C reflect on their performance, pointing out that in contrast to student A, they recorded more general information without explicitly writing the numbers.

Sample 2

D: Yeah, but what about the tools you used to be able to recite later? What tool did you use when you wrote down?

E: Keywords, potentially use an arrow. *[direct; cognitive strategies: focusing on keywords; using symbols]*

F: I just, I shortened sentences. *[direct; cognitive strategy: paraphrasing and abbreviating]*

G: You made sort of like a bullet point list. *[direct; cognitive strategy: systematically organizing information]*

D: Yeah, I do different signs, whether it's a main topic or it's a sub-topic. *[indirect; metacognitive strategy: planning]*

E: Yeah, I do a little spaces for when he changes subject, or if it's something is like a sub subject to put it under, so it makes it more... *[indirect; metacognitive strategy: planning]*

Early in Sample 2, the students E and F are able to express two different preferences in terms of directly interacting with the language they heard: symbols and paraphrases. Later, student G points out that one of her classmates uses bullet points to organize the individual pieces of information. Overall organizational strategies (i.e., using different signs to distinguish between main and supporting ideas and purposefully leaving spaces in notepaper) fall in the categories of indirect, metacognitive strategies and are articulated by students D and E.

Sample 3

G: Yeah because in the end he said "so what have we learned from this?" and then I wrote lessons, question mark. *[direct; cognitive strategy: paraphrasing]*

138   *Embracing dialogic potential of notes*

In Sample 3, student G explains an example of how the cognitive strategy of paraphrasing can be used. She reports what the speaker said and describes how she has truncated the question from seven words to a single word plus a question mark. Her ability to reiterate the speaker's full utterance from a single word suggests this note is successful in stimulating her recall of what she heard.

Sample 4

H: I think it's... I think it's easier if you listen first and when the clip is over, you can write down, like summarize. *[indirect; metacognitive strategy: planning] [indirect; affective strategy: predicting and managing stressful situations] [direct; cognitive strategy: summarizing]*

With this comment, student H implicitly refers to the time pressure listeners face while taking notes. To relieve this pressure, student H plans for the time when he will engage in notetaking, a strategy that serves as both metacognitive planning as well as an affective strategy to manage emotions and relieve stress. The final phrase in the comment ("like summarize") shows H's recognition of the cognitive strategies of summarizing and attending to keywords and themes rather than focusing on every single individual word.

Sample 5

H: But it's just hard to, to find what's important to write down and what's just...You know... *[indirect; affective strategy: expressing anxiety] [indirect; social strategy: seeking reassurance and/or advice from others and seeking personal connections]*.
D: Yeah, I mean, I get better grades when I do notes, but I try to connect what I wrote down with different things that happen. Because it's easier to remember if you have something kind of interesting besides that to like put an anchor at the... *[indirect; social strategy: empathizing] [direct; cognitive strategy: using background knowledge and building associations]*

This exchange demonstrates how affective and social strategies can be activated through discussion about notes. Student H expresses frustration about the difficulty of making decisions on what to take notes on (see Chapter Five for pedagogic activities related to the challenge of making decisions in notetaking). H is able to express his anxiety and simultaneously open up the opportunity for classmates to provide emotional support and/or advice to help H improve. Student D responds with "Yeah," thereby acknowledging H's feelings and also offers advice in the form of the cognitive strategies utilizing background knowledge and connecting what is heard with other information (from which I infer D means: (a) previous information from the immediate lecture, (b) previous life experience, or (c) both).

Embracing dialogic potential of notes 139

Sample 6

I: So, the first thing I paid attention to was that it was going to be about health and happiness. *[indirect; metacognitive strategy: selective attention] [direct; cognitive strategy: identifying keywords; recognizing topic]*

Early in the lecture, Student I recounts how she was able to catch the main topic of the lecture by identifying keywords. She utilized selective attention by recognizing that the main theme of the lecture would likely be introduced early on and knew to pay special attention at that point.

Sample 7

I: I wrote down health and happiness and then I just wrote time, energy, and an arrow pointing to a question mark. What do we put time and energy on? *[direct; cognitive strategy: use of symbols; identifying key words]*

J: Yeah, same thing different words. *[direct; cognitive: comparing information] [indirect; affective: confirming information]*

Student I continues with the strategy of recording only keywords and describes how he condensed the question "What do we put time and energy on?" into two words plus two symbols (i.e., time, energy → ?). In student J's reply, there are both cognitive and affective elements, as the students compare and confirm information. The confirmation aspect can be particularly valuable and allows both students to feel more confident that they have recorded information of importance. With more traditional L2 language learning, such as grammar worksheets or multiple-choice tests, this type of confirmation of "correct" answers can build motivation and self-confidence while reducing anxiety.

Sample 8

J: I didn't pay attention to that part. I started writing about millennials when he mentioned, because I could relate, because we are kind of millennials, I would say. *[indirect; metacognitive: selective attention; ignoring that which we cannot relate to] [direct; cognitive: making associations; using background knowledge]*

In this example, student J explains that he exercised selective attention in *not* paying attention to certain lecture content. After a period of not paying attention, he was then able to recognize a cue to tune back in to the lecture content more carefully and resume taking notes. Associations and background knowledge related to the term "millennial" constituted triggers to do so.

Sample 9

I: Yeah, and then I wrote down that their goals that are most impossible to reach.

J: I wrote that too. *[direct; cognitive: comparing information] [indirect; affective: confirming information]*

140 *Embracing dialogic potential of notes*

K: Same. *[direct; cognitive: comparing information] [indirect; affective: confirming information]*

In this exchange, students J and K confirm that their notes include the same information as I articulates. This joint confirmation can provide a form of verification that all group members attended to and noted the same information, thereby providing a positive confirmative aspect.

Sample 10

J: Yes, because he kind of went over it a lot of times, he repeated himself. So it was really easy. *[direct; cognitive: recognizing repetition] [indirect; affective: positive self-talk]*

Student J recognized that the speaker repeated the same or similar points at multiple times during the lecture. Because of her ability to recognize this pattern, she believes the particular piece of information was easy to understand and record.

Sample 11

I: At the end, yeah. After that I didn't write anything else until the end when he came to the conclusion that good relations bring happiness and health. *[indirect; metacognitive strategy: selective attention] [direct; cognitive: recognizing lecture organization; prediction based on genre]*

Student I recognized the typical generic format of a presentation and knew to expect a conclusion. When that conclusion came, she was ready to reengage with the notetaking act. Student I exercised selective attention by, after a period of not writing "anything else", she returned to her notes when the conclusion began. In sample 6 above, Student I recognized the importance of the introduction to understanding a presentation, and with sample 11, she reinforces this attention to structure by acknowledging the conclusion.

As demonstrated by the transcript extracts above, several relevant types of strategies were manifested during the conversations based on student notes. These findings have pedagogic implications for students and teachers in the EAP and EMI classrooms, which are discussed in the next section.

Discussion and pedagogic implications

In building on the findings of Luo et al. (2016) that collaboration improves note quality, this brief study aimed to shed light on what takes place in L2 student discussions of notes when viewed through the lens of language learning strategy frameworks. Findings showed students engaged in conversations not only about the content of the notes themselves, but indirectly demonstrating strategy use and providing potential learning opportunities through sociocultural frameworks and the ZPD. This section discusses the findings with a view to promoting student discussions about notes as a valuable use of class time for several reasons: social and affective factors, strategy development, and confidence building. While such discussions are likely beneficial in all contexts, some variations due to the differences between EAP preparation courses and tertiary EMI lectures need to be acknowledged. In order to support teachers in implementing these discussions, a set of five prompting questions is provided, although this list is suggestive rather than definitive. The section and chapter conclude with comments on how this initial research can be expanded for the future.

Broad venue for strategy coverage

As demonstrated by the eleven samples above, a wide range of strategies can be found in the discussion data. Strategies matching the various categories introduced by O'Malley and Chamot (1990) and Oxford (1990, 2011, 2017) emerged from the transcripts. Metacognitive, cognitive, and socio-affective strategies (O'Malley & Chamot, 1990) as well as several examples of both indirect and direct strategies (Oxford, 1990) were evident. This range suggests that discussions surrounding notes and notetaking provide students with an expansive canvas on which to describe and articulate their own strategy usage and to listen to and learn from other students about how they approach notetaking in general and the methods they used to record specific information following a particular listening event.

Findings suggest that valuable exchanges can take place in brief discussions following notetaking. Whereas previous research has established that collaboration with classmates and joint review of notes leads to higher achievement on tests of lecture content in L1 contexts (Luo et al., 2016), the findings presented above indicate that L2 EAP students are able to articulate and reflect on their notetaking practices, confirm information, ask for and receive affective support, and develop a collaborative classroom atmosphere. Therefore, post-notetaking discussions, even as short as five min, may prove beneficial, not only as review opportunities but also to alleviate and counteract the isolation and anxiety that notetakers sometimes feel. In other words, overlooking the potential of such discussions would lead to missed classroom opportunities.

Teachers in EAP classrooms tend to recognize that their students are at various stages of L2 English development and thus teachers may need to adjust expectations, adapt teaching and tasks, and so on in order to account for student proficiency levels. The EAP classroom is still recognized as "sheltered" in some ways and students are not meant to have "mastered" the language but are instead working towards goals of becoming increasingly more proficient in L2 English as it relates to the four main language skills. The students involved in this particular dataset are from L2 EAP courses at the high school level in Sweden. As such, they are interacting with academic texts and

142 *Embracing dialogic potential of notes*

their teachers intend to help them develop notetaking skills so that they can succeed in future EMI environments at the tertiary level in the future.

In EAP preparation courses, post-notetaking discussions can provide space for students to: gain confidence, get advice, learn techniques from others, develop notetaking skills, and expand their knowledge and application of both implicit and explicit L2 language learning strategies. In such courses, the actual content of the lecture texts and accurate recording thereof in notes may be less important than developing L2 notetaking skills (from several perspectives, including metacognitive, cognitive, and socio-affective dimensions) for future listening events.

In EMI courses in higher education, students are typically expected to enroll with a high level of proficiency. Lecturers may or may not take L2 English proficiency into account when delivering lectures, setting tasks, and assessing student knowledge of course content. The focus in EMI is on subject content and subject knowledge rather than the development of L2 skills (which in theory would be developed in previous EAP or elsewhere). In these ways, EMI can be viewed as distinct from EAP. If these findings are projected to EMI lectures in higher education, EMI instructors might also incorporate such discussions in their lectures for several reasons, some of which overlap with those for EAP teachers and some that are distinct to EMI.

The university lecture hall can be an intimidating place for L2 English students challenged with listening and taking notes on unfamiliar content (see Chapter Two for a review of challenges such students face). By incorporating post-notetaking discussions, EMI lecturers can provide room for their students to gain confidence in their L2 English listening and notetaking skills, confirm and adjust notes for accuracy, and add to notes based on contributions from peers. Moreover, from social and affective perspectives, discussions can provide a sense of community, increased collaboration, and reductions in anxiety and uncertainty. When such discussions become a regular part of EMI courses, students may look forward to the activity for precisely those reasons, as they will begin to understand that notetaking does not have to entail a sense of isolation.

Limitations

The excerpts presented in this chapter come from relatively mono-cultural classrooms in Sweden. That is, all students shared the same L1 (i.e., Swedish) and most had spent a similar number of years in the Swedish school system. In classrooms that include students from several L1s and/or cultural backgrounds, opportunities for exchanges about notetaking strategies specifically and L2 learning strategies in general would likely increase. This is because of variations in approaches to listening, lecture expectations, recognizing and prioritizing information in lectures, taking notes (both at organizational and more discrete levels), and collaborative practices.

In addition to cultural aspects, L2 proficiency level likely also affects the merits of such conversations. This study included students who are at

Embracing dialogic potential of notes 143

approximately the B2–C1 levels on the CEFR scale. They were able to (a) listen to a text; (b) take notes in English; and (c) conduct the discussions in English, for the most part. Students at lower proficiency levels may need more support for how to compare and discuss their notes. If students share a common L1, these discussions could take place in that language, which would allow for deeper, more meaningful exchanges than would low proficiency L2 interactions. A certain maturity level may also be necessary in order to appreciate the place of notetaking as a core academic skill that can have positive impacts on lifelong learning; this, as opposed to a curt and superficial review of notes.

Suggested prompts

For students who may struggle to have such discussions, the following questions may provide necessary scaffolding. They may be useful for teachers and students, at least in the early going, to stimulate discussion and focus attention on relevant aspects of notes and notetaking.

1   What notes do you have that are the same as and/or different from the other students in your group?
2   If you have the same information noted down, *how* is it written? (word for word, keywords, abbreviations, etc.)?
3   Why did you note down each piece of information? Can you reflect on and justify your choices?
4   In what ways do the notes look the same/different (in terms of format, handwriting, etc.)?
5   Do certain sets of notes appear to be more effective / better than others? If so, why?

As students become accustomed to such discussions, responding to these questions may become inherent and routine, and new prompts, either designed by the teacher or initiated by students themselves, may evolve.

Chapter summary

This chapter aimed to examine one possible avenue for alleviating the often-isolating practice of individual notetaking. Despite notetaking being common practice in rooms full of students, these individuals (and their teachers) do not always capitalize on the collaborative opportunities available to support learning and notetaking. From a sociocultural perspective, this chapter examined peer-to-peer small group discussions based on notes and explored the extent to which strategies emerge during such conversations through the lens of language learning strategy frameworks. Findings from an analysis of the transcriptions demonstrated a range of strategies evident in the student discussions, which can serve several roles in the EAP and EMI classrooms, respectively. The habit on the part of the teacher of allowing for

144 *Embracing dialogic potential of notes*

and encouraging brief discussions following a period of notetaking can lead to increased and deeper content knowledge, expanded techniques for notetaking, and strengthened learning through collaboration.

Students in these discussions occasionally commented on the quality of notes and their preferences for different ways of recording information, both in terms of overall organizational as well as discrete items of information. When it comes to evaluating note quality, many EAP teachers are either required or feel compelled to examine and assess student notes. Such evaluation can take place more formally, in that it generates a letter grade or a certain number of points, or it can happen more informally, manifested in comments about handwriting quality, amount of notes, etc. Making fair and accurate judgments about notes, however, is not as clear and straightforward a task as one may initially think. Therefore, teachers and students would do well to be aware of the various ways that notes can be evaluated and the effects those evaluations may have for individual students. The next chapter turns to the topic of evaluation of note quality and to deliberating what constitutes "good" notes.

References

Chappell, P. (2014). Engaging learners: Conversation- or dialogic-driven pedagogy. *ELT Journal*, 68(1), 1–11.

Chappell, P. (2018). Inquiry dialogue: A genre for promoting teacher and student speaking in the classroom. In A. Burns & J. Siegel (Eds.), *International perspectives on teaching the four skills in ELT* (pp. 97–110). Basingstoke, UK: Palgrave Macmillan.

Graham, S., & Santos, D. (2015). *Strategies for second language listening*. Basingstoke, UK: Palgrave.

Halliday, M. A. (1993). Towards a language-based theory of learning. *Linguistics and Education*, 5(2), 93–116.

Luo, L., Kiewra, K., & Samuelson, L. (2016). Revising lecture notes: how revision, pauses, and partners affect note taking and achievement. *Instructional Sciences*, 44, 45–67.

O'Malley, J., & Chamot, A. (1990). *Learning strategies in second language acquisition*. Cambridge: Cambridge University Press.

Oxford, R. (1990). *Language learning strategies: What every teacher should know*. Boston: Heinle & Heinle.

Oxford, R. (2011). *Teaching and researching language learning strategies* (1st edition). Harlow, UK: Pearson Education.

Oxford, R. (2017). *Teaching and researching language learning strategies* (2nd edition). New York: Routledge.

Richards, J. (1983). Listening comprehension: Approach, design, procedure. *TESOL Quarterly*, 17(2), 219–240.

Richards, J., & Rodgers, T. (2014). *Approaches and methods in language teaching* (3rd ed.). Cambridge: Cambridge University Press.

Rose, H. (2017). Researching language learning strategies. In B. Paltridge & A. Phakiti (Eds.), *Research methods in applied linguistics* (pp. 421–438). London: Bloomsbury.

Rubin, J. (1975). What the "good language learner" can teach us. *TESOL Quarterly*, 9(1), 41–51.

Shabani, K., Khatib, M., & Ebadi, S. (2010). Vygotsky's zone of proximal development: Instructional implications and teachers' professional development. *English Language Teaching*, 3(4): 237–248.

Vygotsky, L.S. (1978). Interaction between learning and development. In M. Cole, V. John-Steiner, S. Scribner & E. Souberman (Eds.), *Mind in society: The development of higher psychological processes* (79–91). Cambridge, MA: Harvard University Press.

Vygotsky, L.S. (1987). Thinking and speech. In R. Rieber & A. Carton (Eds.), *The collected works of L.S. Vygotsky: Vol 1. Problems of general psychology* (pp. 39–285). New York: Plenum Press. (Original work published 1934).

Waldinger, R. (2015). *What makes a good life? Lessons from the longest study on happiness (2015, November)*. *[Video file]*. Retrieved from: https://www.ted.com/talks/robert_waldinger_what_makes_a_good_life_lessons_from_the_longest_study_on_happiness.Main+Learning+From+Longest+Study+into+Happiness+Video+18Elizabeth+Dunn:+Happiness+and+MoneyElizabeth.

Wells, G. (1999). *Dialogic inquiry: Towards a sociocultural practice and theory of education*. Cambridge: Cambridge University Press.

7 Assessing note quality

Introduction

As the previous chapters have emphasized, notetaking ability is crucial to student learning, retention of information, and overall academic success, both for students learning in their L1 or L2. Regardless of the language in which notes are taken, one unresolved issue surrounding notes is determining whether one set of notes is better than another. Defining characteristics that comprise "good" notes is a challenging undertaking. This challenge applies to both the overall organization of the notes (e.g., is the flexible outline better than the Cornell method?) and to discrete points of information (e.g., is recording a fact during a lecture via paraphrasing preferable to drawing a small picture?). Language educators, particularly those in EAP, must be aware of a range of related factors and the need to employ an objective and systematic method for assessing notes in order to avoid subjective judgments.

This chapter examines the issue of assessing note quality by first considering the term "good" and viewing it from multiple perspectives: students, peers, teachers and researchers. The chapter then moves on to provide a brief overview of studies that have focused not on notes themselves but on post-listening tasks for which notes were used. Such studies neglect notes themselves as artifacts of listening comprehension that deserve attention in their own right. Subsequent discussion argues for more attention to the objective assessment of note content itself and reviews several methods for assessing note quality used in L2 notetaking literature, highlighting both strengths and weaknesses of the various approaches. The notion of the "information unit" (IU) is promoted as a viable and relatively objective option for assessing note quality, albeit one with inherent flaws as well (briefly, an IU is "smallest unit [of information] one can judge as true or false" (Anderson, 2014, p. 104; a fuller discussion of IUs is available later in the chapter). The chapter concludes with pedagogic advice for EAP teachers who need to attach grades to student note taking ability as well as broader considerations for any teacher whose students take notes.

"Good" to whom?

A working definition of "good" notes needs to account for notes that select, organize, and elaborate ideas expressed by speakers so that the person taking them can learn in generative and constructive ways. That learning may occur at the encoding stage, the storage stage, or both. In addition, "good" notes presumably capture and preserve information in a form that retains the intended message expressed by the speaker, and stimulates recall of main and supporting details for *the individual notetaker*. From this perspective, "good" notes can be recorded in a variety of formats through any combination of verbatim or generative techniques involving abbreviations, pictures, symbols, and so on. While notetakers have several tools and methods from which to choose, including tradition long-hand and digital options, when one thinks of assessing note quality, at least up till now, it is mostly long-hand pen and paper notes that are evaluated, particularly in L2 contexts (although a small selection of recent studies in L1 contexts (e.g., Mueller & Oppenheimer, 2014; Morehead, Dunlosky & Rawson, 2019) have included digital notetaking). The quality of digital notes has yet to receive the same level of scrutiny in terms of keystrokes, figures, paraphrasing, and so on. All of these factors, either individually or in combination, might precipitate a teacher to classify notes as "good"; however, there is seldom an objective method applied to the evaluation of content and quality of notes.

The quality of notes may be evaluated to some degree by several groups. Notetakers themselves may look at their notes for review and either be satisfied that a piece of information they are seeking does indeed appear in their notes. Alternatively, if one looks back at their own notes hoping to refresh their memory of lecture content and realize that they have missed a point they had wanted to record, they may be disappointed. This is in a way an "immediate, relevant" needs method of assessment. Either the notes contain the desired information, or they do not. From a student perspective, assessment of notes can be used to measure progress and instill a goal to achieve.

Assessment of notes also helps to justify the valuable class time devoted to the skill; that is, if the results of notetaking are not evaluated in any meaningful manner, one might question the need for in-class instruction altogether. At times, student peers evaluate note quality, such as when a classmate who missed a lecture borrows notes to learn what they missed, or when small groups of students meet to review their notes. If one's notes are taken systematically in easily accessible ways, they are likely to be viewed in positive ways, accompanied by compliments like "Wow, you took good notes!" or "Thanks, I want to just copy this section since I missed it."

Notes are also important to teachers, although a focus on note quality often arises only in EAP-type contexts. In EAP, teachers often monitor student ability and progress with notetaking to ensure that they are capturing increasingly more information presented in lecture format. EAP students are learning and

148 *Assessing note quality*

practicing notetaking, and therefore the monitoring of quality and performance is a crucial aspect of teaching and assessment. EAP teachers may check student notes and make assessments of note quality, either based on intuition or using an a priori set of criteria. They may classify notes as "good" for a number of reasons: Notes that are written in clearly legible and attractive handwriting, well organized on the page, make effective use of space and margins, and are potentially useful on upcoming tasks such as summary writing or comprehension questions may warrant praise and/or high marks. Several of these aspects, such as legible handwriting and "effective" use of margins are rather subjective and standards may differ depending on the teacher. Apart from presentation, the efficiency of notes, in that they include a maximum amount of information in the fewest possible tokens, may also be considered "good" notes, can contribute to note quality, although this is sometimes overlooked in classroom practice.

By the nature of EAP courses, and their explicit purpose of developing academic skills to cope with and learn from English-based material, instructors who focus on notetaking often encourage (or in extreme cases, demand) that their students adopt a specified notetaking system. This statement is made based on intervention studies, which have emphasized a single notetaking format as well as on a review of commercial notetaking materials for the L2 classroom that often provide explicit practice in one or a limited range of notetaking systems. When EAP teachers introduce and provide practice opportunities for discrete notetaking strategies like abbreviating or paraphrasing, they typically expect students to demonstrate their ability to use such techniques when taking notes, whether the students want to or not. These observations suggest that notetaking in EAP is at a superficial level in some ways; that is, students are meant to "display" their notetaking ability in line with specific instructional objectives outlined by their teacher. Demonstrating the ability to listen to and take notes in L2 English according to prescribe styles could be recognized by high grades or point values regardless of whether the information in those notes is actually used for learning content.

In contrast, for EMI teachers, note quality is less of an explicit concern. Their priority is to encourage student learning and one visible and influential way to accelerate that learning is by having students take notes. The format of those notes and the techniques contained within them are likely of little importance to EMI lecturers. So long as students can master the content, the methods they use to take notes (or even to learn the material in the absence of taking notes) are irrelevant in light of the final goal: learning the material. EMI lecturers are less concerned with students' ability to adopt a particular method, to paraphrase a concept in an efficient manner, or consistently use symbols and abbreviations in their notes than many EAP practitioners. Yes, lecturers in EMI settings probably hope their students take notes, but these educators rarely check the content and quality of their students' notes, if ever. Quality notes to an EAP teacher would likely involve showing listening comprehension and a well-organized archive of as much information as possible. For EMI teachers, taking notes is often assumed and rarely checked. Their intentions are for deeper intellectual engagement with and learning of the material they present rather than the form in which that information is represented in notes.

The various perspectives described above lead to a conclusion that, beyond the individual notetakers themselves, EAP teachers often have a vested interest in evaluating the quality of the notes their students take. Many teachers are required to assign grades to student notes and to monitor students ability to put into practice certain systems and/or techniques introduced in class. As students become more proficient in these and are able to demonstrate them consistently, grades and scores likely increase. Teachers may pay attention to both quantity and quality of notes. Quantity can be measured by, for instance, the total number of words written or the percentage of key ideas a student has recorded. Quantity often impacts evaluation as well, as teachers may be pleased to see more (rather than fewer) words on the notetaker's paper. Quality can mean recording a maximum amount of information in the most efficient ways possible (which could lead to a *lack* of quantity), such as paraphrasing in clever ways, linking various pieces of information to one another, and avoiding redundancy in notes.

While differing depending on school, many EAP instructors may be required to formally evaluate student notes and assign grades to them. In these cases, grading policies may be determined centrally by course coordinators and/or administrators. In other situations, teachers may be left on their own to develop individualized ways of grading student notes. Some teachers have expressed displeasure and resistance related to grading policies imposed on them. Such resentment may originate from: (a) a reluctance to provide a subjective judgment on work that is meant to be meaningful to the person taking the notes; or (b) grading notes may deviate from a teacher's instructional goals for teaching notetaking. That is, perspectives on whether the process or the product of notetaking should be the focus of grading is open to question.

Should teachers award high grades for students who adopt certain instructed formats or techniques? What happens if a student takes notes that capture all relevant content but that student neglects to include any of the instructed frameworks? Does their grade suffer despite the high information content of their notes? Beyond the process-product issue, another point of contention to consider is whether the notes are recorded in the L2 or the L1 (e.g., Tsai & Wu, 2010; Siegel, 2020), as well as the degree of tolerance the teacher has for notes in the L1. If a student takes copious notes in the instructed frameworks while listening to academic content in L2 English but records the notes in L1 orthography, what marks will they receive?

These are the types of issues that EAP teachers encounter when trying to assess student notes. An outside reader of someone else's notes may not be able to extract the same information as the notetaker because the outside viewer: (a) was not present with the notetaker at the encoding stage and/or (b) was not privy to the notetaker's thought processes and reasoning when encoding the information. Of course, teachers must be clear to students about grading criteria and expectations; however, since notetaking has for so long been an "assumed skill," in my experience topics such as these are often left

150 *Assessing note quality*

unresolved in EAP classrooms. They can be difficult to grapple with and challenging to resolve due to the potential friction between students' taking notes with their own preferred methods and teachers who are tasked with providing set frameworks and assessing students ability to adhere to those frameworks. And the notes themselves may not be the ultimate object of evaluation.

"Good" notes and task relation

To determine what constitutes either "good" or subpar notes, the purpose for notetaking is likely an influencing factor. Purposes can range from an individual intrinsic desire to record, learn, and preserve content to external pressure to perform to a predetermined standard on a define task or tasks following the listening and notetaking event. These task(s) and the roles the notes need to fulfill can affect the way in which listeners take notes. For example, if students know they will use their notes on, or to study for, a discrete item multiple-choice test related to a lecture, they may try to record as much information verbatim as possible. This approach would be valuable for lectures that contain lots of discrete facts that are not open to interpretation such as mathematical formulas, historic dates, or chemical combinations.

On the other hand, if students know they need notes to write a summary of lecture content, they may elect to note broad themes and paraphrase lecture content, an approach which may lend itself to lectures on more abstract themes. For many lectures, the content is often a mixture of both abstract concepts and theories and how they are realized in practical terms in the real world. Since the content is often a mixture, understanding the purpose for taking notes and expectations of any post-listening tasks can aid the notetaker in taking *good notes for a given task.*

Furthermore, since many students rely on their notes either to study for or directly answer comprehension questions or to write a summary, teachers may feel that grading the end task rather than the notes (which have an intermediary function) is more relevant and appropriate (i.e., if the student can perform well on the end task based on their memory capacity and "poor" notes, should they be penalized for those subjectively "poor" notes?). This view of notes applies to EMI instructors who are concerned with performance in relation to the learning of course content rather than to the EAP instructor's priority of developing a set of transferable academic skills that can be applied regardless of the target content. In other words, the EAP teacher usually wants to see evidence of listening comprehension in notes, the ability to take those notes in L2 English per a prescribed system and/or techniques, and performance on post-listening activities that demonstrate content understanding. The priorities attached to these three aspects vary by course, context, and individual student. The EMI instructor is only interested in the demonstration of understanding irrespective of how that knowledge was gained.

Several previous studies on L2 notetaking have concentrated on post-listening task rather than note quality per se (Siegel, 2018a). That is, they have focused on analyzing task performance on which notes were used rather

Assessing note quality 151

Table 7.1 A selection of studies that include transfer of information from notes to a task (adapted from Siegel, 2018a)

Study	Purpose of study	Post-notetaking task
Dunkel et al. (1989)	To examine the strength of the encoding effect	30-item multiple choice test
Hayati & Jalilifar (2009)	To examine differences between uninstructed notetakers, Cornell method notetakers, and non-notetakers (see Pauk & Owens, 2014, for a comprehensive explanation of the Cornell method)	TOEFL listening test
Tsai & Wu (2010)	To examine how language (L1 or L2) of notes affects comprehension	Comprehension test
Lui & Hu (2012)	To examine how notetaking affects comprehension test and summary writing performance	Comprehension test; Summary writing task
*Kiewra et al. (1995)	To examine how notetaking format can affect performance testing	Comprehension tests
*Mueller & Oppenheimer (2014)	To compare pen and paper to computerized notes	Factual-recall questions and conceptual application questions
*Bui & McDaniel (2014)	To examine how learning aids (e.g., skeleton outline, illustrative diagram, etc.) affect learning	Free recall test; short answer test
*Luo et al. (2018)	To compare pen and paper to computerized notes; to compare the process and review functions of notes; to explore images in notes	Multiple choice test consisting of questions related to facts, relationships, and recognition of new examples; other aspects of the study focused on note quality (e.g., total words, verbatim overlap, images, and idea units)
*Morehead et al. (2019)	To replicate Mueller & Oppenheimer (2014) and extend their work by including an eWriter group	Factual-recall questions and conceptual application questions (a replication of Mueller & Oppenheimer, 2014; thus, the questions were exactly the same as in that study); other aspects of the study focused on note quality (e.g., total words, verbatim overlap, and number of idea units)

Note: Studies marked with (*) focused on L1 notetaking.

152 *Assessing note quality*

than on the quality of the notes themselves (see Table 7.1 for an overview of such studies). By focusing on the post-notetaking task, these studies focus on the transfer of information from notes (or the listener's memory) to the various tasks, all of which require slightly different methods of knowledge expression. As such, they are less concerned with "good" notes than with quality performance that may or may not be supported by notes. Strong performances in many of these cases could be linked to working memory capacity, previous background knowledge of the topic, clever test-taking strategies, strong ability in certain L2 skills (e.g., reading and/or writing), or just plain luck (particularly on multiple-choice tests).

As Siegel (2018a) observes, examination of student notes themselves is likely a more accurate method for assessing lecture comprehension than post-listening tests for several reasons. Firstly, comprehension tests are created by a test writer who may have different priorities than a lecturer and/or notetakers. Therefore, it is the test creator who determines what is important in the lecture rather than the speaker and/or listeners. Students may well have written good and accurate notes with large coverage of the lecture topic; however, test items may not have included much of that information.

Apart from the caveats mentioned above (e.g., potential effects of working memory, guessing, the quality of test questions, etc.), such studies typically do not account for the possibility that two students could get the same result on a comprehension test but have vastly different notes and could have used those notes to varying degrees. What is more, students may have information in their notes above and beyond what the test questions ask for, yet they do not receive recognition for these notes. Therefore, the studies often make generalizations about notetaking without focusing enough attention on the notes themselves.

I would suggest that more attention to notes themselves, possible via mixed methods research that accounts for both the notes *and* for task performance accompanied by notes would place much-needed emphasis on the notes as products of listening comprehension that can be used in a variety of ways and to various extents. Research approaches such as these seem to overlook the fact that many students often use their notes in multiple ways at different times during a period of tuition. For example, a student may take notes in order to write a summary based on their notes immediately following a lecture and then use the same notes to review for a summative multiple-choice test at the end of the semester. Limiting research to a single task, albeit possibly for time constraints or challenges in retaining participant engagement, fails to reflect authentic patterns of note usage.

Furthermore, there is an issue of the good *note user* in contrast to the good *notetaker*. While a student may take accurate, efficient, and clearly-organized notes, the ability to transfer that information into another usable form is a distinct academic skill. That usable form could include embedding the information in memory, using the visual cues in notes to stimulate recall, and/or locating and applying information within the notes on a task. The good note user is one who can locate information in notes and use it to, for instance, answer a multiple-choice or short answer question. An ineffective note user might have recorded relevant information in their notes but fail to locate and use that information to provide a correct answer. In such a case, the student may demonstrate being an astute listener and an adequate notetaker but may also fail to utilize their notes for maximum positive effect. In a sense, the studies outlined in Table 7.1 focus on students as note *users* in that the notes taken are not the objects of study; instead, it is the use of notes on an external task that has received most of the researchers' attention.

Prioritizing note quality

Rather than focus on students as note users, other studies have concentrated either solely or partially on notes themselves. In some cases, these studies have adopted dual foci of post-listening tasks as well as notes with equal emphasis on both (see Table 7.2). As detailed in the table below, several different methods for examining and evaluating note content and quality are evident, most of them involving quantitative measures of total numbers or ratios of words or IUs recorded to the total number of words or IUs possible in a given text. Other more qualitative measures relate to how note content corresponds to test questions and task requirements. Table 7.3 provides definitions and further description of several of the methods.

Several of the methods listed in Table 7.2 are relatively transparent and likely familiar to teachers (e.g., total number of words; highlights; arrows). The notion of the IU, however, requires further explanation in order for the IU method to be compared and contrasted with others. Siegel (2018a, p. 87) defines IUs as follows, influenced largely by Anderson's (2014) use of the term but applying it directly to notetaking:

"An IU is...defined by Anderson (2014) as 'the smallest unit of knowledge that can stand as a separate assertion...the smallest unit one can judge as true or false' (p. 104). IUs typically contain a combination of at least two words, abbreviations, pictures, and/or symbols, which may include an agent or actor (noun), an action (a verb), and/or a description (an adjective or adverb), the combination of which creates a complete proposition that is explicit and relies more on the written notes themselves rather than on memory to stimulate recall."

Morehead et al. (2019) included "idea units" in their analysis of L1 notes taken by students in long-hand, laptop, and eWriter groups. Luo et al. (2018) also adopted the "idea unit," following Bui, Myerson and Hale (2013). Bui et al. (2013) qualify idea units by awarding a full point for an entire idea unit and half a point for an incomplete but partially correct idea unit, and notes were scored by two different raters at adequate levels of inter-rater reliability. However, neither a definition of "idea unit" nor illustrative examples of the term are provided in these papers, leading to a lack of clarity about what constitutes an "idea unit" in their studies. In L2 contexts, Sakurai (2018) measured "key points...[such as] sleep deprivation, effects on the brain, [and] get lower grades...[, which] represented important concepts or facts for the main and supporting ideas of the lecture, and were selected and confirmed

154 *Assessing note quality*

Table 7.2 Studies from L2 notetaking that include explicit evaluation of notes

Study	Purpose of study	Methods for evaluating notes
Dunkel (1988)	To establish and examine differences in L1 and L2 notetaker ability	Total number of words; total number of IUs; test answerability; completeness; efficiency (also included a post-lecture comprehension test)
Clerehan (1995)	To compare L1 and L2 note quality in terms of hierarchical structure	Number of words; hierarchical structure; organization
Song (2012)	To examine effects of different notetaking formats	Note quality compared to a hierarchical system of lecture points (also included a post-lecture comprehension test)
Crawford (2015)	To examine the effects of notetaking practice	Number of content words; notations; abbreviations; highlights; arrows
Siegel (2016)	To examine the effects of systematic teacher-led notetaking instruction using semi-authentic listening materials	Number of IUs
Sakurai (2018)	To measure the effects of a pedagogic intervention	Total number of English/Japanese words; symbols; abbreviations; key points; hierarchical structure analysis (following Song, 2012) (also included a post-lecture comprehension test)
Siegel (2018b)	To examine the effects of systematic teacher-led notetaking instruction using authentic listening materials	Number of IUs (also included a post-lecture comprehension test)
Kusumoto (2019)	To examine the effects of systematic teacher-led notetaking instruction using authentic listening materials	Number of IUs (also included a post-lecture comprehension test)

by three EFL teachers" (p. 9). One could speculate that "idea units," "key points," and IUs all have much in common and are nearly synonymous.

The variety of approaches for judging note quality listed in the last column of Table 7.2 suggests a single objective measure of note quality is debatable. Without a standard consensus among researchers as to which measure is

Table 7.3. Methods for assessment of L2 student note quality (from Siegel, 2018a)

Method	Definition	Strengths	Weaknesses
Total number of notations	All marks made on a student's paper, including words (in L1 or L2), abbreviations, symbols, and punctuation (Crawford, 2015)	A full accounting for all visual efforts made by the notetaker on paper.	Treats all notations with equal importance; fails to attach significance to each notation; A high number of notations does not necessarily mean notes are comprehensible and meaningful.
Total number of words	Total number of words, abbreviations, symbols and illustrations (Dunkel, 1988)	Relatively objective, as general consensus as to what constitutes a "word"; Straightforward to assess.	Assumes each word has equal importance; Uncertainty with how to account for misspellings; Paraphrasing may cause confusion in assessment.
Total number of content words	Total number of nouns, verbs, adjectives, and adverbs (those that typically carry significant meaning) (i.e., not function words) (Crawford, 2015)	Focus on words that carry meaning.	Recording a list of content words may not facilitate accurate understanding or recall.
Information units	The smallest detached information that in itself can be judged as true or false (e.g., water freezes at 0 degrees C) (Dunkel, 1988; Siegel, 2018b)	Aims to capture intended meaning; Allows for combinations of words, symbols, illustrations to generate meaning.	Fails to assign importance to each unit; Potential disagreement about what constitutes an information unit, and which units are crucial to record.
Tiered rating of information units	Based on the notion of information units, but adds a 3-point system indicating importance of item (Siegel et al., 2020)	Accounts for varying levels of importance of information; Adds flexibility to the notion of information units.	Potential disagreement when assigning levels of importance.
Completeness	A ratio of recorded information units to possible information units (Dunkel, 1988; Siegel, 2016)	Generates a useful ratio that can be tracked and compared; Encourages the recording of ideas rather than single words.	Same as for Information Units described above.

156 *Assessing note quality*

preferable, it can be difficult to compare results between studies or to replicate previous findings in different contexts.

Several methods have been applied in L2 notetaking research to determine the quality of student notes, each with its own pros and cons. Table 7.3 is based on a review of relevant L2 notetaking studies (Siegel, 2018a). Definitions of several methods, along with strengths and weaknesses are also presented, allowing readers to consider which system or adaptation thereof may be most applicable to their own teaching context and learners' notetaking goals.

To illustrate how these various methods for evaluating notes can be applied to notes, Siegel (2018a) employed several measurements to analyze the same authentic sets of student notes. Results of those comparisons indicate that the IU method captures more comprehensive meanings than other methods such as the total number of words, which may or may not be linked in any meaningful ways. A study by Siegel (2018a) applied several of these methods to the same textual samples in order to demonstrate the ways in which results generated by certain methods can be more robust or misleading. The study compared authentic extracts from student notes to excerpts of lecture transcripts. Depending on the notes, a wide range of results was revealed. For example, one illustrative sample contained the following: 11 total notations; 9 total words; 6 total content words; and 1 information unit (Siegel, 2018a, p. 91). According to Siegel (2018a), the number of total notations and words may be misleading, as only a single comprehensive idea was included in the notes, suggesting that when recognizing and awarding complete ideas contained in notes, the IU may be a measure preferable to other options.

The IU method, however, entails several drawbacks that need to be addressed. First, it is challenging to reach a consensus on precisely what qualifies as an IU (or an "idea unit" or a "key point"). Students, teachers, and speakers themselves may have different notions and interpretations of how many IUs are present in any given lecture. Sakurai (2018) took steps to account for this variation by including three EFL teachers, who selected and identified "key points" for her analysis. Along the same lines, steps can be taken to offset the weaknesses related to some of the methods outlined in Table 7.3. These steps include collaboration in scoring notes (e.g., determine if a "word" should be awarded a point or if a questionable phrase deserves to be labeled an "information unit"). Rather than having a single teacher or researcher assess a set of notes, measures such as inter-rater reliability (in which multiple persons score the same notes using the same procedures, and then compare results) can bolster confidence in the assessments made.

To improve analysis methods that incorporate IUs, groups of researchers (e.g., Siegel et al., 2020) have attempted to address challenges faced when determining the level of importance of IUs in lecture (i.e., TED Talk) transcripts. In that study, a team of five teacher-researchers independently assigned an importance level of 1–3, with three being the most important, to the information units in two transcripts. Results showed that raters' views differed noticeably for some of the IUs, suggesting that procedures and expectations for rating need to be clear and that norming sessions among groups of teachers who score notes are highly recommended. A related caveat is that it is rarely the speaker, particularly in EAP courses that utilize pre-recorded lectures (e.g., from commercial textbooks or authentic materials such as podcasts, webinars, or TED Talks), who analyzes the notes. Regardless of how many collaborators focus on a single speech or set of notes, they will most likely not include the original speaker. Background knowledge and interpretation will likely vary within the group, thereby adding additional layers to an opaque operation.

An individual EAP teacher, or even a group of qualified EAP teachers and/or applied linguistic researchers, cannot know precisely how the original speaker would label the importance of each piece of information, meaning that while collaboration is a promising endeavor, it cannot meet requirements of objectivity and accuracy unconditionally. While the notion of evaluating notes using IUs is an improvement on more rudimentary methods like tallying words or notations, or on methods in which note content is dependent on its relation to arbitrary test questions (i.e., test-answerability), the IU method continues to evolve and be refined in order to address issues of consistency.

Pedagogical perspectives on note assessment

In terms of pedagogy, EAP teachers can demonstrate to their students how to improve their notetaking ability and achieve higher results on measures of note quality, which in turn would lead to higher grades for notetaking in the EAP classroom. For instance, activities for paraphrasing and simplifying strategies can help students record notes more efficiently and effectively than writing verbatim, thus increasing efficiency. Siegel (2019) outlines a three-step approach for teaching simplification in notetaking that includes a warm-up phase (priming for producing easier versions of more complex input), a transition phase (in which students work with short bursts of academic English texts and then reflect on the paraphrases they made), and a real-time phase (where students are challenged to maintain simplification strategies for longer stretches of text).

Another pedagogic technique teachers can employ is to demonstrate how different styles of notetaking can match post-listening tasks. For example, notes with a focus on details (e.g., names, dates, definitions) can be helpful on comprehension tests, whereas noting major ideas, topic shifts, and intonation can prove more valuable for summarization purposes and/or determining the speaker's attitude towards a particular topic than an abundance of discrete facts. In addition, teachers who prepare students specifically for English proficiency tests such as TOEFL iBT or IELTS, which encourage notetaking during certain portions, can cater notetaking instruction and assess note quality with those end uses in mind (i.e., what sorts of information that would likely be most useful to succeed on the types of tasks on these tests should be recorded in notes, and how those notes be used to the best effect to achieve the highest score possible).

Chapter summary

To sum up, assessment of note quality is a complex topic that can be viewed from a number of perspectives. Notions of "good" notes may differ depending on whether the evaluation comes from the notetaker him/herself, an EAP teacher, or an outside researcher. An important distinction has been made in this chapter between research studies that focus on the transfer of information from notes to other tasks and those that place a central focus on the notes themselves. When considering note quality, it is essential that the emphasis be placed on the notes themselves, particularly in EAP courses in which developing notetaking ability is a core objective. Teachers can employ assessment methods that revolve around the IU to get a better sense of their students' current abilities as well as to monitor the improvement of notetaking (i.e., not the improvement of test taking or completion of other tasks) in relation to lecture listening. To help students understand teachers' expectations of how to demonstrate "good" notetaking abilities, teachers need to make these expectations clear and provide examples of stronger and weaker notetaking, which can be used as springboards to stimulate conversations about the skill.

References

Anderson, J. (2014). *Cognitive psychology and its implications* (8th edition). New York: Worth.

Bui, D., & McDaniel, M. (2014). Enhancing learning during lecture note-taking using outlines and illustrative diagrams. *Journal of Applied Research in Memory and Cognition*, 4, 129–135.

Bui, D. Myerson, J., & Hale, S. (2013). Note-taking with computers: Exploring alternative strategies for improved recall. *Journal of Educational Psychology*, 105(2), 299–309.

Clerehan, R. (1995). Taking it down: Notetaking practices of L1 and L2 students. *English for Specific Purposes*, 14(2), 137–155.

Crawford, M. (2015). A study on note taking in EFL listening instruction. In P. Clements, A. Krause, & H. Brown (Eds.), *JALT2014 Conference Proceedings* (pp. 416–424). Tokyo: JALT.

Dunkel, P. (1988). The content of L1 and L2 students' lecture notes and its relation to test performance. *TESOL Quarterly*, 22(2): 259–278.

Dunkel, P., Mishra, S., & Berliner, D. (1989). Effects of note taking, memory, and language proficiency on lecture learning for native and nonnative speakers of english, *TESOL Quarterly*, 23(3), 543–549.

Hayati, A. M., & Jalilifar, A. (2009). The impact of note-taking strategies on listening comprehension. *English Language Teaching*, 2(1), 101–111.

Kiewra, K., Benton, S., Kim, S., Risch, N., & Christensen, M. (1995). Effects of note-taking format and study technique on recall and relational performance. *Contemporary Educational Psychology*, 20, 172–187.

Kusumoto, Y. (2019). EFL students perception of note-taking and the effect of note-taking instruction. *The Kyushu Academic Society of English Language Education Bulletin*, 47, 47–56.

Lui, B., & Hu, Y. (2012). The effect of note-taking on listening comprehension for lower-intermediate level EFL learners in China. *Chinese Journal of Applied Linguistics*, 35(4), 506–518.

Luo, L., Kiewra, K. A., Flanigan, A. E., & Peteranetz, M. S. (2018). Laptop versus longhand note taking: effects on lecture notes and achievement. *Instructional Science*, 46(6), 947–971.

Morehead, K., Dunlosky, J., & Rawson, K. A. (2019). How much mightier is the pen than the keyboard for note-taking? A replication and extension of Mueller and Oppenheimer (2014). *Educational Psychology Review*, 31(3), 753–780.

Mueller, P., & Oppenheimer, M. (2014). The pen is mightier than the keyboard: Advantages of longhand over laptop note taking. *Psychological Science*, 25(6), 1159–1168.

Pauk, W., & Owens, R. (2014). *How to study in college* (11th edition). Boston, MA: Wadsworth Cengage Learning.

Sakurai, S. (2018). Promoting skills and strategies of lecture listening and note-taking in L2. *Fukuoka University Journal of Humanities*, 49(4), 1019–1046.

Siegel, J. (2016). A pedagogic cycle for EFL note-taking. *ELT Journal*, 70(3), 275–286.

Siegel, J. (2018a). Did you take "good" notes? On methods for evaluating student notetaking performance. *Journal of English for Academic Purposes*, 35, 85–92.

Siegel, J. (2018b). Teaching lecture notetaking with authentic materials. *ELT Journal*, 73(2), 124–133.

Siegel, J. (2019). Notetaking in EFL: A focus on simplification. *The Language Teacher*, 43(3), 20–24.

Siegel, J. (2020). Appreciating translanguaging in student notes. *ELT Journal*, 74(1), 86–88.

Siegel, J., Crawford, M., Ducker, N., Madarbakus-Ring, N., & Lawson, A. (2020). Measuring the importance of information in student notes: An initial venture. *Journal of English for Academic Purposes*, 43. DOI: https://doi.org/10.1016/j.jeap.2019.100811.

Song, M. Y. (2012). Note-taking quality and performance on an L2 academic listening test. *Language Testing*, 29(1), 67–89.

Tsai, T., & Wu, Y. (2010). Effects of note-taking instruction and note-taking languages on college EFL students' listening comprehension. *New Horizons in Education*, 58(1), 120–132.

8 Key insights from classroom research and final thoughts

Main messages: Looking back and forward

The main motivation for collecting the perspectives and evidence, conducting the classroom research, and engaging in the topics in this book has been to bring notetaking in an L2 in to clearer focus for students, teachers, and researchers than it has been in the past. My enthusiasm for and interest in the topic began from the perspective of an EAP teacher; specifically, I felt I was under-delivering in terms of notetaking instruction and was not accurately understanding the complexity of the task when I assumed an instruction like "take notes" was sufficient. My hope is that the book helps shed light on the experiences of and options available to EAP students and others either preparing to take or currently taking notes in an L2 in academic situations. An additional ambition has been to provide some guidance to EAP teachers, if not necessarily to adopt all of the particular teaching techniques introduced here, then at the very least to better appreciate the extents to which notetaking presents challenges both from instructional and operational positions.

Despite the lengthy history of the act of notetaking (that is, humans have been recording images and words in order to remind them of certain things for centuries), it continues to evolve. Traditional ideas of academic notetaking involve a pen, paper, and an attentive and able listener. While these elements remain prominent, notetaking continues to be in a transitional phase, one marked by technological strides and the effects those endeavors have on teaching in and learning from academic lectures. Methods and tools for notetaking have developed from writing utensils to laptop computers, to tablets and styli that aim to simulate the feel of a pen and paper but embrace modern technology. Options for teachers and students, like providing Powerpoint slides via lesson management platforms, have also altered how notetaking is viewed and practiced. Last but certainly not least is the language used to deliver academic content. Whereas in the past, a large number of students would expect to study at tertiary level in their respective L1s, many around the world study at least at some point in an L2, which is English more often than not. As educators, we need to keep these shifting factors in mind and consider how they may reflect, or be reflected in, student notes.

Key insights from classroom research and final thoughts 161

Early on in the book, I presented and promoted the definition that notes are "short condensations of a source material that are generated by writing them down while simultaneously listening" (Piolat, Olive & Kellogg 2005, p. 292). Throughout the book, I have considered what these "short condensations" are and the various ways that a single item can be represented in diverse ways within multiple overarching frameworks. Various samples and related discussion have demonstrated how students prefer to, and in reality do, record information in "short condensations". Issues pertaining to specific notetaking techniques (e.g., generative or non-generative, verbatim or paraphrased, etc.) have been raised, as have pros and cons of various organizational systems (e.g., the Cornell system, the outline format, etc.). In addition to these areas that relate to the encoding function of notes, the roles of storage and review have also been discussed. The function of notes in EMI and other L2 content learning needs more careful consideration, in particular to identify how L2 students use notes after taking them, and what roles notes may play in the consolidation of information.

Another main message I hope readers take away from this book is an appreciation for the full set of complex behaviors that goes in to notetaking during academic discourse, particularly when one is operating in an L2. Further, notetaking and academic listening are not synonymous; in fact, far from it, although admittedly these two distinct actions intermingle. Listening certainly plays a crucial role in the early stages of the notetaking act but there is much more than meets the eye. As established earlier, not only listening but also decision-making steps at various levels (what, how, and when to record), as well as physical activities of writing or typing, are heavily involved. Thus, there are visible as well as cognitive aspects of notetaking that deserve attention in the L2 classroom.

Even before one commences the notetaking process, making the conscious decision to take notes, considering which format to use, and finding and bringing the appropriate notetaking tools factor into the metacognitive preparation that can affect success. Every stage of the notetaking procedure deserves coverage in academic preparation courses, though time spent on each particular stage may vary depending on the L2 language proficiency, educational background, and academic acumen of the students involved. This list of stages and procedures may not be comprehensive, and I welcome further attention to this area that would help to identify, articulate, explore, and provide scaffolded training for any steps I have failed to acknowledge.

Readers in Japan and Sweden, the two countries that are described in most depth, may be able to apply findings and pedagogic suggestions described here to their respective contexts with little to no change. Those working in other contexts might consider how the findings and suggestions may need to be modified within their existing contextual frameworks (e.g., course goals, numbers of students, access to materials, etc.). Regardless of the context in which one is teaching, this book should be seen as providing a basic understanding of the complexity of L2 notetaking and how L2 English students approach the task.

An overview

The book began with general comments about notetaking before putting a clear focus on notetaking during the academic lecture given in an L2. Various aspects of notetaking, including generative and non-generative practices, different methods and techniques available, and the combination of skills involved were introduced and defined. Notetaking was also discussed within EMI, a broader framework of L2 usage and one that continues to expand. Chapter Two reviewed relevant research from both L1 and L2 contexts, highlighting areas of particular interest for EAP and L2 notetaking. Intervention studies in L2 contexts were a point of emphasis meant to stimulate readers to trial and adopt systematic instruction that focuses on encoding. For those for whom the pedagogic suggestions may not be possible or preferable, the hope is that at least teachers reflect on, articulate, and justify how they approach notetaking in their classrooms.

Student perspectives, and the understanding thereof, were at the forefront of Chapter Three, which summarized previous survey research on student views and habits related to notetaking. In addition, findings from an international survey involving EFL students on multiple continents were shared in an effort to show where notetaking practices and viewpoints converge and diverge, providing readers with an more global perspective on L2 notetaking. This international survey stands in contrast to the often limited national contexts in which previous survey research has been conducted. The latter part of Chapter Three drew on a number of authentic note samples and discussed the pros and cons of certain methods of using and organizing note paper in addition to various approaches for recording particular items of information.

In response to the raising interest in and need for commercial EAP notetaking materials produced by international publishing houses, Chapter Four promoted an objective and pragmatic list of evaluation criteria. This list or a modified version thereof can be employed by teachers, course coordinators, and/or administrators in order to make the evaluation and selection of L2 notetaking textbooks more transparent. Included in the chapter was a sample evaluation that demonstrated the many strong points of commercial materials, which have certainly improved in recent years. To fill the potential gaps in textbooks as well as to make notetaking instruction more "teacher-centered" (in the sense that the teacher is necessary for input and not just providing materials and practice, managing audio material, and checking answers), Chapter Five introduced and described a multiple-step teaching cycle for L2 notetaking. This description included theoretical explanations and justifications for each stage in the process accompanied by explicit classroom activities for teachers to apply in their classrooms.

Chapter Six built on previous work by exploring and promoting the potential for discussions based on notes in the EAP classroom, both for learning of content and for the development of notetaking strategies. Evidence from recordings made between small groups of EAP students showed that a

Key insights from classroom research and final thoughts   163

number of language learning and notetaking strategy types (e.g., metacognitive, cognitive, social, and affective) were present in the discussions. Advice for how teachers can organize and facilitate similar conversations among their students was also provided. The issue of what constitutes "good" notes was the topic of Chapter Seven, which reviews different options and makes a distinction between general expectations of EAP and EMI teachers when it comes to notetaking. After summarizing and contemplating different ways of evaluating notes, the "information unit" (IU) was put forth as a viable option that can have positive implications for classroom teaching and learning, albeit with some caveats related to consistent application.

Revisiting the EAP and EMI relationship

This book has spent a considerable amount of time on notetaking in academic contexts where an L2 is being used, most often within EMI, which is itself set within broader ELF frameworks on tertiary campuses. To prepare for EMI, many students and teachers work on notetaking abilities in EAP courses. An important distinction between the roles of notetaking in these two contexts needs to be reemphasized. Notetaking in EAP is for developmental purposes. A general aim is for teachers to support students in the development and expansion of notetaking capacity and techniques so they are ready to grapple with authentic situations where they really need to take notes for learning.

In a sense, EAP is sheltered and involves *display* of notetaking ability; in other words, teachers often want to see that students are able to take notes in English while listening to English, regardless of the content of the text. The purpose is to show teachers that students have or are in the process of improving their ability to do so. Seldom are students responsible for learning the actual content of the texts to which they listen. Commercial materials used for notetaking in EAP provide scaffolded support, simplified and/or abbreviated texts that align nicely with certain notetaking techniques, and teachers and students can check "correct" answers to such activities. Thus, the skill of notetaking is in focus.

In contrast, the focus of EMI is on content learning in whatever ways the student can accomplish that learning. Most often, in university settings, that learning can be facilitated at least in part by attending and listening to lectures, taking notes, reviewing, and possibly using those notes later. Successful notetaking in EMI, then, is the goal for which many EAP courses aim. EMI teachers often assume that students who attend their courses have the L2 English listening, notetaking, and productive capacities to learn from and contribute to their courses. The EMI teacher seldom sees part of their role to support students' notetaking skills, apart from planning and delivering their lectures in ways that make the content clear and cohesive. EMI teachers probably do not spend class time on specific notetaking skills. Instead, their main focus is on transmitting course content for student learning.

164 *Key insights from classroom research and final thoughts*

The onus is on the students to learn that material using their own academic and linguistic resources. Issues related to individual EMI lecturers' English usage (e.g., pronunciation, rate of speech, lexical choices, confidence, idiosyncratic patterns, etc.) as well as cultural expectations both on the parts of the teacher and students can affect student notetaking ability and learning in EMI lectures.

Insights from classroom research

Based on the review of previous research, ideas, and findings presented in the previous chapters, as well as on my own reflections thereof, the following 12 key insights from classroom research are presented as core "take away" ideas:

1 **Notetaking is generally effective in facilitating better learning and performance than not taking notes.** As such, it is recommended that EAP teachers dedicate class time to support student notetaking in as comprehensible a manner as possible and to be explicit about the benefits of efficient and accurate notetaking. Most research has demonstrated that taking notes is valuable, and students also recognize the importance of notetaking. On surveys, students have consistently indicated that taking notes in L2 English is a valuable skill to have not only for academic purposes but in future professional careers as well.

2 **Teachers may need support in teaching notetaking in scaffolded and systematic ways.** While it is clear that notetaking is crucial for L2 students in academic contexts, teachers need more support. This is particularly evident when one considers the vast array of factors that impact notetaking performance (e.g., L2 listening proficiency, metacognitive planning, writing speed, working memory, strategies for using notes for learning, language choice, etc.).

3 **The encoding function needs explicit attention.** Given the variety of ways a single item can be recorded in notes, students should be exposed to the number of strategies available to them. Teachers can engage students in discussion of preferable methods and notetaking efficiency in relation to different methods. Students should aim to extend their pallet of strategies and techniques for encoding, and teachers should be equipped to help them do so.

4 **The storage function storage deserves explicit attention.** This point is often overlooked in L2 contexts but is crucial because just taking notes does not guarantee learning. Instead, students need to revisit and work with the notes they have taken in multiple ways. Teachers can incorporate different ways of utilizing and reviewing notes (e.g., rewriting, discussing, quizzing) into notetaking practice. The EAP classroom can be a useful place to exercise the storage function.

5 **Interventions can be effective for improving L2 notetaking performance.** As evidenced in several different L2 contexts, interventions have helped students become aware of, learn, practice, and apply a range of

Key insights from classroom research and final thoughts **165**

notetaking systems and techniques for encoding. I am especially supportive of those that focus on decision-making stages and that focus on the recording of individual items as opposed to promotion of overall systems.

6 **Students bring their own styles and preferences.** Since most if not all students will have taken notes in some way at some time prior to any given course, their individual styles and preferences need to be acknowledged. Teachers can find out from students, by a notetaking sample activity, a survey, and/or a discussion, how the individuals in a class tend to and prefer to take notes. Based on those responses and trends, teachers can develop supportive instructional content and strategies that align with rather than alter student preferences.

7 **Traditional pen and paper remains the most common method for taking notes.** Therefore, the traditional method should occupy significant class time dedicated to notetaking. However, as technology continues to impact notetaking, various digital options need to at least be acknowledged as possibilities. Differences between traditional and digital methods and tools can also be incorporated into class discussions. Use of technology for L2 notetaking should be a major avenue for research to explore in the future.

8 **Some overlap exists between L1 and L2 notetaking ability.** Teachers should not assume that students are starting from scratch and that students are taking notes for the first time in an EAP course. They might be taking notes *in L2 English* for the first time, but many if not all will already have established some routines and preferences in the L1. Teachers can try to incorporate these as well as raise awareness of which strategies from the L1 can be transferred to L2 notetaking.

9 **Notetaking textbooks should be examined with care.** Commercial notetaking materials need to be examined in their own right utilizing objective evaluative criteria that focus specifically on theoretical and practical aspects of the notetaking act. While most textbooks also include audio and/or video material that accompany notetaking activities, when evaluating and selecting materials for notetaking, the listening components should be secondary, with a primary focus on how the activities are designed to support notetaking.

10 **Discussions based on notes provide an untapped resource for notetaking development and learning.** Teachers should take advantage of students' desire to "check" their notes with peers, opportunities that allow students to confirm, revise, and discuss their notes, thereby strengthening their learning both in the present and in future instances of note review. Such discussions also allow for the development of and exposure to multiple perspectives on and strategies for notetaking.

11. **Evaluation and judgment of notes need to be done with care.** If necessary, notes should be judged with as objective and transparent methods as possible, while still considering inevitable individual differences such as format, encoding, and language choices. The IU was proposed and

166 *Key insights from classroom research and final thoughts*

promoted in this book as one relatively objective and transparent option that is teacher- and student-friendly in terms of classroom instruction and demonstration (which eventually lead to evaluation).

12. **A focus on content and quality should be paramount.** When looking at student notes, the actual information included in those notes should be the main focus. Has the student accurately recorded the essential points from a given lecture? Is the information recorded in ways that will stimulate later recall? Do the "short condensations" reflect an ability to make accurate decisions about what to record and then to do so in efficient and "terse" ways? My view is that these should be points of emphasis for teachers and students rather than adoption (sometimes forced) of a particular style or technique.

Unresolved issues and future avenues

While the increased visibility and prominence of L2 academic notetaking is welcome, a number of unresolved pedagogic issues have arisen. Among the most important to investigate and address is who has responsibility for supporting student development in regards to notetaking? When it comes to L2 proficiency itself, the responsibility lies in large part with the L2 instructor (coupled of course with the L2 learner along with their motivation, effort, and study skills). However, in terms of notetaking as an academic skill that has considerable overlap in the L1 and the L2, teachers in L1 contexts earlier in the educational process may influence how a student eventually takes notes in the L2.

If L1 content teachers spent some class time focusing on notetaking formats and strategies for their own subjects, by the time students entered EAP or EMI courses in high school or tertiary levels, L2 instructors would not feel the need to start from scratch. Instead, they could build on the notetaking background, techniques, preferences, and experiences students already had, either from L1 or previous L2 instruction. EAP teachers may be under the (sometimes false) assumption that all students in their courses have already developed notetaking abilities "somewhere else" (Siegel, 2018). This issue of who is responsible for notetaking instruction and when it should ideally begin is an area worth future research and pedagogic attention.

A second debatable topic is whether teachers should be dictating predetermined note formats in their EAP courses or whether students should be allowed to take notes in their own individualized manners. The prevalence of intervention studies in EAP contexts that promote a single format (e.g., the formal outline or the Cornell system) may cause undue stress or pressure some students to use formats with which they are not comfortable. Students might then only adopt the highlighted format in order to please their teacher and/or get a good grade in the immediate term rather than focusing attention on techniques that they will utilize after the EAP course ends. Furthermore, given the range of methods for recording specific pieces of information, teachers may wish to allow for variation rather than prescription. In addition, language choice and the option of translanguaging in notes in L2 academic contexts are areas in need of further exploration. Given the range of options available to notetakers, it is important for teachers to understand the effects their classroom choices and promotions can have on student performance and attitudes.

Choice of materials for notetaking instruction and practice represents another unresolved issue. Commercially published materials for EAP notetaking are readily available and are often accompanied by convenient lecture listening materials. At the same time, many EAP teachers prefer to select authentic materials (e.g., TED Talks, podcasts, news broadcasts, etc.), which their students listen to and take notes on. Both the more controlled and systematic textbook approach and the less rigid more open procedures enabled by authentic materials have pros and cons. Yet the effects of these frameworks for notetaking instruction have not been elucidated clearly based on classroom evidence and the issue of which approach is preferable in certain contexts for particular reasons remains unanswered (Siegel, 2018).

Technology and its role in notetaking in general and in L2 notetaking specifically is a largely untapped area. In theory, technological advancements, such as laptops, tablets, and electronic writing instruments (e.g., the stylus), are meant to make notetaking faster, easier, and more convenient at the encoding stage. These tools are also meant to make storage, filing, and retrieval of notes simpler and more secure. While technology and notetaking has begun to receive attention in L1 contexts (e.g., Mueller & Oppenheimer, 2014; Luo, Kiewra, Flanigan & Peteranetz, 2018; Morehead, Dunlosky & Rawson, 2019), there is a clear dearth of studies examining the impact of technology in L2 notetaking. Such L1 research has demonstrated some benefits of technology compared to traditional long-hand, although the evidence at present is not conclusive. This avenue of research needs to be replicated in L1 contexts as well as actively pursued in relation to L2 notetaking.

While this book has aimed to bring to light the complexity of L2 notetaking through examples and discussion of classroom research, and has presented a number of principles based on those lines of inquiry, the fledging state of notetaking research and the complexity of the skill necessitate more wide-ranging appreciation, recognition, scholarly study, and pedagogic attention. The issues outlined above in particular represent areas of immediate need but this list is clearly not comprehensive. As more theoretical considerations and classroom research is undertaken, additional and more sophisticated research agendas will surely develop.

Beyond academic contexts

The focus of this book has been squarely on L2 notetaking in academic contexts. It has centered in large part on the relationship between the preparatory aspects of EAP at the secondary and "bridge" levels with a final destination of success in listening to, taking notes during, and learning from EMI content lectures. In doing so, the book has summarized and commented on research from both L1 and L2 academic contexts, drawn on perspectives from EAP student and teachers, and presented findings from classroom investigations, including samples of EAP students notes and transcripts of interactions related to notes.

Many students taking such EAP and/or EMI courses have goals beyond their formal education and are motivated to find jobs and establish careers that may, to varying degrees, involve both L2 English and notetaking. As described in Chapter One, people take notes in any number of personal, academic, and professional settings. Depending on the field one finds oneself working in, notetaking can take a number of forms, some of them not particularly linked to academic formats. Among professional genres in which notetaking often occurs are the formal meeting (involving multiple people listening and responding to others' output, often with distinct goals to express opinions, garner support, reach consensus, etc.) and the individual consultation (such as between a doctor or counselor and patient or between a lawyer and a client).

As articulated by Mueller and Oppenheimer (2016), the goals and usage of notes taken in such professional arenas can differ greatly, especially in relation to academic notetaking, which most often occurs as a single person taking notes for their own personal use for the purposes of learning content and/or performing well on assessments in order to get grades or academic credit. In a work meeting, for example, one person might be designated to take notes of the entire multiparty interaction so that others (both present and absent) have a record of what occurred. These notes may only be referenced later for confirmatory purposes or to update colleagues who missed part or all of the meeting. In medical settings, notes on patient history and condition are certainly important but also need to be taken in ways that do not disrupt personal rapport and comfort levels. The common goal for these professional situations, as well as in academic notetaking, is "creating an external record for one's future reference" (Mueller & Oppenheimer, 2016, p. 140). However, purposes for and uses of the external record, along with the level of detail and the explicitness or discreteness of the notetaking act will often differ.

Unlike in academic lecture situations where notetakers typically focus on a single speaker (i.e., the lecturer), those taking notes in professional contexts often face a choice between taking copious notes in a timely fashion and participating in the conversation. It is often a tradeoff, where a person may struggle to write or type while also injecting their own opinions and thoughts. This challenge, the inclusion of dual-roles of notetaker and active participant, combined with more participants speaking in a meeting, can make notetaking in meetings a particularly stimulating environment, from a research perspective. Add to the mix language choice, personal relationships, and so on, and the context becomes only more fascinating. Since many students will move on from EAP and EMI to careers where English is used, understanding how notetaking occurs in such professional settings can provide valuable information and experience that can feed back into the preparatory stages.

Final thoughts

Everyone at one time or another depends on notes to compensate for memory limitations. Notes help us preserve meaning for stimulation of recall and later use of information. Learning and success in academic contexts often depend on the ability to take accurate and useful notes. A number of factors and skills interact when listening to and taking notes in an L2, making the task much more complicated than one might assume on the surface. A careful consideration of what a teacher expects and assumes when they say "take notes" reveals a labyrinth of challenges, any of which can potentially confound notetaking success. Development of sound notetaking skills and strategies can lead to favorable outcomes not only in academic life but in the workplace as well.

As a teacher, I initially struggled to teach L2 notetaking in same theoretically sound and pedagogically justifiable ways that I taught other L2 skills. After discussing this challenge with colleagues and consulting the literature, I realized many teachers could relate to my troubles and that too little attention was being allocated to this crucial academic ability. I seek to better understand the options available to notetakers, the notetaking act itself, and perspectives from L2 students on how they approach notetaking in EAP and EMI. This understanding promotes and leads to better and more informed classroom practice.

Notetaking will maintain its status as an unavoidable, invaluable, and constructive skill in academic settings, even as technology continues to offer additional options and tools. The identification of relevant information in any given listening text and the ability to make sound decisions about what information to include in notes, along with when to record and how to do so will always be important and worthy of class time allocation. The focus for both teachers and their students should always be on the ability to take notes in ways that stimulate one's own individual recall in the most efficient and effective ways possible.

References

Luo, L., Kiewra, K., Flanigan, A., & Peteranetz, M. (2018). Laptop versus longhand note taking: Effects on lecture notes and achievement. *Instructional Science*, 46, 947–971.

Morehead, K., Dunlosky, J., & Rawson, K. (2019). How much mightier is the pen than the keyboard for note-taking? A replication and extension of Mueller and Oppenheimer (2014). *Educational Psychology Review*, 31, 753–780.

Mueller, P., & Oppenheimer, M. (2014). The pen is mightier than the keyboard: Advantages of longhand over laptop note taking. *Psychological Science*, 25(6), 1159–1168.

Mueller, P., & Oppenheimer, D. (2016). Technology and note-taking in the classroom, boardroom, hospital room, and courtroom. *Trends in Neuroscience and Education*, 5, 139–145.

Piolat, A., Olive, T., & Kellogg, R. (2005). Cognitive effort during note taking. *Applied Cognitive Psychology*, 19, 291–312.

Siegel, J. (2018). Notetaking in ELT: Highlighting contrasts. *TESOL Journal*, 10(1), 1–5.

Index

Page numbers in *italics* refer to content in *figures*; page numbers in **bold** refer to content in **tables**.

abbreviation 4, 7, 15, 32, 34, 39, 42, 63, 65, 68, 92, **102–104**, 112, 132, 143, 148, 153, **154–155**
academic lectures: L2 notetaking materials 93, **101**; sequence 26, 93–94, **101**
academic notetaking 8–10, 88; collaboration 9; interaction lacking between speaker and listener 9; takes place in isolation 9
academic performance 1, 51, 88
academic skills **57**, 61, 63–64, 68, 69, 84, 97, 150, 152, 164, 166; notetaking 1–24
accents 17, 18, 27, 28, **56**, 62, 69
acquiescence bias 69
administrators 17, 108, 149, 162
affective strategies 134, 135, 138–140
Africa 18, 52
Airey, J. 27
alignment principle 89, 95
Anderson, J. 153
annotating 30, 100, **102, 103**
anxiety 45, 129, 135, 138, 139, 141, 142
apps 4, 44–46
arrows 10, 39, *72, 73, 74,* 75, 79, **102,** 112, 137, 139, 153, **154**
Artz, B. 44
Asia 17, 52
association (of ideas) 70, 138, 139; *see also* arrows
attention xi, 5, 13, 14, 19, 45, 60, 129, 139–140
audio xii, 20, 41, 106, 108, 165

Badger, R. 36, 37, 47
Barbier, M-L. 37, 62–63

Beretta, A. 26–27
Bolton, K. 18, 28
Boyle, J. 35
Bui, D. 36–37, 44, **151**, 153
bullet points 31, 32, 37, *73,* 73, 74, 137

Cameroon **53–58**, 65
Canagarajah, S. 64
Carter, S. P. 43
CEFR (Common European Framework for Reference of Languages) 41, 42, 59, 100, 113, 114, 120, 143
Chakrabarty, P. 70, 77, 85, **122,** *122–124*
Chamot, A. 25, 99, **105**, 133, 136, 141
Chang, W. C. 35
Chang, Y. Y. 28
Chappell, P. 132
charts 12, 15, 42, 92
chunking **41**, 67, 68, 90, 91, 114, **115,** *115,* 116, *119,* 120, *121,* 124–126, 135
classroom discussions 3, 20, 113, 132–133, 142–144, 165
classroom research xii, 118–127, 160, 164–168
Clerehan, R. 32, **154**
cloud computing 19, 43
cloze exercises 34
CLT (Communicative Language Teaching) 129
cognition 12–13, 109, 116, 134
cognitive effort 5, 7, 23, 36, 63, 84, 97
cognitive load 5, 33, 60
cognitive skills 2, 60, 69, 90, 110
cognitive strategies 99, **105**, 133–135, 138–142, 163

172 *Index*

collaborative notetaking 16–17, 30, 34, 69, **105**, 111, **115**, 116–118, 120, 127, 129–145, 147, 162–163, 165; broad venue for strategy coverage 141–142; comparing information 139–140; confirmation aspect 139–140; findings 136–140; findings (limitations) 142–143; pedagogic implications 140–143; research methodology 136

compensation strategies 134, 135

comprehension 5, 7–9, 13, 16, 18, 19, 21, 26, 27, 38, 60, 125, 135, 148

comprehension tests 40, 42, 118, 120, **151**, 157

concentration xii, **54**, 60, 61, 69, 135

confidence 7, 14, 27, 139, 141, 142, 156, 164

Conteh, J. 64

content words 39, 112, 124, **154–155**, 156

contrast groups 39, 41

control groups 39–42, 119, 120

conversations 3, 9, 26, 129, 132, 136, 140, 143, 158, 163, 168

Cornell method *11*, 11–12, 22, 31, 35, 39, 40, 51, 111–112, 126, 146, **151**, 161, 166

course planners 87, 95, 106, 108

Crawford, C. C. 30–31, 34

Crawford, M. 28, 29, 39, 46, 51, 59, 60, 65, 68, 69, 112, **155**; evaluation of notes **154**

creative-construction hypothesis 89

culture 18, 28, 30, 32, 142, 164

Dearden, J. 17

decision-making 6, 10, 13, 33, 37, 39, 43, 47, **53**, 64, 67, 75, 87, 88, 94, 96, 97, **102–103**, 109, 110, 113, 114, 117, 124–126, 132, 138, 161, 165, 169

DeKeyser, R. 38, 116

depth of processing: definition 7

design 89–90, 93, 94

detail 10, 12, 31, 37, 74, 76, 83, 90, 92, 95, **103**, 110–112, 147, 157, 168

digital notetaking 3–4, 14, 25, 29, 33, 41, 46, 61, 69, 96, **102**, **105**, 108, 147, **151**, 160, 165; drawbacks 43

DiVesta, F. 7, 34

Donohoo, J. 11

drawing effect (type of encoding) 33

Dunkel, P. 28–29, 31–32, 46, **151**, **154–155**; "terseness of notations" 32

EAP (English for Academic Purposes) 2, 9, 18, 25, 30, 31, 38, 40, 46, 47, 58, 62, 63, 69, 70, 84, 168, 169; listening and notetaking book 126; notetaking abilities (developmental purpose) 163; notetaking materials 162; pedagogic approaches to L2 notetaking 108, 110, 111, 113–114, 125–126; pedagogical perspectives on note assessment 157; teacher expectations 163

EAP courses xii, 8, 17, 29, 33, 36, 37, 44, 66, 67, 165, 166; notetaking textbooks (evaluation) 87–98 *passim*, 106

EAP students 160, 162–163; collaborative notetaking 136–144; collaborative notetaking (emergent strategy use) 137–140; note quality 146–150, 157, 158

EAP teachers 20, 26, 51, 52, 60, 66, 125, 126, 142–150 *passim*, 157, 158, 160, 164, 166, 167; "must be concerned with notes" 61

Eddy, M. D. 30

educational psychology 130–133

EFL (English as Foreign Language) 45, 52, 65–66, 68, 70; students 39–41, 162; teachers 154, 156

ELF (English as Lingua Franca) 2, 18, 31, 163

ELT (English-Language Teaching) 20

EMI (English-Medium Instruction) xii, 9, 20, 21, 30, 46, 58, 62, 63, 69, 70, 84, 161, 162, 168, 169; note quality 148–150; notetaking 17–18; notetaking (focus on content learning) 163–164; relationship with EAP 163–164; teacher expectations 163

EMI courses 38, 67, 68; notetaking textbooks (evaluation) 87, 89, 92–94, 106

EMI lecturers 2, 37, 51, 52, 60, 61, 66; not interested in how student knowledge is gained 150; post-notetaking discussions (value) 142

EMI lectures 8, 17, 25, 64; genre and norms 26–28

encoding 29, 31, 33, 44, 51, 71, 91, 92, 94, 98, 132; effectiveness 32; textbooks 96–97

encoding effect 7, 28, 29, **151**

encoding function 6–8, 25, 30, 34, 46, 47, **102–103**, 116, 117, 125, 161,

162, 165; "needs explicit attention" 164; research 31–33
encoding stage 147, 149, 167
encoding techniques 32, 89
engagement 7, 27, 59, 90, 99, **103**, 149, 152; *see also* sociocultural engagement
ESL (English as Second Language) 34, 37, 47, 52, 68
ESP (English for Specific Purposes) 31
evaluation 134, 135
eWriters 34, 43, 45, 153, 167
exchange students 18, 28

feedback xi, xii, 90, 110, 113, 118, 121, 132
flexible outline method 36, 146
Flowerdew, J. 8
Forchelli, G. 35
Forsberg [initial/s n.a.] 17
four skills 87, 126, 144

Gallini, J. 15
García, O. 64
gender 36
genre model 89
Gobet, F. 116
grammar 15, 100, 139
Gray, S. 7, 34
Griffiths, R. 26–27

Halliday, M. A. 131
Halo Effect 69
Hamp-Lyons, L. 10, 12, 76–77, 87, 91–92, 96, 98, 106–108
handwriting 15, 19, 36, 96, 134, 143, 144, 148, 161
handwriting speed 4, 14, 19, 36, 73, 164
Harwood, N. 87, 93, 94
Hawthorne Effect 69
Hayati, A. M. 38–39, 46, 111, **151**
headings 4, 32; and subheadings 10, 15
higher education 1–3, 21, 30, 142, 163; notetaking 8–10
highlighting 3, 35, 39, 73, 77, 91, 97, 100, **102–103**, 153, **154**
high schools *see* upper secondary schools
Hu, Y. **151**

iBT 157
ichthyology 77–78
idea units (Morehead *et al.*) **151**, 153, 154, 156
IELTS 157

illustrations 65, **155**
illustrative diagrams 36–37
images 4, 19, 33, 45, **151**; pictures 15, 78, 97, 98, 123, 146, 153
indentation 10, 31, 73
individual flexibility **103**
Indonesia **53–58**, 61
informal outline 100, **102**, **104**
information hierarchy 10, **41**, 70, **115**, 117, 131, 132, 142, **154**
information processing 9, 33
information retention theory 47
information transfer 6, 30, 91, **151**, 152, 158
input-output process 89
inquiry dialogue 132
interactive lecturing 26
internet 18, 43, 108, 114, 129
interventions *see* pedagogic interventions
interviews 36, 46, 110–111, 125
iPad 43, 60
İpek, H. 60
isolation 129, 141–143
IU (information unit) 40–42, 45, **115**, 116, 119, 120, 146, **154**, 154, 158, 163, 165–166; definition 118, 153; tiered rating **155**
IU method 153; drawbacks 156–157

Jalilifar, A. 38–39, 46, 111, **151**
Japan 17, 18, 29, 39, 41, 113–114, 161; EFL learners 59–60, 68, 120; L2 notetaking (five-stage pedagogic cycle) 118–121, *121*; L2 notetaking survey **53–58**, 65
junior schools 1, 20, 126

key points 153, **154**, 154, 156
keywords xii, 11, 21, 35, **41**, 96, **102–104**, 110, 112, **115**, 137–139, 143
Kiewra, K. 36, **151**
Klesch-Kincaid Grade Level **122**
knowledge storage systems 61
knowledge transfer goal 8
Kobayashi, K. 29–31, 34
Kovacs, G. 114
Ku, Y. M. 35
Kusumoto, Y. 41–42, 63–64, 66, 68, 118, 120, 125; explicit evaluation of notes **154**
Kuteeva, M. 18, 28

L1 (first language) xi–xii, 2, 11–12, 16, 17, 20, **102**, 110, 135, 141–143,

147, **155**, 160, 167, 168; language choice in notetaking 62–64; research on technology in notetaking 44–45
L1 content teachers 126, 166
L1 courses 89, 92
L1 English 62–63
L1 notes 130, 153
L1 notetaking 25, **154**; *see also* language choice
L1 Spanish 62–63
L1 Swedish 79
L2 (second language) 4, 11, 14, 17, 27, 97; language choice in notetaking 62–64; obstacles to student comprehension 17; research on technology in notetaking 45–46
L2 English 9–10, 38; proficiency 41–42
L2 French 62–63
L2 learning strategies 99, 133–136, 143; definitions 134; explicit and implicit 142
L2 listening xii, 96, 110, 135–136, 164
L2 note quality **154**
L2 notetaking 2–8, 25; academic purposes 10; definition 16; instructional cycle 109; moving forward 106; pedagogic approaches 26, 108–128, 162; pre- and post-intervention samples 121–124; unique skill 16
L2 notetaking abilities 127, **154**
L2 notetaking (five-stage pedagogic cycle) 109–110, 113–118, 162; findings from classroom research 118–121, 127
L2 notetaking materials: broader criteria 93–97; case for evaluation 88–90; previous evaluations 91–93; roles of other language skills 100, **105**
L2 notetaking materials (design criteria) 93–97; accounting for typical lecture sequence 93–94, **101**; building on previous skills 95–96, **102**; encoding and storage 96–97, **102**; genre of academic lecture 93, **101**; notetaking-specific goals 95, **102**; range of systems and techniques 96, **102**; syllabus itself *versus* "pick and choose" 95, **101**; teacher and student roles 94, **101**
L2 notetaking materials (procedural criteria) 97–100; generative and non-generative notetaking 97, **103**; language skills 100; individual flexibility 98, **104**; "notetaking" *versus* "listening comprehension" 99,

104; specific stages of notetaking 97–98, **103**; strategies 99, **105**
L2 notetaking skills: beyond academic contexts 167–169; conclusions 3, 21, 114, 160–170; EAP and EMI relationship 163–164; further research required 165–167; insights from classroom research 164–166; main messages 160–161; overview 162–163; unresolved issues 166–167
L2 notetaking textbooks (evaluation principles) 2–3, 20, 21, 84, 87–107, 162; application of criteria 100–105; *see also* L2 notetaking materials
L2 strategy taxonomies 133–136
L2 students xi–xii, 8, 129
language choice 16–17, **57**, 62–66, 164, 168
language skills 2, 14–16, 100, **105**; listening 14–15, 133; reading 15–16, 133; speaking xi, 133; writing xi, 15, 133
laptop computers 19, 31, 34, 41, 43–45, 58, 60, 153, 167
Lau, K. 28
learning xi, 3–5, 7, 8, 16, 27, 29–34, 51, 62, 89, 147; goals 21; outcomes 36; theory 116; words plus images 15
learning disabilities 35
lecture culture 18, 28
lecture handouts 15, 60, 61
lecture listening course 88
Lecture Ready 2 (Sarosy and Sherak, 2013) 100, **101–105**, 106, 108
lecture signposts 95
lecture structure 18, 93, 140
lectures 2–4, 7, 11, 13–15, 18, 21, 68, 69, 89–90, 129; components 27–28; main ideas (difficulty for L2 notetakers to discern) 32; purpose 94; requirements 8; typical sequence 93–94; styles 26; "value-laden discourses" 26
Lee [initial/s n.a.] 26
lesson management platforms 160
lesson management systems 60
lexical segmentation 114, 116, 124, 126
Likert scales 119
Linder, C. 27
lines (indicating relationships between pieces of information) 12, *75–76*, *115*, 116–117, 123, *123*
linguistics 131; applied linguistics 43, 61, 157

listening xi, xii, 3–9, 13, 18, 35, 36, 68, 89, 148; distinct skill 90–91; language skill 14–15

listening comprehension 37, 41, 84, 88, 91, 98, 150, 152; *versus* "notetaking" 99, **104**, 106, 161; obstacles 62; skills 100, **105**; test scores 38–39

Listening & Notetaking Skills, Level 2 [Lim and Smalzer, 2014] 72

listening process 116

listening skills 2, 36, 135

listening strategies **101**, **103**; bottom-up *versus* top-down 13

Lui, B. **151**

Luo, L. 33, 34, 45, 46, 130, 140, **151**, 153

Lynch, T. 26

margin use 3, 12, 61, 148

marking transcript (with symbols) **115**, *115*, 116, 117, *119*, 120, *121*

Mayer, R. 15

McDaniel, M. 36–37, **151**

memory 7, 8, 16, 32, 33, 36, 62, 90, 134, 135, 152, 153, 164

memory limitations 4, 169

meta-analyses 29–31

metacognition 13–14

metacognitive strategy 75, 99, **105**, 133–142 *passim*, 161, 163, 164

Miller, L. 8

mind map 12, 75–76, *76*

minutes (formal meetings) 168

mobile telephones 19, 43, 44, 108

monitoring 134, 135, 158

Morehead, K. 12, 31, 33–34, 37, 45–47, 52–58, 60, **151**, 153

motivation 36, 45, 61, 62, 64, 133, 139, 166, 168

Mueller, P. 44–46, **151**, 168

multiple choice 34, 91, 92, 99, 130, 139, 150, **151**, 152

Murata, K. 18

Nekoda, H. 42

non-notetakers 31, 34, 37, 39, 58, 111, **151**, 164

notation 32, 39, **154**–**155**, 156, 157

note content 37, 153

note quality 3, 21, 42, 47, 51, 61, 64, 90, 99, 131, 144, 146–159, 163; assessment methods 146, 153, **155**; choice of language (L1 or L2) 63; completeness **155**; definition of "good" 146–150; evaluation

165–166; influence of five-stage pedagogic cycle 118; mixed-methods research 152; "no single influencing factor" 62; pedagogical perspectives 157; post-notetaking tasks (selection of studies) **151**; prioritizing 153–157; studies that include explicit evaluation **154**; task relation 150–153

note quantity 14, 16, 45, 61, 84, 118, 149, 153, **154**; *see also* word count

notes: definition 3, 161; evidence of lecture comprehension 46; focus on content and quality "should be paramount" 166; functions 7; objects of study 46; summary 4–5; types and functions 1–3

notes (dialogic potential) 3, 21, 69, 129–145, 162–163; educational psychology 130–133; L2 learning strategies 133–136; L2 strategy taxonomies 133–136

note samples 21, 40, 41, 52, 110, 112, 113, 156, 161, 162, 165, 168; five-stage pedagogic cycle (findings from classroom research) 118–127; five-stage pedagogic intervention (impact) 121–124, *122–124*; organizational options 70–84, *71–83*; same information, different notes 77–84; strategy use 137–141; student practices 70–84, *71–83*

notetakers: direct and indirect strategies 135, 137, 141; *versus* "note-users" 152–153

notetaking: academic 8–10; "assumed and misunderstood skill" xi; background knowledge (importance) 83, **103**, **105**, 138, 139, 152, 157; benefits (improved learning and performance) 164; choice of language **151**; combination of cognitive and physical skills 4, 110, 117, 168; completeness scores 130; context 8; definition 5; direct *versus* indirect strategies 138–140; "distinct skill" 90–91; encoding and storage functions 6–8; "essential skill" xi; five R's 111; four-stage pedagogic sequence 40, **41**; gateway academic skill 1–24, 168, 169; generative and non-generative 5–7, 29, 47, 89, 97, **103**, 136, 147, 161, 162; individual flexibility 98; intervention and non-intervention

176 *Index*

conditions 29–30; key ideas captured 149; L1 and L2 149; *versus* "listening comprehension" 99, **104**, 106; multiple steps 4; number of words 149; pedagogic perspectives 20; process and product elements 8, 29, 36, 130, 149; in same language as speaker 16, 36, 39, 64, 65; specific stages 97–98, **103**; style and formats 10–12; yields better results than not taking notes 39

notetaking (student practices) 70–84; organizational options 70–77, 84; same information, different notes 77–84

notetaking (subskills and impacting factors) 12–17; cognitive aspects 13; language choice 16–17; language skills 14–16; listening 14–15; metacognition 13–14; physical factors 14; reading 15–16; writing 15

notetaking ability 38, *119*, 120, *121*, 121, 125, 129, 131, 136, 157; context (EAP *versus* EMI) 163; L1 and L2 overlap 165, 166

notetaking act 2, 14, 31, 51, 52, 61, 70, 71, 83, 91, 99, **103–104**, 117, 121, 130, 134, 135, 140, 160, 161, 168, 169

notetaking activities 42, 89, 92, 95, 98, **104**, 118, 165

notetaking audience 16–17

notetaking in English 2, 63–64, 68, 84; *see also* L2 notetaking

notetaking in everyday life 1–2

notetaking formats 36, 38, 47, 99, **102**, 135, 143, **151**, **154**; student preference 166–167

notetaking instruction 39, 40, **41**, 41, 42, 47, 58, 63, 68–69, **154**, 162; choice of materials 167; impact on notetaking ability 66–67; L2 student's perspective 65–66

notetaking in L1 and L2 contexts: differences between L1 and L2 notetaking 37–38; effectiveness of notes 34–35; encoding research 31–33; historical perspective 30–31; individual differences 36–37; previous research 2, 3, 7, 19, 21, 25–50, 52, 67, 162; review articles 28–30; storage research 33–34

notetaking from L2 student's perspective 2, 21, 38, 51–86, 162; instruction 65–66; instruction

(impact on notetaking ability) 66–67; translanguaging 64–65; views on pedagogic approaches 67–70

notetaking from L2 student's perspective (survey research) 52–64; benefits to concentration **54**, 61; language choice **57**, 62–66; mode of notetaking **53**, 61; obstacles to effective notetaking **56**, 62; original survey research in L2 contexts 60–61; reasons for taking notes **55**, 61–62; student habits 59–60, 68; student views and beliefs 61–62, 68; teacher potential **58**, 66–68, 84

notetaking pedagogy 106; four-step approach (Siegel) 67

notetaking performance 38, 40, 114, 118, **133**, 135, 136

notetaking research: fledgling state 167; reflections 46–47; strands 25–26

notetaking skills 142; complexity 167, 169; textbooks 95–96

notetaking strategies 38, **102**, 131, 162–163; textbooks 95–96

notetaking systems 36, 47, 96, 148

notetaking techniques 38, 39, 47, 99, **102**, 135, 161; textbooks 95–96

notetaking textbooks 108–109, 126; "should be examined with care" 165; *see also* L2 notetaking textbooks

O'Malley, J. 25, 99, **105**, 133, 135, 141

objectivity 76, 84, 87, 106, 108, 146, 147, 154, **155**, 157, 162, 165–166

Oppenheimer, M. 44–46, **151**, 168

organizational options 70–77, 84, 89, 96; columns *75*, 75; drifting notes *74*; hierarchy of significance 76–77; mind map or word web 75–76, *76*; notes taken in short bursts, left to right 71–72; notes with arrows *72*, 72; notes with bullet points *73*, 73, 74; notes with spaces *71*; notes with spaces and summary words 71, *72*; vertical orientation *73–74*, 73–74; vertical pattern with arrows *74*

organizational skills **54**, 61

outline format 10–12, 31, 36–37, 51, 60, 92, **102**, 114, 126, 161, 166; sample *10*

Owens, R. 11, *11*, 39, **151**

Oxford, R. 25, **105**, 136, 141; direct and indirect L2 learning strategies 134–135

paraphrase 5, 7, 29, 31, 33, 34, 40, 45, 59–61, 95, 97, **103**, 132, 134, 137, 138, 146, 148, 149, **155**, 157, 161
Pauk, W. 11, *11*, 39, **151**
pedagogic approaches: L2 student's perspective 67–70
pedagogic interventions 25, 29–31, 60, 118–120, 148, 162; effective for improving L2 notetaking performance 164–165; effects on note quality **154**; L2 notetaking 38–42; research 46–47
pedagogic techniques: research literature 110–113
pedagogy 11, 12, 35, 39, 95; for notetaking 9–10; "good language learner" (Rubin) 133; L2 notetaking 3, 21, 67, 84, 106, 108–128; note assessment 157; perspectives on notetaking 20; pre- and post-intervention notetaking samples 121–124; unresolved issues and future avenues 166–167
pedagogy (five-stage cycle of L2 notetaking) 109–110, 113–118, 127; findings from classroom research 118–121; further development 124–125; unresolved issues 126
peer-to-peer interaction 62, 113, 117, 143
pen and paper notetaking 31, 41, 43, **53**, 60, 61, 77, 96, **102**, 147, **151**, 160, 165; "longhand" 33, 34, 44–45, 153, 167
phonemes 6, 15, 27–28, 90
photographs 19, 43, 44
Piolat, A. 3, 36
planning 135, 137, 138
plus signs (+) (to show relationships) **102**
podcasts 125, 126, 157, 167
post-listening tasks 25, 146, 150–153, 157, 158
post-listening tests 31, 47, **154**
post-notetaking activity 59, 92, **103**
post-notetaking discussions 144; benefits 142; scaffolding 143; suggested prompts 143
PowerPoint 15, 19, 58–60, 106, 117, 160
practice 38, 41, 42, **115**, 117, 120, **154**
pragmatic force modifiers 28
prediction 6, 11, 99, **101**, **103**, **105**, 135, 138, 140

prestige bias 69
Princeton University 44
problem-solving 117, 131
procedure 89, 90
professional arenas 168–169
proficiency 20, 25, 26, 29, 35, 37, 38, 41, 42, 59, 88, 94, 99, 108, 113–133 *passim*, 141–143, 149, 157, 161, 164, 166
pronunciation 95, 164
punctuation **155**

qualitative research 36, 136, 153
quantitative measures 153
quizzes 30, 33, 94, 164

rate of speech 14, 17, 27, 28, **41**, 41, **56**, 62, 69, **115**, **122**, 164
reading 3, 35, 88; language skill 15–16
reading skills 100, **105**
recall xi, 7, 8, 16, 29–36 *passim*, 44, 73, 83, 96, 138, **151**, 152, 153, **155**, 166, 169
reciting 111, 137
recording *see* verbatim recording
Reddington, L. 36
reduction 111, 113
reflection 42, 133, 137, 143, 162
review (of notes) 33–34, 44, 59, 71, 91, 96–97, **103**, 131, 141, 147, 164, 165
review exercises 89
review function 161
rhetorical signals 93
Richards, J. 89, 90, 94, 129, 135
Rodgers, T. 89, 90, 94, 129
Roy, D. 45–46
Rubin, J.: "What 'good language learner' can teach us" (1975) 133

Sakurai, S. 153–154, **154**, 156
Sarosy, P. 100, **101–105**
scaffolding 11, 20, 26, 37, 42, 46, 63, 69, 98, **101**, 109, 113, 116, 120, 129–130, 161, 163
schema: definition 90
Scotland 30
selective attention 133, 139, 140
self-confidence 139
self-deception bias 69
Seychelles **53–58**, 65
Sheldon, L. 87
Sheppard, B. 27–28
Sherak, K. 100, **101–105**
Shields, A. **122**, *122–124*

178 *Index*

shopping lists 1, 10, 51
short condensations 3–4, 161, 166
Siegel, J. 6, 9, 16, 23–24, 33, 37–39, **41**, 41, 42, 46, 51, 58, 64–68, 85, 90–91, **154–155**, 156, 159, 166, 167, 170; definition of IU 153; as EAP teacher xi, 160; explicit evaluation of notes **154**; L2 notetaking (five-stage pedagogic cycle) 109–110, 112–119; L2 notetaking (pedagogic approaches) 110–119, 126, 128; L2 notetaking (post-listening tasks) 150–153; simplification of notes (three-step approach) 157
Siegel, J. (*Developing Notetaking Skills*): book aim 10; book focus 20; book purpose 160; major drive for book 20
silence 18, 129
simplification of notes **41**, 42, 67–68, **103**, 113, **115**, *115*, 116, 117, *119*, 120, *121*, 121, 125, 126; three-step approach (Siegel 2019) 157
simultaneity 3–4
skeleton notes 92, 113–114
skeleton outlines 40, **151**
skill acquisition theory 38, 116, 117, 127
slides 15, 19, 59–61, 106, 111, 114, 117, 160
socio-affective strategies 99, **105**, 133–135, 138, 141, 142, 163
sociocultural engagement (dialogic potential of notes) 129–145, 162–163; findings 136–140; pedagogic implications 140–143; research methodology 136
sociocultural theory 117–118, 129, 131, 136, 143
Song, M. Y. 37, 47, **154**
space and spacing 11, 12, 32, 39, *71–72*, *73*, 75, 79, 137, 148
Spain 53–58
spelling 15, 64, 77–78, 80
spray chart 12
Springpad 46
storage function 6–8, 25, 29–31, 47, 71, 91, 94, **102**, 125, 147, 161, 167; "deserves explicit attention" 164; research findings 33–34; textbooks 96–97
stress 14, 99, 138, 166
students 45, 47; habits 59–60, 68; roles 94, **101**; styles and preferences

165; views and beliefs 61–62, 68; *see also* notetaking from L2 student's perspective
stylus 19, 43, 160, 167
subjectivity 146, 148–150
summarizing 7, 16, 33, 91, 94, 112, 138, 148, 150, **151**
survey research: "inherent flaws" 69
Sweden 17, 18, 33, 40, 65–66, 161; collaborative notetaking 136–44; EAP students 59; L2 notetaking (five-stage pedagogic cycle) 118–121, *119*; L2 notetaking survey results **53–58**, 61, 67; Ministry of Education 114; national curriculum 66; notetaking (same information, different notes) 77–84; notetaking pedagogy 67–68; pre- and post-intervention notetaking samples 121–124
Swedish language lectures 27
syllabus 90, 95, **101**
symbols 4, 15, 42, 67, 68, 79, 83, **102–104**, 116, 137, 139, 153, **154–155**
systematic approach xi, xii, 9, 11, 30, 37, 39, 63, 92, **102**, 106, 108–110, 124–125, 127, **134**, 135, 137, 146, 147, **154**, 162, 164, 167

tables of contents 93, 95, 96, 100, **101–102**, 109
tablet computers 4, 31, 41, 43, **53**, 58, 167; photograph-taking 19; writing utensils 43–44
Taiwan 29, 35, 67
"take notes" (injunction) xii, 4, 9, 12, 20, 21, 25, 70, 88, 98, 110, 120, 127, 160, 169
teacher expectations 62, 158
teacher potential in notetaking **58**, 66–68, 84
teacher roles 94, **101**, 109
teachers xii, 87–88, 108–111, 125, 162, 163
technology 18–20, 25, 58, 60, 167, 169
technology in notetaking: L1 contexts 44–45; L2 contexts 45–46; research 43–46
TED Talks 40, 41, 44, 45, 67, 70–71, 109–110, 113–117, 121, 125, 126, 136, 156–157, 167
test creators 152
test performance 32, 34, 35, 37, 42, 46
tests 44, 62, 69, 141, 153
T-format notetaking 12, 36, 92

Index 179

time 8, 33, **41**, **56**, 62, 68, 72, 81–83, 93, **102–103**, 111, 113, **115**, 116, 117, **122**, 125, 130, 131, 135, 139, 141, 147, 157, 161, 163–166, 169
time-efficiency 42
time pressure 4, 7, 13, 14, 16, 21, 36, 44, 138, 152
TOEFL 38–39, **151**, 157
Tomlinson, B. 89
top-down *versus* bottom-up processing 6, 13, 90–91
transcripts: interactions relating to notes 168
translanguaging 16, 24, 37–38, *65*, 65, 79, 81, 167; definition 64; L2 student's perspective 64–65
transparency 34, 153, 162, 165–166
Tsai, T. 35, 37, 39, 111–112, **151**
Turkish university L2 English students 60
typing xi, 15, 96, **105**, 134, 161
typing speed 4, 14, 19, 43, 45

Ubernote 46
uncertainty 65–67, 77, 78, 142, **155**
underlining 3, 10, 30, 32, 73, 91
uninstructed notetakers 39, 111, 121, **151**
United Kingdom 36, 47
United States 30, 35–37, 45; L1 notetaking habits 52–58; L2 notetaking survey 53–58
Universitets Läraren 17
universities 8, 30, 33
upper secondary schools (high schools) 8, 20, 33, 40, 59, 60, 65–67, 70, 114, 118, 119, 136, 141–142;

pre- and post-intervention notetaking samples 121–124

verbatim notes **115**, *115*, 116, 117, *119*, 120, *121*
verbatim overlap 63, 151
verbatim recording 3, 5–7, 29, 30, 32, 33, 37, 40–43, 45, 59–61, 67–68, 79, 83, 97, 103, 143, 147, 150, 161
vertical orientation *122*, 123
video 19, 20, 41, 44, 46, 108, 125, 126, 165; split-screen 106
visual forms 102, 104
vocabulary 14, 33, 59, 95, 132
Vygotsky, L. S. 117, 131–132

Wagner, E. 69
Wall Street Journal 45
Wammes, J. 33
Wells, G. 131, 132
word count 34, 149, **151**, 153, **154–155**, 157; *see also* word quantity
words: definition (for notetaking) 4
word substitution 7, 80, 81, 83, 84, 97
word web 75–76, *76*
"write down keywords" xii, 21, 110
writing xi, 3–4, 88, 96, 161; language skill 15
writing skills 2, 100, **105**
Wu, Y. 35, 37, 39, 111–112, **151**

Young, L. 27

ZPD (zone of proximal development) 117, 131–132, 141; definition (Vygotsky) 131

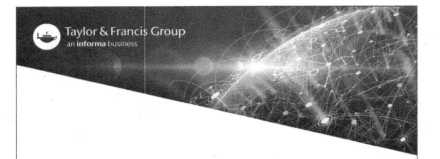